Introducing Art

ABOUT THE PROGRAM

Introducing Art has a thematic focus. It presents a wide range of artworks and styles and groups them by the themes that served as inspiration for the works.

People, places, animals, and nature. Artists have used these themes as subjects for their art since the beginning of man. Animals and stick people appeared on the walls of caves more than twelve thousand years ago. They remain today as a visual link to our forebears.

Celebrations and events are commemorated in paintings, sculpture, and photographs. Fantasy is a powerful stimulus for the creative process. These and other themes in *Introducing Art* will bring creative inspiration to the classroom.

ABOUT THE COVER ILLUSTRATION

St. Basil's Cathedral. Begun in 1554 by Ivan the Terrible from the plans of architects Barma and Postmik. Completed in 1679. Red Square, Moscow. Images © 1996 Photodisc, Inc.

St. Basil's Cathedral, now a museum in Moscow, appears on the cover. Its colorful onion domes and patterned exterior are testament to the fact that even public buildings can be whimsical creations of an inspired artist.

Introducing Art

Gene Mittler, Ph.D.
Professor Emeritus
Texas Tech University

Rosalind Ragans, Ph.D.
Associate Professor Emerita
Georgia Southern University

Jean Morman Unsworth, M.F.A.
Professor of Fine Arts Emerita
Loyola University of Chicago

Faye Scannell
Specialist, Technology
Bellevue, Washington Public Schools

Glencoe McGraw-Hill

New York, New York   Columbus, Ohio   Woodland Hills, California   Peoria, Illinois

ABOUT THE AUTHORS

Gene Mittler

Gene Mittler is one of the authors of Glencoe's middle school/junior high art series, *Introducing Art, Exploring Art,* and *Understanding Art.* He is also author of *Art in Focus,* a chronological approach to art for Glencoe's senior high program, and *Creating and Understanding Drawings.* He has taught at both the elementary and secondary levels and at Indiana University. He received an M.F.A. in sculpture from Bowling Green State University and a Ph.D. in art education from the Ohio State University. Dr. Mittler is currently Professor Emeritus at Texas Tech University.

Jean Morman Unsworth

Jean Morman Unsworth, author, teacher, and consultant, is one of the authors of Glencoe's middle school/junior-high book *Introducing Art.* Educated at the Art Institute of Chicago, University of Notre Dame, and the University of Georgia, she has taught elementary through graduate levels and was Professor of Fine Arts at Loyola University of Chicago until 1987. She initiated and designed Chicago Children's Museum and the Interdisciplinary Arts Masters program at Columbia College in Chicago. She now gives full time to writing and consulting.

Rosalind Ragans

Rosalind Ragans is one of the authors of Glencoe's middle school/junior high art series, *Introducing Art, Exploring Art,* and *Understanding Art.* She served as senior author on the elementary program *Art Connections* for the SRA division of McGraw-Hill, and wrote the multi-level, comprehensive *ArtTalk* text for Glencoe's senior high program. She received a B.F.A. at Hunter College, CUNY, New York, and earned a M.Ed. in Elementary Education at Georgia Southern College and Ph.D. in Art Education at the University of Georgia. Dr. Ragans was named National Art Educator of the Year for 1992.

Faye Scannell

Faye Scannell is an art specialist, lead art technology teacher, and teacher educator in the Bellevue, Washington Public Schools, the Bellevue Art Museum, and through Seattle Pacific University. She has written technology activities for Glencoe's *Introducing Art, Exploring Art, Understanding Art,* and *ArtTalk.* She was educated at Kutztown State University of Pennsylvania, Lesley College, and several Washington universities. In 1993 she received the Art Educator of the Year Award from the Washington Art Education Association.

ABOUT ARTSOURCE®

ART SOURCE

The materials provided in the Performing Arts Handbook are excerpted from *Artsource®: The Music Center Study Guide to the Performing Arts,* a project of the Music Center Education Division. The Music Center of Los Angeles County, the largest performing arts center in the western United States, established the Music Center Education Division in 1979 to provide opportunities for lifelong learning in the arts, and especially to bring the performing and visual arts into the classroom. The Education Division believes the arts enhance the quality of life for all people, but are crucial to the development of every child.

Glencoe/McGraw-Hill

A Division of The McGraw-Hill Companies

Copyright © 1999 by Glencoe/McGraw-Hill. All rights reserved. Except as permitted under the United States Copyright Act, no part of this publication may be reproduced or distributed in any form or by any means, or stored in a database or retrieval system, without prior written permission of the publisher.

Send all inquiries to:
Glencoe/McGraw-Hill
21600 Oxnard Street, Suite 500
Woodland Hills, CA 91367

ISBN 0-02-662363-3 (Student Text)
ISBN 0-02-662364-1 (Teacher's Wraparound Edition)

Printed in the United States of America.

3 4 5 6 7 8 9   004/043   03 02 01 00 99

EDITORIAL CONSULTANTS

Claire B. Clements, Ph.D.
Specialist, Special Needs
Associate Professor and Community Education
  Director at the Program on Human Development
  and Disability
The University of Georgia
Athens, Georgia

Robert D. Clements, Ph.D.
Specialist, Special Needs
Professor Emeritus of Art
The University of Georgia
Athens, Georgia

Cris Guenter, Ed.D.
Specialist, Portfolio and Assessment
Professor, Fine Arts/Curriculum and Instruction
California State University, Chico
Chico, California

Dede Tisone-Bartels, M.A.
Specialist, Curriculum Connections
Crittenden Middle School
Mountain View, California

Kathleen Laya
Educational Publishing and Curriculum Consultant
Wilmette, Illinois

CONTRIBUTORS/REVIEWERS

Max A. Butler
Fine Arts Instructor
Cedar Valley Middle School
Austin, TX

Gail F. Enkey
Art Teacher
Chiaravalle Montessori School
Evanston, IL

Stacey Hendrickson
Art Instructor
Gates Intermediate School
Scituate, MA

Joy Jones
Art Teacher
Chisholm Trail Middle School
Round Rock, TX

Cathy J. Kiser
Art Teacher
Jesse Stuart Middle School
Louisville, KY

Barbara A. Perez
Art Teacher
St. Athanasius School
Evanston, IL

Irene Wettermark Porter
Visual Arts Teacher
Hayes Middle School
Birmingham AL

Teri Power
Art Specialist & G&T Coordinator
East Elementary School
New Richmond, WI

Margaret Powers
Art Teacher
McAdory Elementary School
McCalla, AL

Wandra Merritt Sanders
Art Teacher
Hyde Park Elementary
Jacksonville, FL

Beverly N. Silletto
Art Teacher
Southern Middle School
Louisville, KY

Sylvia L. Thompson
Art Instructor
Cammack Middle School
Huntington, WV

PERFORMING ARTS HANDBOOK CONTRIBUTORS

Joan Boyett
Executive Director
Music Center Education Division
The Music Center of Los Angeles County

Melinda Williams
Concept Originator and Project Director

Susan Cambigue-Tracey
Project Coordinator

Arts Discipline Writers:
    Dance—Susan Cambigue-Tracey
    Music—Rosemarie Cook-Glover
    Theatre—Barbara Leonard

STUDIO LESSON CONSULTANTS

The authors wish to express their gratitude to the following art teachers who participated in field testing the Studio Lessons with their students.

Debra Belvin
Bearden Middle School
Knoxville, TN

Jeff Bender
Park Plaza Middle School
Evansville, IN

Ashley S. Benkwith
McAdory High School
McCalla, AL

Barbara Bugg
Westport Middle School
Louisville, KY

Gail F. Enkey
Chiaravalle Montessori School
Evanston, IL

Miranda Grubisich
Weber Middle School
Port Washington, NY

Stacey Hendrickson
Gates Intermediate School
Scituate, MA

Joy Jones
Chisholm Trail Middle School
Round Rock, TX

Natalie Jones
Oak Hill Middle School
Evansville, IN

Cathy J. Kiser
Jesse Stuart Middle School
Louisville, KY

Audrey Komroy
Akron Central School
Akron, NY

Pamela Layman
Bardstown Middle School
Bardstown, KY

Charles L. Osten
Whittle Springs Middle School
Knoxville, KY

Catherine K. Pate
Sneed Middle School
Florence, SC

Barbara A. Perez
St. Athanasias Grammar School
Evanston, IL

Irene Wettermark Porter
Hayes Middle School
Birmingham, AL

Margaret Powers
McAdory Elementary School
McCalla, AL

Mary Rokitka
Medina High School
Medina, NY

Gloria Santilli
Winman Junior High School
Warwick, RI

Faye Scannell
Cherry Crest Elementary
Bellevue, WA

Beverly N. Silletto
Southern Middle School
Louisville, KY

Lisa Solomon
Medina High School
Medina, NY

Sylvia L. Thompson
Cammack Middle School
Huntington, WV

Curtis R. Uebelhor
Perry Heights Middle School
Evansville, IN

TABLE OF CONTENTS ILLUSTRATION CREDITS

Lisa Pomerantz/Deborah Wolfe, Ltd.

STUDENT CONTRIBUTORS

The following students contributed exemplary work for the Studio Lesson pages:

Fig. 1–13, Dustin Keaton, Bardstown Middle School, Bardstown, KY; Fig. 1–19, Keyanda Brown, Bardstown Middle School, Bardstown, KY; Fig. 2–5, David Burkes, Plaza Park Middle School, Evansville, IN; Figure 2–13, Crystal Latham, McAdory Middle School, McCalla, AL; Fig. 3–7, Jack Nondorf, St. Athanasius School, Evanston, IL; Fig. 3–11. Cathleen Cramer, St. Athanasius School, Evanston, IL; Fig. 3–17, Nancy Gardner, Whittle Springs Middle School, Knoxville, TN; Fig. 4–9, Kathryn Ross, Cammack Middle School, Huntington, WV; Fig. 4–11, Mandy Grisham, Plaza Park Middle School, Evansville, IN; Fig. 4–13, Florian Kimpel, Plaza Park Middle School, Evansville, IN; Fig. 4–13, Jing Liu, Plaza Park Middle School, Evansville, IN; Fig. 5–6, Kate Morrison, St. Athanasius School, Evanston, IL; Fig. 5–10, Katie Harr, St. Athanasius School, Evanston, IL; Fig. 5–16, Andrew Zangerle, Medina High School, Medina, NY; Fig. 5–16, Jason A. Weeks, Medina High School, Medina, NY; Fig. 5–20, Caitlin Bradley, Oak Hill Middle School, Evansville, IN; Fig. 6–5, Emilia Hofmeister, St. Athanasius School, Evanston, IL; Fig. 6–9, Abby Taylor, St. Athanasius School, Evanston, IL; Fig. 6–13, Katie Miskel, Gates Intermediate School, Scituate, MA; Fig. 6–17, Kate Feeney, Cherry Crest Elementary, Bellevue, WA; Fig. 7–5, Caitlyn Lillo, Chisholm Trail Middle School, Round Rock, TX; Fig. 7–9, Deborah Laranjeira, Chisholm Trail Middle School, Round Rock, TX; Fig. 7–13, Alex Dorsey, Southern Middle School, Louisville, KY; Fig. 7–17, Brandie Rawlinson, Perry Heights Middle School, Evansville, IN; Fig. 7–17, Darrell Ray Morris, Perry Heights Middle School, Evansville, IN; Fig. 8–5, Jennifer Sturgill, Jesse Stuart Middle School, Louisville, KY; Fig. 8–9, LaToya Jackson, Southern Middle School, Louisville, KY; Fig. 8–13, Jimmy Crouch, Jesse Stuart Middle School, Louisville, KY; Fig. 8–17, Paul Bolling, Southern Middle School, Louisville, KY; Fig. 9–5, Bradley Camp, Westport Middle School, Louisville, KY; Fig. 9–10, Lorin Wilkie, Perry Heights Middle School, Evansville, IN; Fig. 9–14, Ai-ling Chang, Westport Middle School, Louisville, KY; Fig. 9-18, Rie Fujii, Bearden Middle School, Knoxville, TN; Fig. 10–5, Lisa Marie Rivera, Bearden Middle School, Knoxville, TN; Fig. 10–9, Susan Peng, Cammack Middle School, Huntington, WV; Fig. 10–13, Ashley Revell, Sneed Middle School, Florence, SC; Fig. 10–17, Stephen Schleh, Cherry Crest Elementary, Bellevue, WA; Fig. 11–5, Michael Kennedy, McAdory Middle School, McCalla, AL; Fig. 11–9, Joshua R. Reynolds, Whittle Springs Middle School, Knoxville, TN; Fig. 11–13, Nicholas Dutton, McAdory Elementary, McCalla, AL; Fig. 11–16, J. T. Helms, Sneed Middle School, Florence, SC; Fig. 12–5, LaToya Jackson, Southern Middle School, Louisville, KY; Fig. 12–8, Laura Jeanne Post, Chiaravalle Montessori School, Evanston, IL; Fig. 12–13, 9th grade art students, Beacon School, Port Washington, NY; Fig. 12–17, Matt Carlisle, Whittle Springs Middle School, Knoxville, TN; Fig. 13–5, Jessica Abbs, Keena Burgess, Ericka Chadsey, Sarah Chaffee, Lauren Cierniak, Danelle Edwards, Steven Frey (Director), Bill Gibson, Dawn Graham, Andrea Halbach, Iwona Klapa, Annette Koszuta, Rochelle Leiker, Sarah Linneman, Christina Lucciano, Susan Morris, Nickole von Ohlen, Jennifer Ormsby, Jamie Palfi, Scottie Rovito, Andrea Sagerman, Melissa Stone, Laurie Summers, Katie Tordy, Beth Tripi, Lauren Whelan, Fallan Winter, Akron Central School, Akron, NY; Fig. 13–9, Tina Sheppard, Hayes Middle School, Birmingham, AL; Fig. 13–13, Julia Bess Good, Chiaravalle Montessori School, Evanston, IL; Fig. 13–17, Dante Rhodes, Hayes Middle School, Birmingham, AL; Fig. 14–5, Brandie Rawlinson, Perry Heights Middle School, Evansville, IN; Fig. 14–9, Paul Goderis, St. Athanasius School, Evanston, IL; Fig. 14–13, Brittney Sohn, Whittle Springs Middle School, Knoxville, TN; Fig. S–1, Sarah Rosenfeld, Cherry Crest Elementary, Bellevue, WA; Fig. S–2, Sean Kebely, Clay Cuttitte, Kyle Kashiwagi, Matt Colville, Ryan Anderson, Lauren Marrs, Jessie Allen, Andrea Wilkerson, Sarah Rosenfeld, Cherry Crest Elementary, Bellevue, WA; page 278, Lindsay Dillon, Medina Elementary, Bellevue, WA.

CONTENTS

Credit line on page 48.

Credit line on page 76.

Credit line on page 138.

Credit line on page 153.

Credit line on page 254.

Credit line on page 228.

Figure 1–1 Notice the colors, lines, and shapes the artist used to create these figures. What has she done to make them come alive as dancers?

Miriam Schapiro. *Pas de Deux*. 1986. Acrylic & fabric on canvas. 228.6 × 243.8 cm (90 × 96″). © Miriam Schapiro. Private collection. Courtesy Steinbaum Krauss Gallery, New York, New York.

CHAPTER 1

The Elements of Art

Most people look at a blank surface and see nothing. The artist looks at the same surface and sees an exciting challenge. This is the challenge to create.

Study the painting at the left. Here are some questions the artist asked herself as she created the work: What colors and shapes will I use? How will those colors and shapes be arranged? Is my goal to suggest a feeling or to capture a lifelike image?

In this book, you will learn more about these and other questions artists ask themselves. You will also learn how you can use these questions yourself to better understand art.

OBJECTIVES

After completing this chapter, you will be able to:

- Name and describe the elements of art.
- Describe the different types of line.
- Identify the properties of color.
- Experiment with various elements to understand their role in making art.

WORDS YOU WILL LEARN

artist
color
elements of art
form
hue
intensity
line
line quality
negative space
portfolio
shape
space
still life
texture
value

PORTFOLIO IDEAS

You may be asked to keep your art projects in a portfolio. A **portfolio** is *a carefully selected collection of artwork kept by students and professional artists.* Keeping a portfolio will give you the opportunity to

- hold your artwork in one place and in good condition.
- show that you can apply art concepts, techniques, and skills.
- demonstrate your growth as an artist.

The Language of Art

Have you ever heard a person described as "wearing many hats"? Saying a person wears many hats means he or she is good at a number of things. An **artist**—*a person who uses imagination and skill to communicate ideas in visual form*—wears many hats. Among the hats artists wear is one labeled "scientist." Wearing this hat, artists experiment with the effects of light on objects. Wearing the mathematician's hat, they carefully measure distances between objects. Wearing the hat of writer, they tell stories and record events.

In this book, you will learn about the different ways in which artists have used these skills over the centuries. You will also meet specific artists and learn about their creations.

THE ARTIST'S LANGUAGE

Like other professionals, artists "speak" a language all their own. Just as the mathematician uses numbers, so the artist uses *line*.

Much in the way musicians communicate through notes and sounds, artists speak in *color* and *shape*. The writer relies on words, sentences, and paragraphs, the artist on *form*, *space*, and *texture*.

These six terms—line, color, shape, form, space, and texture—make up the artist's vocabulary. The terms are grouped together under the heading **elements of art.** These are *the basic visual symbols an artist uses to create works of art.* An artist's success depends on how well he or she uses these elements.

Using the Artist's Vocabulary

When you look at an artwork, it is not always clear where one element ends and another begins. Study the artworks in Figures 1–2 and 1–3. You do not see the elements of form and color in the first or the element of line in the second. Instead, you see the works as a whole. As you examine each, your eye

Figure 1–2 **Does the artist use a single color to show an object? Do the objects look real? What does this artwork "say" to you?**

Paul Cézanne. *The Basket of Apples*. c. 1895. Oil on canvas. 65.5 cm × 81.3 cm (25¾ × 32"). Art Institute of Chicago, Chicago, Illinois. Helen Birch Bartlett Memorial Collection.

"reads" all the elements together. In fact, it is the careful blending of elements that allows you to see an artwork as the artist meant it to be seen. Taken together, the elements in Figure 1–2 "add up" to a basket of apples and a bottle. The lines in Figure 1–3 cleverly suggest a familiar farm animal. Can you identify it?

"Reading" the Artist's Vocabulary

Think back to when you first learned to read. You did not start with a book. Rather, you began by reading a word at a time. This is how you will learn the vocabulary of art. You will learn about the elements of art one at a time.

Each of the remaining lessons in this chapter treats one or more elements. In later chapters, you will learn about other terms that are central to the practice and study of art.

Check Your Understanding

1. Define *artist*.
2. Name the six elements of art.

STUDIO ACTIVITY

Making a Viewer

To learn how a clock works, you might take it apart and study the pieces. The same is true of a work of art. By studying the elements, or "pieces," you learn what makes the work "tick." One tool that can help you sharpen your awareness of the elements of art is a viewfinder. You can easily make a viewfinder by following the directions in Technique Tip 8 on page 283. Make a viewfinder and use it to focus on familiar objects in your community, such as a tree or a building. Keep a sketchbook in which you record your findings. As you learn more about the elements of art later in this chapter, return to these drawings.

PORTFOLIO

Select your best sketch, and date and sign it. Write a short evaluation on the back of the sketch and put it in your portfolio.

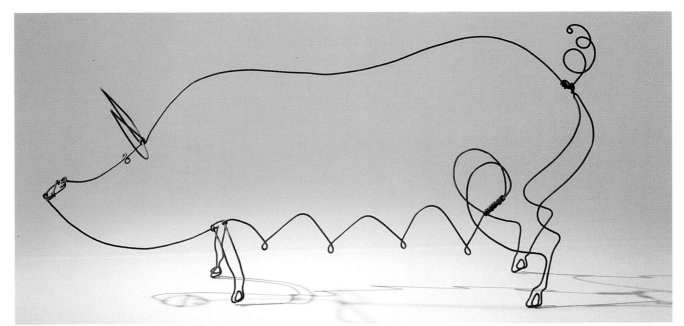

Figure 1–3 **What are some of the questions you think the artist asked himself while he was creating this work?**

Alexander Calder. *Sow*. 1928. Wire. 19.5 × 43.2 × 7.6 cm (7⅔ × 17 × 3"). The Museum of Modern Art, New York, New York. Gift of the artist. © 1997 Artists Rights Society (ARS), New York/ADAGP, Paris

Line

It might be said that all art begins with a line. You see lines everywhere in your daily life. As you ride in a car along a highway, the edges of the road straight ahead of you form two lines that meet in the distance. The edge of each wall of your classroom is a line. So are the curves that make up the letter *s*.

To the artist, a **line** is *the path of a dot through space.* In this lesson, you will learn about different kinds of lines. You will see how these lines can be used to suggest specific feelings and ideas.

KINDS OF LINE

By definition, every line goes somewhere. A line may "travel" up, down, or across. It may move at an angle, or it may curve back on itself. Each type of line carries a different message to the viewer.

There are five main kinds of line. These include:

Horizontal

Horizontal lines run from side to side. Lines of this type seem to be at rest. They may suggest peace and quiet. Think of the line of a calm lake where the water meets the sky (Figure 1–4).

Figure 1–4   **Horizontal line.**

Vertical

Vertical lines run up and down. They never lean. Lines of this type seem to be standing at attention. Artists use vertical lines to show strength and permanence. Picture the soaring lines of a skyscraper (Figure 1–5).

Figure 1–5   **Vertical line.**

Diagonal

Diagonal lines are straight lines that slant. Lines of this type suggest a sense of movement and excitement. They seem to be rising or falling. Diagonal lines are used to give a sense of movement.

Curved

Curved lines are lines that change direction little by little. Wiggly lines are made up of two or more curves. Spirals and circles also begin with curved lines. Like diagonals, curved lines express movement, but in a more graceful way.

Figure 1–6   **Curved line.**

Zigzag

Zigzag lines are formed by joining together several diagonals that move in different directions. The diagonals form sharp angles that make lines change direction suddenly. Zigzag lines create confusion. They suggest action or nervous excitement (Figure 1–7).

Figure 1–7   Zigzag line.

LINE QUALITY

Think about the crease in a pair of freshly ironed trousers. Would you describe this "line" as smooth or rough? How about a line made with chalk? Smoothness, roughness, thickness, and thinness each represent a different **line quality.** This quality is *the unique character of any line.*

How a line appears depends on several factors. These include:

- *The tool used.* A crayon produces a slightly ragged line. A paintbrush dipped in ink produces a line that narrows and trails off.
- *The pressure of the artist's hand.* Pressing down on a tool creates a thicker line.

Using less pressure creates a thinner line. How would you describe the quality of the lines in Figure 1-8? Are the lines smooth or rough? Are they thick or thin?

✔ Check Your Understanding

1. Name the five directions a line can take.
2. Tell how each of the line types can make a viewer feel or react.
3. What is line quality?

Figure 1–8   **How many different kinds of lines has the artist used? Describe the quality of these lines.**

Vincent van Gogh. *Corner of a Park at Arles (Tree in a Meadow).* 1889. Reed pen and black ink over charcoal. 49.3 × 61.3 cm (19⅜ × 24"). Art Institute of Chicago, Chicago, Illinois. Gift of Tiffany and Margaret Blake, 1945.3

LESSON 3

Color

Imagine a world without color. Like lines, color surrounds us. It is in the reds and purples of the sky at sunset. It is in the lush green of a well-tended lawn. Our moods even have "color." We describe someone who is angry as "seeing red." A happy, carefree person is said to be "in the pink."

In this lesson, you will learn about the way color is used in art. In the next lesson, you will practice using color yourself.

PROPERTIES OF COLOR

Have you ever tried to find a pair of matching socks on a dark winter morning? It is not easy. Without light, all colors look the same. Scientists and artists have long understood this. Both know that **color** is *what the eye sees when light is reflected off an object.*

Some artists use color boldly. Others use it softly. To get these results, artists need to understand the three main properties of color. These are hue, value, and intensity.

Hue

Hue is *a color's name.* Orange, green, and violet are all hues. The relationship among hues is shown in the color wheel in Figure 1–9. Three of the hues in the wheel—red, yellow, and blue—are known as the primary, or pure, hues. *Primary* means "first." They are called

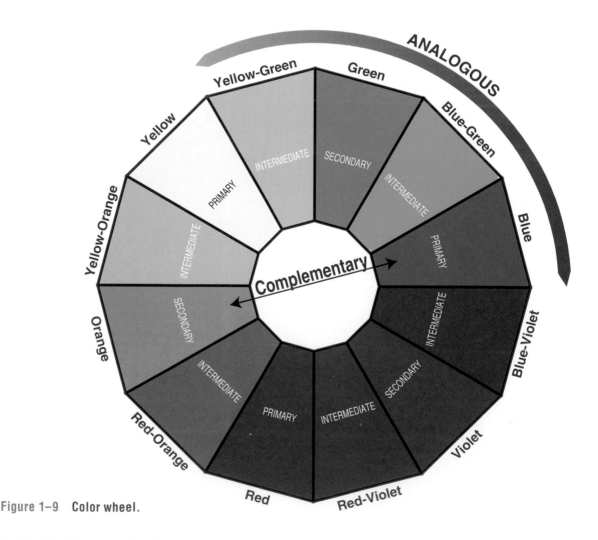

Figure 1–9   **Color wheel.**

Figure 1–10   What color questions do you think the artist asked herself? How did she portray the figures in this painting?

Helen Hardin. *Robed Journey of the Rainbow Clan.* 1976. Acrylic. 47 × 76.2 cm (18½ × 30″).
© 1996 Helen Hardin, © 1999 Cradoc Bagshaw.

this because these three are mixed to create all the other hues. Mixing the two primary colors of yellow and blue gives green, a *secondary* color. Mixing a primary color like red with a secondary color like orange gives red-orange, an *intermediate* color. Look at the painting in Figure 1–10. The artist has overlapped hues to capture all the colors of the rainbow. Match the hues in the painting with those on the color wheel. Has the artist used any primary hues? Which secondary hues has she used? Which intermediate hues has she used?

Value

A second property of color, **value,** is *the lightness or darkness of a hue.* You can change a hue's value by mixing in white or black. When white is added to a hue, the resulting color is said to be a *tint.* When black is added, the result is called a *shade.* Pink is a tint of red. Maroon is a dark shade of red. These and other values of red appear in the "value scale" in Figure 1–11a.

SHADE

TINT

Figure 1–11a   Value scale.

HIGH INTENSITY   LOW INTENSITY

Figure 1–11b   Intensity scale.

Intensity

Some colors appear lively and brilliant. Others look murky or dull. The difference is called the color's **intensity.** This is the *brightness or dullness of a hue.* A strong, bright hue is said to be "high-intensity." Pure green is such a hue. A faint, dull hue is said to be "low-intensity." Olive green is a hue that fits this description. The intensity scale in Figure 1–11b shows some intensities of green.

One way of lowering a hue's intensity is by mixing it with its *complementary,* or opposite, hue on the color wheel. Look once again at the color wheel on page **8.** Find the hues at either end of the double-headed arrow. If you mix these hues, you get a neutral color such as gray or brown. The same is true if you mix any other complementary hues.

COMBINING COLORS

You may have heard the term *loud* used to describe outfits of clothing. The term also refers to a combination of colors that clash. Art, like clothing, makes use of color combinations, or *schemes.* Different color schemes give different effects. Some color schemes are quiet. Others are exciting.

The following are some common color schemes used by trained artists:

Monochromatic

A monochromatic (**mah**-noh-kroh-**mat**-ik) color scheme uses different tints or shades of a single hue. Such a combination can help bring together the parts of a work.

Monochromatic color schemes must be used with caution, however, because they can produce a dull, uninteresting effect. See an example of a monochromatic color scheme in Figure 1–11c.

Analogous

An analogous (uh-**nal**-uh-gus) color scheme uses hues that are side by side on the color wheel and share a hue. (See Figure 1–11d.) Analogous color schemes relate objects in a work. Look at the color wheel shown in Figure 1–9 on page **8** and find the colors analogous to yellow. What hues would be included in an analogous color scheme based on red?

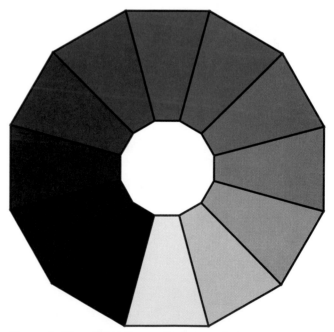

Figure 1–11c   Monochromatic color scheme.

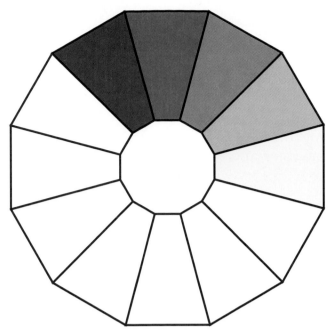

Figure 1–11d Analogous color scheme.

Complementary

As its name suggests, the complementary color scheme (Figure 1–11e) uses opposite hues on the color wheel. It makes for the most striking color combinations. As with monochromatic colors, care must be taken when combining complementary colors. Placing high-intensity complementary colors close together in an artwork can create an unusual flickering effect.

STUDIO ACTIVITY

Experimenting with Color Combinations

Gather sheets of colored cellophane. Cut circles or other shapes from each sheet. Experiment with different color combinations by overlapping the shapes in a clear plastic folder. Secure the edges of the folder. Then hold it up to the light. In your sketchbook, note combinations that are especially pleasing to your eye. Repeat the experiment, this time overlapping more colors. Try more than one layer of a single color to deepen it. Last, try making combinations of *warm colors*—red, yellow, and orange—and of *cool colors*—blue, green, and violet. Think about scenes in which you might be likely to use a warm color scheme. How might you use a cool color scheme?

P O R T F O L I O

On a separate piece of paper, list the color combinations that made your favorite warm color and your favorite cool color. Put this paper in your portfolio for use in an upcoming project.

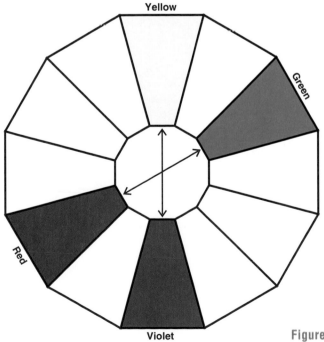

Figure 1–11e Complementary color schemes.

✔ Check Your Understanding

1. Define the term *hue.*
2. What are the three properties of color?
3. Where do you find complementary colors on the color wheel?

Mixing Colors

Artists look at the world around them and see far more than a blue sky and green grass. Claude Monet was called an *Impressionist* painter because he looked at the landscape at different times of day and saw every color of the rainbow. At dawn he found purples, pinks, and blues in the farmer's wheat stacks. At noon these stacks appeared to be blazing oranges and yellows. He painted "impressions" of the wheat stack in Figure 1–12 by laying strokes of many colors on his canvas. As we look at his paintings, our eyes "mix" the strokes of color together. Look for the brush strokes in the haystack and elsewhere.

WHAT YOU WILL LEARN

You will discover colors by mixing tempera paints. You will use two *primary* colors and white. Each time you add a stroke of one of these colors and blend it on your paper, you can make a new color. When you have filled your paper, you will have a rich painting. Try to mix as many variations of your two colors as possible.

Figure 1–12 **What kind of color scheme has the artist used in this painting? How would you describe the intensity of the colors?**

Claude Monet. *Stack of Wheat.* 1891. Oil on canvas. 65.6 × 92 cm (25¾ × 36"). Art Institute of Chicago, Chicago, Illinois. Restricted gift of the Searle Family Trust; Major Acquisitions Centennial Endowment; through prior acquisitions of the Mr. and Mrs. Martin A. Ryerson and Potter Palmer Collections; through prior bequest of Jerome Friedman, 1983.29

WHAT YOU WILL NEED

- White drawing paper, 9 x 12 inches (23 x 30 cm)
- Tempera paints—two primary colors and white
- Wash or bristle brush
- Cup of water, paper towels

WHAT YOU WILL DO

1. On a plastic plate, take spoonfuls of two primary colors and white tempera paint. Your teacher will divide the class into three groups and give red and yellow to one, red and blue to another, and yellow and blue to the third.
2. Wet your brush, squeeze the water out of it with your fingers, and dip it into one primary color. Paint an area on your paper. Rinse your brush and dry it with the towel before you start using a new color.
3. Dip into the second primary and begin blending the two colors on your paper until you get the *secondary color*—green or orange or purple.
4. Continue adding more of each primary color as you fill your paper, trying to make new colors each time. Blend the colors into each other.
5. When you have mixed many new colors, begin adding white to all of your colors to get *tints*.

EXAMINING YOUR WORK

- **Describe** Point out on your painting the secondary color you mixed and the many variations you blended. Locate the tints you made by mixing white with your colors.
- **Analyze** Discuss the experience of discovering new colors. What happened when you blended the colors longer with your brush?

Figure 1–13 **Student works. Mixing primary colors.**

STUDIO OPTIONS

Try This!

■ Add the third primary to your palette and mix the three colors right on the palette. You will find that you get a neutral brown. Do another painting in all neutral tones, adding more of each of your colors as you paint. You have now changed the *intensity* of your colors.

■ Make a class color wheel by arranging groups of paintings on a bulletin board. One painting from each group will give you all the colors of the color wheel. Put a neutral painting in the center.

Shape, Form, and Space

Here is a riddle. What do *you*, a stop sign, and a rubber ball have in common? You all exist in—and are set off by—space. This is true of all objects. Some objects are recognizable because of their shape or form alone. Even without seeing the letters or red color, you could identify a stop sign. You would recognize its octagonal shape. Even in the dark, you could identify a rubber ball. You would feel its round form.

Shape, form, and space are closely related. In this lesson, you will learn about these elements and their special place in art.

SHAPE

To an artist, a **shape** is *an area clearly set off by one or more of the other five visual elements of art*. Shapes exist in two dimensions. They have length and width but not depth. Shapes are flat.

All shapes are one of two types:

- **Geometric Shapes.** Geometric shapes are precise, mathematical shapes. They look as though they were made with a ruler, compass, or other special tool. The square, circle, and triangle are among the most common geometric shapes. The rectangle and oval are others. Geometric shapes are mostly, though not always, made by people. Examine the painting in Figure 1–14. Which geometric shapes has the artist used? How many of each of these shapes can you find in the work?
- **Free-form** or **Organic Shapes.** Free-form shapes are not regular or even. Such shapes are found throughout nature.

Figure 1–14   The title of this work mentions a free-form shape from music. Can you find this shape?

Roy Lichtenstein. *Modern Painting with Clef.* 1967. Oil and synthetic polymer and pencil on canvas. 252.4 × 458.2 (100⅛ × 180⅜"). Hirschhorn Museum and Sculpture Garden, Smithsonian Institution, Washington, D.C. Gift of Joseph H. Hirshhorn, 1972.

The outline of a lake is a free-form shape. So is the outline of your hand. The artwork in Figure 1–3 on page **5** is made up of a number of free-form shapes. How many different shapes can you find?

FORM

Like shapes, forms have height and width. Unlike shapes, they also have a third dimension: depth. **Form** is *an element of art that refers to an object with three dimensions.* When you hold a book in your hand, you are experiencing its form in three dimensions: height, width, and depth.

Forms are grouped as geometric or free-form, much as shapes are. An aluminum can is an example of the geometric form called *cylinder.* Rocks and clouds, by contrast, are free-form. So is the stack of wheat in Figure 1–12 on page **12.**

In art, a close relationship exists between shapes and forms. A two-dimensional circle and three-dimensional sphere have the same round outline. A two-dimensional square can be "stretched" into a third dimension to become a cube. These and other shape-form relations are shown in Figure 1–15.

SPACE

All objects take up space. **Space** is *the distance or area between, around, above, below, and within things.* Space is empty until shapes or forms fill it.

In some works of art, space is real. In others, it is only suggested. Compare the artworks in Figures 1–16 and 1–17 on pages **16–17.** The first is an example of sculpture. It exists in three dimensions. If you were viewing this work in person, you could walk around it. You could enter its space and appreciate its form.

The second work of art is a painting. The scene looks very realistic and lifelike. If you tried to move forward into it, however, you would bump into a flat surface.

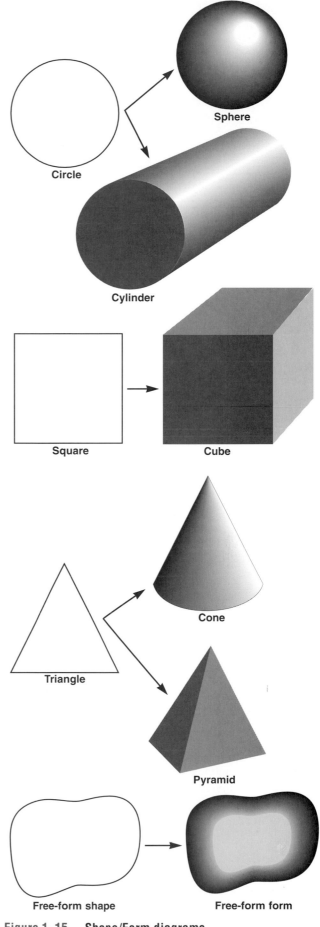

Circle → Sphere

Cylinder

Square → Cube

Triangle → Cone

Pyramid

Free-form shape → Free-form form

Figure 1–15   Shape/Form diagrams.

Space Techniques in Two-Dimensional Art

The artist who painted the street scene in Figure 1–17 used several techniques to capture the feeling of deep space. Artists have developed a number of such techniques. These include the following:

- **Linear perspective.** The lines of buildings, roads, and similar objects are slanted. This makes them appear to come together or meet in the distance.
- **Size.** Distant objects are made smaller than objects that are close up.
- **Overlapping.** Nearer shapes and forms overlap, or partly cover, those meant to appear farther away.
- **Placement.** Distant objects are placed higher up in the picture. Closer ones are placed lower down.

- **Intensity and Value.** The colors of objects meant to appear in the distance are lower in intensity than objects meant to appear nearer. They are also lighter in value.
- **Detail.** More detail is added to closer objects and less detail is added to those in the distance.

Which of these techniques was used in Figure 1–17? What other steps has the artist taken to make forms seem to stand out in space?

Negative Space

When it comes to the element of space, there is one question every artist must answer. That is the question of how much negative space to build into a work. **Negative space** is the *empty spaces between the shapes or forms in two- and three-dimensional art.*

Figure 1–16 **What makes this work a form rather than a shape? Has the artist used real or suggested space?**

Henry Moore. *Reclining Figure.* 1939. Elmwood. 94 × 200.7 × 76.2 cm (37 × 79 × 30"). Detroit Institute of the Arts, Detroit, Michigan. Founders Society Purchase with funds from the Dexter M. Ferry, Jr. Trustee Corporation.

How the artist answers the question about negative space will affect the viewer's reaction to the work. Look back at the artwork in Figure 1–3 on page **5**. There is far more negative space than form to this work. The abundance of negative space gives it a light, airy feel. Contrast this with the negative space in Figure 1–16. This sculpture seems heavier and more compact because there is less negative space.

Little negative space in a painting or drawing makes the work look busy. A lot of negative space can express calm, peace, or even loneliness.

✔ Check Your Understanding

1. What is shape?
2. Define *form.* What forms are closely related to the circle?
3. Identify and describe at least three techniques artists use to suggest space in two-dimensional art.

STUDIO ACTIVITY

Sketching a Still Life

Look back at the painting of apples in Figure 1–2 on page **4**. This work is an example of a type of art called *still life.* A **still life** is *a painting or drawing of non-living objects.* What nonliving objects besides fruit did the artist choose for this still life? What techniques did he use to achieve a sense of space?

Plan a still life of your own by gathering several familiar objects. Use books, pencils, and other materials found in the classroom. Arrange these on a table. Study the arrangement from different angles. Make pencil sketches from several different views. Be sure to use techniques such as overlapping to capture a feeling of space.

P O R T F O L I O

Save your best sketch for Lesson 6. Put it in your portfolio.

Figure 1–17 What techniques has the artist used to give a feeling of space?

Richard Estes. *Paris Street Scene.* 1972. Oil on canvas. 101.6 × 152.4 cm (40 × 60″). Virginia Museum of Fine Art, Richmond, Virginia. Gift of Sydney and Frances Lewis. © 1998 Richard Estes/Licensed by VAGA, New York, NY/Courtesy Marlborough Gallery, NY

LESSON 6

Drawing a Still Life

Ordinary objects can become exciting shapes and forms when an artist sees them. Janet Fish arranged these glasses in front of a window and painted *Spring Evening* (Figure 1–18). Look at all the colors and shapes she found in the reflections. Notice how she used lines, colors, shapes, forms, and space to provide realism.

WHAT YOU WILL LEARN

Select the best of the still-life sketches you did in Lesson 5. Do an oil pastel drawing of it. You will use the space techniques you learned in Lesson 5 as you draw the objects and choose oil pastel colors. Look back at page **12** and study the way Claude Monet mixed colors in his painting *Stack of Wheat.*

Figure 1–18 **Notice how the artist has overlapped the objects in this still life to show distance. Which objects are farthest from the viewer?**

Janet Fish. *Spring Evening.* 1977. Oil on canvas. 111.8 × 162.6 cm (44 × 64"). Rose Art Museum, Brandeis University, Waltham, Massachusetts. Herbert W. Plimpton Collection.

WHAT YOU WILL NEED

- Pencil, sketch paper, eraser
- White or colored drawing paper, 12 x 18 inches (30 x 46 cm)
- Oil pastels

WHAT YOU WILL DO

1. Study your sketches and choose the one you like best. Notice that drawings from different angles will show different arrangements of the same objects.
2. On your drawing paper, draw the objects lightly with pencil.
3. Begin applying colors lightly with the oil pastels, building up color as you go. Look for reflections, shadows, and changes in color on your objects.

EXAMINING YOUR WORK

- **Describe**   Point out the ways in which you used size, overlapping, and placement in your drawing. Show the way you used intensity and value in coloring your objects in the foreground and background.
- **Explain**   Tell what effect you were trying to create as you chose which colors to use. How did you use color to set off the objects in the foreground?

4. Choose background colors that will set off the objects in the foreground.
5. Fill the entire surface of your paper with color.

Figure 1–19   **Student work. A still life.**

STUDIO OPTION

■ Look down a street in your neighborhood or outside your school. Can you see the street appear to narrow in the distance as it does in *Paris Street Scene*,

Figure 1–17 on page **17**? Do a sketch of the street. Notice that the buildings in the distance seem smaller. Try closing one eye to see the narrowing lines of the street.

Texture

His beard was *rough as sandpaper.* The lake was smooth as glass. You have probably read and maybe even written descriptions like these. The descriptions are effective because they bring to mind the sense of touch. They remind us of familiar textures. As an art element, **texture** is *how things feel, or look as though they might feel if touched.*

Like space, texture in art can be *tactile,* texture that can be touched, or *visual.* In this lesson, you will learn about the double role of texture as an element.

TEXTURE

Imagine the smoothness of mashed potatoes, the brittleness of a wheat cracker. Our sense of touch is always alert to the things around us. It helps us identify them and enjoy their feel. It also helps us avoid unpleasant touch sensations. Such an unpleasant sensation is suggested by the sentence that opens this lesson.

Artists take advantage of our experience with textures to enrich their works. How an artist uses texture depends on whether he or she is working in two or three dimensions.

Tactile Texture

Sculptors, you may recall, work in real space. They also work in real texture. Refer back to the sculpture in Figure 1–16, page **16.** How do you think this work would feel to the touch? Contrast that sensation to the one you might get touching the work in Figure 1–20. This sculpture of a horse is life-size. It is made of mud and tree branches. What words would you use to describe its texture? What do you think it would be like to ride this horse?

Sometimes artists use texture to capture visual designs in three dimensions. The sculpture in Figure 1–21 is such a work. Have you ever touched a raised design in fabric? Do you think the "clothing" worn by this guardian would feel smooth or rough to the touch?

Visual Texture

Artists are aware that we experience texture not only through our sense of touch, but also through our sense of *vision.* Look back at the painting in Figure 1–18 on page **18.** The glassware has been painted in a very lifelike fashion. Each facet, or cut design in the glass,

Figure 1–20 Would you expect to see a horse that looks like this one? What materials has the artist used for texture?

Deborah Butterfield. *Horse.* 1977. Mud and sticks. Life-size. Zolla/Lieberman Gallery, Chicago, Illinois.

looks real enough to touch. Yet, a viewer touching the surface would feel no such facets. The surface instead would feel flat. It would also feel slightly grainy rather than smooth. This is because the work was done on canvas, a coarse material.

This painting makes use of *visual texture.* We "feel" the texture with our eyes. Look back at the realistic street scene in Figure 1–17 on page **17.** How many different textures has the artist recorded? Which of these would feel smooth?

Figure 1–21   Describe the use of color and texture in this work. Notice the work's title and size. Why might the artist have made the sculpture so large?

Thailand. *Guardian Figure.*

STUDIO ACTIVITY

Making Rubbings for Texture

Explore your classroom and the school grounds for objects with uneven, hard textures. These might include coarse stones and grainy wood. Gather several different surfaces. Place a sheet of drawing paper over each. If possible, secure the paper with masking tape. Using the side of an unwrapped crayon, do a rubbing of each surface. Press down just hard enough to capture the texture.

Use the best of your rubbings as the basis for a still life. Refer to the sketch you did in Lesson 6. For this still life, however, cut the shape of each object from one of your rubbings. Try several arrangements of visual textures before you glue the pieces in place. Decide whether you need areas of solid color. If so, add these.

P O R T F O L I O

Compare this still life with the sketch you did for Lesson 6. Write a paragraph telling whether you were successful in using your previous sketch as a basis for this Studio Activity. Put this paragraph in your portfolio with the still life.

✔ Check Your Understanding

1. What is texture?
2. Which of our senses experience texture?
3. What are the two kinds of texture used in art?

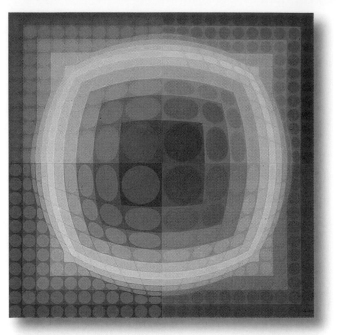

Victor Vasarely. *Paz-Ket*. 1969. Oil on canvas. No measurement available. Museo de Bellas Artes, Bilbao/Bridgeman Art Library. © 1997 Artists Rights Society (ARS), New York, NY

How Does the Eye Perceive Color?

Have you ever told a friend, "I like that blue sweater" only to find that your friend thought the sweater was green? Why did you and your friend see two different colors?

The way you perceive color depends on the way your brain responds to the signals from your eyes. When your eyes focus on an object, such as an orange basketball, you are actually seeing the light reflected from the ball. When light enters the eye, it lands on the retina. The retina contains rods and cones, which are cells that detect light. The rods allow you to see at night, and the cones sense color.

Light travels as electromagnetic waves. Each color in the spectrum is part of a range of wavelengths. The term *blue*, for example, refers to a series of colors. Your friend's sweater may not have been blue or green. Instead, it may have been turquoise or aquamarine, which are in the range of colors between blue and green.

Color is one of the six elements of art. Victor Vasarely used color as an important element in *Paz-Ket*. The placement of the dots in the work affects the way our eyes perceive the colors.

MAKING THE CONNECTION

✔ Besides color, what other elements of art did Vasarely use in this work?

✔ What is the purpose of rods and cones in the eye? In what part of the eye are they located?

✔ Learn more about the eye. Draw a picture of an eye and label its parts.

INTERNET ACTIVITY

Visit Glencoe's Fine Arts Web Site for students at:

http://www.glencoe.com/sec/art/students

◆ BUILDING VOCABULARY

Number a sheet of paper from 1 to 10. After each number, write the term from the box that matches each description below.

color	shape
elements of art	space
form	still life
line	texture
negative space	value

1. The path of a dot through space. *line*
2. A painting or drawing of nonliving objects. *still life*
3. The basic visual symbols an artist uses to create works of art. *elements of art*
4. An area clearly set off by one or more of the other five visual elements of art. *shape*
5. The lightness or darkness of a hue. *value*
6. The distance or area between, around, above, below, and within things. *space*
7. An element of art that refers to an object with three dimensions. *form*
8. Empty spaces between the shapes or forms in two- and three-dimensional art. *neg space*
9. What the eye sees when light is reflected off an object. *color*
10. How things feel, or look as though they might feel if touched. *texture*

◆ REVIEWING ART FACTS

Number a sheet of paper from 11 to 15. Answer each question in a complete sentence.

11. What emotion or feeling is suggested by horizontal lines? What feeling do diagonal lines communicate to the viewer? *calm* *movement excitement*
12. What is the relationship between primary and secondary colors?
13. Under what circumstances might an artist choose to use complementary colors in a work? *bold thickness* *2 dimension 3 dimension*
14. In what ways are shape and form alike? In what ways are they different?
15. Name and explain three techniques artists use to achieve a feeling of deep space. *distant objms. overlap distant less detail before on page*

💡 THINKING ABOUT ART

On a sheet of paper, answer each question in a sentence or two.

1. **Analyze.** Imagine that you were asked to design the cover for a book about a basketball legend. What kind of color scheme would you choose for the cover? What kind of lines would you use for the illustration? Explain your choices.

2. **Interpret.** In this chapter, you learned about techniques for giving depth to forms in works of art. Yet, some artists— cartoonists, for example—purposely do not work at achieving depth. Why do you think this is so?

MAKING ART CONNECTIONS 🎥

1. **Science.** Artists, as you learned, sometimes "wear the hat" of scientist. Using an encyclopedia or on-line research tool, look up *optics.* Explain what this science is, and what contributions scientists have made through the ages. Conclude by explaining the role of optics in art.

2. **Music.** Music, like art, suggests moods and sensations. Think about the way sound captures certain sensations. Fast music, for example, can be "lively." Then make a three-column chart. Head the first column *Color*, the second *Line*, the third *Sound*. Choose at least three moods or sensations. For each, write the type of color, line, and sound it captures.

Figure 2–1 How would you describe the overall "feeling" or "mood" of this painting? Notice the role line plays in creating this feeling. What other factors contribute?

Zanbur the Spy. Mughal period, reign of Akbar (1556–1605) c. 1561–76. Tempera on cotton cloth mounted on paper. 74 × 57.2 cm (28⅛ × 22½″). The Metropolitan Museum of Art, New York, New York. Rogers Art, 1923.

The Principles of Art

To solve a jigsaw puzzle, you need to fit the pieces together just so. Only when you follow the puzzle maker's plan can you fit the pieces together properly and see the whole picture.

The same is true of looking at works of art. Every artwork is based on an overall plan, or design. The puzzle "pieces" are the elements of art. Only by understanding how the artist has organized these pieces can you fully appreciate works like the one at the left.

In this chapter you will learn about the rules artists use to plan their works. You will learn how to use these rules yourself to see the "whole picture."

PORTFOLIO IDEAS

You will often begin an artwork in a sketchbook. A **sketchbook** is *a pad of drawing paper on which artists sketch, write notes, and refine ideas for their work.* Sketchbook ideas can become plans for finished artwork that will go into your portfolio.

OBJECTIVES

After completing this chapter, you will be able to:

- Define the term *principles of art.*
- Explain the three kinds of balance.
- Tell how artists use the principles of variety, harmony, emphasis, proportion, movement, and rhythm.
- Explain how a work achieves unity.
- Practice organizing elements and principles in original works of art.

WORDS YOU WILL LEARN

balance
emphasis
harmony
movement
picture plane
principles of art
proportion
rhythm
sketchbook
unity
variety

The Language of Design

Have you ever tried to learn another language? To do so, you need to know more than vocabulary. You also need to know the rules of grammar. These rules govern how words go together.

The language of art has its own set of rules. These rules are called **principles of art.** They are *guidelines that govern the way artists organize the elements of art.* In all there are seven such principles. They are: balance, variety, harmony, emphasis, proportion, movement, and rhythm. In this lesson, you will meet the first of these principles, balance.

THE PRINCIPLE OF BALANCE

You have probably lost your balance at one time or another. Maybe it was when you were riding your bicycle.

In art, as in life, balance is important. To an artist, **balance** is *a principle of art concerned with arranging the elements so that no one part of the work overpowers, or seems heavier than, any other part.* Artists speak of three types of balance:

- **Formal balance.** In art that has formal balance, one half of a work is a mirror image of the other half. Formal balance can give a feeling of dignity to a work of art. Notice the decorated screen in Figure 2–2. With your finger, trace a vertical line that divides the work in half and compare the two halves. Notice how they are alike. Can you find other examples of formal balance within this same work?

**Figure 2–2
Imagine that the panel on the right is not there. What would happen to the balance in this work?**

Ramon José Lopez. *Santa Maria y Jesus.* Altar screen (reredo). 1981. Hand-adzed pine painted with natural pigments. 2.4 × 2.7 m (8 × 9'). Collection of the artist.

- **Informal balance.** Imagine yourself on a seesaw with a much heavier person. To balance the two sides, you might ask the heavier person to move closer to the center. In art, the problem of balance is solved through the use of color and other elements. A small, brightly colored shape or form in one area of a work will balance a larger, dull one elsewhere. The two shapes carry the same "visual weight." Works of this type are said to have informal balance. Look at the painting in Figure 2–3. What single large form is your eye drawn to? What smaller, brighter forms command the same attention?
- **Radial balance.** In art with radial balance, shapes or forms are arranged around a central point. Snowflakes exhibit radial balance. So do bicycle tires. For an example of radial balance in art, look again at Figure 2–2. Notice the half circles at the top of each panel. See how the gold-colored teardrop shapes in each seem to extend outward from an invisible point.

STUDIO ACTIVITY

Sketching Shapes with Balance

Look around your home, school, and community for objects with formal, informal, and radial balance. Be creative in your search. With pencil and a sketch pad, make sketches of at least three items. Share your sketches with classmates. Challenge them to identify the type of balance in each sketch.

P O R T F O L I O

Label and date your sketches of formal, informal, and radial balance. Put the sketches in your portfolio for future reference.

✔ Check Your Understanding

1. Define *principles of art.*
2. List the principles of art.
3. Describe the three kinds of balance.

Figure 2–3 Where does your eye travel first in this painting? Where does it look next? Why is this so?

Sondra Freckelton. *Winter Melon with Quilt and Basket.* 1977. Watercolor on paper. 117.5 × 112 cm (46⅛ × 44⅛″). Virginia Museum of Fine Arts, Richmond, Virginia. Gift of Sydney and Frances Lewis.

Making a Mask with Formal Balance

Think about masks you have seen or worn. Like the one in Figure 2–4, these masks probably exhibited formal balance. It is the nature of masks to do so. This is because the faces they are meant to cover also have formal balance.

The mask shown in Figure 2–4 was created by the Yaware people of Africa. It was carved from wood that was polished to a high sheen. Notice the assortment of shapes and forms the artist has used for the facial features. Some of these are geometric. Others are free-form. Can you find examples of each type in the work?

WHAT YOU WILL LEARN

You will design a mask using formal balance. The mask will be created using papier-mâché (**pay**-puhr muh-**shay**). This is a sculpting technique using newspaper and liquid paste. You will add interest to your work by using geometric shapes for facial features and decorations. (Note: For additional information on working with papier-mâché, see Technique Tip **20** on page **287.**)

WHAT YOU WILL NEED
- Pencil and sketch paper
- Newspaper
- Scissors
- Masking tape
- Dish for paste
- Cellulose wallpaper paste
- Water
- Tempera or school acrylic paint and brushes
- Polymer gloss medium (optional)
- Found objects, such as feathers and ribbon

Figure 2–4 How many geometric shapes do you find in this Yaware mask? How many free-form shapes do you see?

Africa. Yaware People. *Face Mask.* Early twentieth century. Wood. 50.8 × 22.8 cm (20 × 9″). Private collection.

WHAT YOU WILL DO

1. Do several pencil sketches of mask designs. Let your imagination guide you. Each design should have formal balance. The facial features and any other details are to be geometric shapes. Choose your best sketch.
2. Cover your desk with layers of newspaper.
3. Fold two sheets of full-size newspaper lengthwise down to two inches. Fit it around your face and attach the ends with masking tape. Lay the oval shape on your desk. This will be the frame of your mask.
4. Crumple up sheets of newspaper and fill the center of your frame with them. Then place a final sheet of newspaper over the filled-in frame, gluing its edges to the frame.
5. Begin cutting small pieces of newspaper. Fold them to make the facial feature shapes on your best sketch. Attach them to the mask with tape to make raised three-dimensional details. Add more forms around the frame if you choose.
6. Tear strips of newspaper (with the grain) about 2 inches wide and 6 inches long. Dip one strip at a time into the bowl of paste. Run it lightly between your fingers to remove the extra paste. Lay each strip on the mask. Work from the frame into the center. Overlap the strips to cover all parts of your mask. Smooth out the edges of the strips where they overlap.
7. When your mask is finished, allow it to dry thoroughly. This will take several days.

EXAMINING YOUR WORK

- **Describe** Point to the different facial features of your mask. Identify the colors you used in your mask. What shapes did you use?
- **Analyze** How have you created balance in your mask design?

8. When your mask is dry, transfer the geometric face features and other details from your sketch to your mask. Paint the mask. The painted design, like the mask itself, should show formal balance. If you want your mask to have a high luster, apply the polymer gloss. Allow the mask to dry again, then add feathers, ribbons, or other materials as you choose.

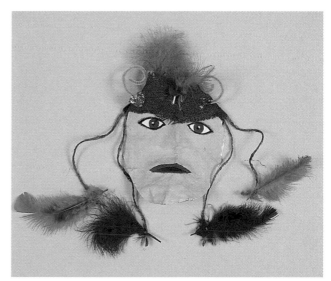

Figure 2–5   Student work. Mask with formal balance.

Try This! STUDIO OPTION

■ Use a plastic gallon milk bottle to make a mask. The bottle's handle can be the nose. Add other features using cut paper, yarn, and any other materials you can find.

Variety, Harmony, Emphasis, and Proportion

"Variety is the spice of life." Are you familiar with this saying? It means that a break from humdrum routines makes life more interesting.

This wise saying applies not only to life but also to art. In this lesson, you will learn how variety and three other principles—harmony, emphasis, and proportion—add interest to artworks.

THE PRINCIPLE OF VARIETY

Think about your favorite TV show. Suppose you were forced to watch this show for hours. In time, you would become bored. You might even grow to dislike the program.

Like TV viewing habits, art needs variety. In art, **variety** is *combining one or more elements of art to create interest.* A splash of brilliant color will add zest to a painting that has mostly dull tones. A free-form shape adds pep to a work done with mostly geometric shapes. Study the unusual painting in Figure 2–6. How many different textures can you find? What else has the artist done to add variety?

THE PRINCIPLE OF HARMONY

Just as you can have too little of a good thing, you can also have too much. In art, an excess of variety can be offset by using the principle of harmony. **Harmony** means *combining the elements of art to accent their similarities.* Look again at the painting in Figure 2–6. This time, study its **picture plane.** This is *the flat surface of a painting or drawing.* Find the horizontal line that divides the upper and lower halves of the picture plane. It runs through the center of the comb. Do you recall from Chapter 1, Lesson 2, the effect horizontal lines have on the viewer? What other lines has the artist used to bring harmony and order to this active painting?

Figure 2–6 Notice the work's title. What statement might the artist be making about morning routines? What clues are provided by the running feet of the figure in pajamas, the orange, and the comb?

James Rosenquist. *Early in the Morning.* 1963. Oil on canvas. 241.3 × 142.2 cm (95 × 56″). Virginia Museum of Fine Arts, Richmond, Virginia. Gift of Sydney and Frances Lewis.

THE PRINCIPLE OF EMPHASIS

To attract a viewer's attention to an important part of a work, artists use emphasis. **Emphasis** is *making an element or an object in a work stand out.* One way artists create emphasis is through contrast. Examine the sculpture in Figure 2–7. Notice how the artist uses contrasting bold colors to draw the viewer's eye into and around the dancing figures. What object or element is emphasized in the work in Figure 2–6?

THE PRINCIPLE OF PROPORTION

As an art principle, **proportion** is *how parts of a work relate to each other and to the whole.* One might say that the proportion or amount of red in a painting is greater than the proportion or amount of the other colors. A large shape in a picture filled with smaller shapes would stand out because of the different proportions in size. Look once more at the sculpture in Figure 2–7. Notice how the larger-than-life size of the figures adds to their importance and interest.

STUDIO ACTIVITY

Painting a Still Life with Emphasis

Arrange several everyday objects on a table or other flat surface. Plan a painting in which you give emphasis to one of the objects. You will do this by using one or more of the elements of art. Use acrylic paints to complete your picture. Share your still life with classmates, challenging them to identify the way or ways you achieved emphasis.

PORTFOLIO

Sign, date, and title your artwork. Put it in your portfolio.

✔ Check Your Understanding

1. Name two ways artists can achieve *variety* in their work.
2. How do artists achieve *harmony*?
3. Explain the principle of *proportion.*

Figure 2–7 Why do you suppose the artist chose to make the dancing partners so large? Why do you think she chose the colors she did?

Miriam Schapiro. *Anna and David.* 1987. Painted stainless steel and aluminum. 10.6 × 9.4 × .23 m (35′ × 31′ × 9″). Steinbaum-Krauss Gallery, New York, New York.

Lesson 3 *Variety, Harmony, Emphasis, and Proportion* **31**

Movement and Rhythm

Have you ever heard a book described as a "page turner"? This label is given to books with exciting stories. The writer's skill takes you beyond the mere words on the page. It permits you to see vivid, fast-paced action as though it were happening before your eyes.

The same may be said for some skillfully done works of art. Through the careful use of elements such as line, shape, and color, the artist captures movement.

In this lesson, you will learn about movement as a principle of art. You will also learn about a companion principle, rhythm.

THE PRINCIPLE OF MOVEMENT

When you meet a person for the first time, what feature do you notice first? Experts tell us that we look at a person's eyes. Then our gaze moves outward to take in the shape of the person's face. All of this happens in less than a second!

Figure 2–8 **Imagine that this work is a "freeze frame" from a motion picture. What do you think will happen in the next instant?**

Katsushika Hokusai. *Fishing Boats at Choshi in Shoshu.* c. 1833. Woodblock print. 18.9 × 25.8 cm (7½ × 10½"). The Art Institute of Chicago, Chicago, Illinois. The Kate Buckingham Fund, 1983.583

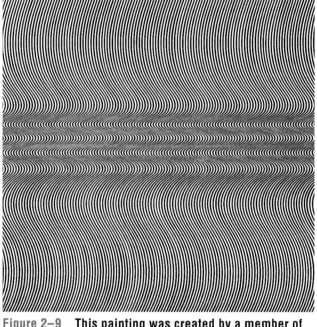

Figure 2–9 This painting was created by a member of a group of artists who called their work "Op art." *Op* is short for a word meaning "eye." Why do you suppose they called their work by this name?

Bridget Riley. *Current*. 1964. Synthetic polymer paint on composition board. 148.1 × 149.3 cm (58⅜ × 58⅞"). The Museum of Modern Art, New York, New York. Philip Johnson Fund.

Although you may not be aware of it, the same thing happens when you look at a work of art. Your eyes focus on one part. Then they move to the next. This visual journey takes place thanks to **movement**. This is *the principle of art that leads the viewer to sense action in a work, or it can be the path the viewer's eye follows through the work.*

Artists create movement through a blending of elements. Look at the artwork in Figure 2–8. Notice how the fishing boats seem to toss and rock. See how the giant waves churn and foam as they swell and curl high above the boats. What elements of art are used to create this sense of motion?

Artworks do not need recognizable subjects to communicate a sense of motion. Study the painting in Figure 2–9. Notice how the curves in this work seem to dance and shimmer. It is as though the painting were alive!

THE PRINCIPLE OF RHYTHM

Do you have a favorite recording artist? If you do, chances are you are a fan of the

person's or group's rhythm. Rhythm is the beat we feel and hear when we listen to music.

In art, **rhythm** is *the repetition of an element of art to make a work seem active*. Look again at the painting in Figure 2–9. The artist achieves rhythm by carefully spacing the curves at equal distances from one another. What kind of rhythm do you detect in Figure 2–8?

STUDIO ACTIVITY

Creating a Rhythmic Drawing

Bring a copy of your favorite compact disc or audiotape to class. Play a few selections. Your classmates will do the same. Choose one selection as it is playing, and attempt to create a "picture" of the sound. Again, your classmates will do the same. Use colored markers, crayons, or any other drawing tool you wish. Repeat colors, shapes, and lines to match the rhythm of the music. Draw to a second, different musical selection. Mount your completed works on the bulletin board with those made by other students. See if you can guess which musical selection each student "drew."

P O R T F O L I O

Write a paragraph that *assesses*, or evaluates, the success of your use of the principle of rhythm in this activity.

Check Your Understanding

1. What is movement in art?
2. Define *rhythm* in art.
3. How do artists create movement and rhythm?

Making a Tessellation

A term often tied to rhythm in art is *pattern*. Patterns, as you know, are made up of repeating shapes or forms. In some patterns, the same shape or form repeats over and over. In others, it varies.

The interesting artwork shown in Figure 2–10 contains an example of a type of pattern called *tessellation*. This is a pattern of shapes that fit together in a way that leaves no space in between. The term comes from the Latin word *tessella*, meaning "tile." Perhaps you have seen floors surfaced with tiles. Look closely at Figure 2–10. On the right side of the work, white birds fly over a small town surrounded by farmlands and a river. On the left side, black birds fly over a mirror image of the same scene. Together, the two flocks form a tessellation. The white birds serve as background for the black birds, and the black birds become a background for the white birds.

WHAT YOU WILL LEARN

You will design a *motif* (moh-**teef**), or basic shape, to be used in a tessellation. You will repeat the motif to fill an entire page. Using your imagination, you will add details to your motif. These details will change the shape into a fantasy creature. You will complete your design by using colored markers.

WHAT YOU WILL NEED

- Scissors
- Squares of 3-inch (7.7-cm) oak tag
- Transparent tape
- Ruler
- Sketch paper
- Pencil
- Drawing or construction paper, 12 x 18 inches (30 x 46 cm)
- Colored markers

WHAT YOU WILL DO

1. Cut a shape from one side of an oak tag square. Carefully tape the shape to the opposite side of the square in the same position (see Figure 2–11).
2. Cut a shape from a third side. Tape it to its opposite side. You will have a shape that looks something like a jigsaw puzzle piece. This is called a template. Turn the shape you have created. Examine it from different sides and angles. Picture fantasy creatures that might be formed by adding details. Draw around the template on sketch paper, and record some of your

Figure 2–10 **Notice that the birds blend not only with each other but with the plowed fields below. Could this scene really exist? Why or why not?**

M.C. Escher. *Day and Night.* 1938. Woodcut in black and gray printed from two blocks. 39.1 × 67.7 cm (15⅜ × 26⅔"). © 1996 Cordon Art, Baarn, Holland. All rights reserved.

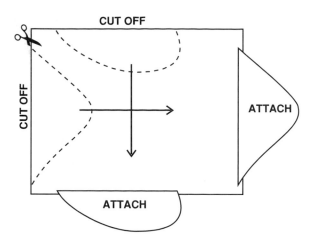

Figure 2–11   Cut off shape and attach to opposite side.

- **Describe**   Explain how you made your motif.
- **Analyze**   Tell what details you added to make a fantasy creature.

ideas in pencil. You may have to experiment with several squares until you have a shape you like.

3. Place your template so that it lines up with the upper left-hand corner of the paper. Using a pencil, carefully draw around all edges. Move the shape to the right. The cutout on the left side of the cardboard should line up with the bulge on the right of the first shape drawn. Draw around it again until you have completed one row.

4. Move the template underneath the first shape you made. (See Figure 2–12). Draw around the edges with the pencil. Continue in this fashion until you have completed a second row. Keep making rows until you have covered the entire paper.

5. Refer to the sketches you made. Choose details for your fantasy creature. Transfer these features to each of the motifs with colored markers.

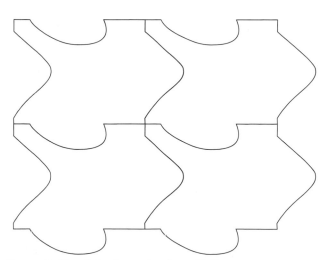

Figure 2–12   **A design using tessellation.**

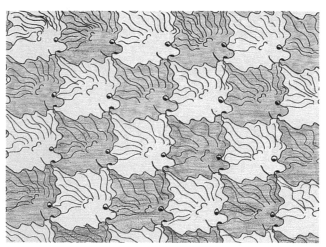

Figure 2–13   **Student work. A tessellation.**

COMPUTER OPTION

Try This!

■ Select the Rectangle or Hexagon shape tool and no-fill color. Draw an open square, rectangle, or hexagon. Choose the Pencil tool and draw a varied line from the top corner of one side, ending at the bottom corner of the same side. Use the Lasso selection tool to select the side. Make a copy and paste the copy on the opposite side of the shape. This makes a slide translation. Erase the unneeded lines with the Eraser tool. Beginning on a third side, make a second slide translation using the same steps. Title and save. Add details, texture, and color to describe the real or imaginary object. Retitle and save. Choose the Lasso selection tool to select, copy, paste, and arrange multiple copies next to each other like pieces of a puzzle. Retitle, save, and print.

Unity in Art

You have probably witnessed the pluses of teamwork. When members of the school basketball team play as one, they usually win. When members of the marching band are "in sync," they put on a great performance.

This idea of acting as one is important in art, too. When you look at a successful work of art, you do not see parts. You see a well-designed whole that has **unity.** This is *the arrangement of elements and principles of art to create a feeling of completeness or wholeness.*

UNITY

You have probably had toys or other possessions that were broken. Sometimes, a broken object can be glued back together so that the cracks are invisible. In an artwork with unity, the "cracks" are likewise invisible. You cannot point to unity as you can an element or principle. You can sense it, however. You can also sense its absence.

Examine the painting in Figure 2–14. This powerful work shows a fierce storm. Much of the picture is given over to a sweeping

Figure 2–14 **How would you describe the feeling conveyed by this painting? What principles of art have been used to create this feeling?**

Joseph M. W. Turner. *Valley of Aosta: Snowstorm, Avalanche, and Thunderstorm.* 1836–37. Oil on canvas. 92.2 × 123 cm (36⅓ × 48"). Art Institute of Chicago, Chicago, Illinois. Frederick T. Haskell Collection, 1947.513

curve of wind and snow. Can you find the people in this picture? Their tiny forms, along with that of a small animal, appear huddled in the lower right corner. The artist achieves unity in this work in the following ways. He:

- uses *proportion* to contrast the vast fury of the storm with the small people.
- captures vivid *movement* through the careful use of line and color.
- adds excitement and suspense through informal *balance.*
- draws the viewer's eye from one part of the work to another through *variety* in shape, form, and color.

Look back at the painting that opened this chapter on page **24.** What arrangement of principles and elements did the artist use to achieve unity?

Recognizing Unity

One way of recognizing unity in an artwork is by using a checklist like the one in Figure 2–15. For each element used, you would make a check mark in the box under the principle or principles the artist has used to organize each element.

STUDIO ACTIVITY

Identifying Unity

Copy the checklist in Figure 2–15 onto a blank sheet of paper. Look back at Figure 2–8 on page **32.** Go through the checklist one element at a time. For each element found, identify the principle or principles used. Remember that not all artworks use all elements and principles. When you have finished, share and compare your checklist with those of classmates.

P O R T F O L I O

Put the list in your portfolio. Make another copy of the checklist to keep in your portfolio. Use it to analyze your own artworks.

Check Your Understanding

1. Define *unity.*
2. Explain how an understanding of unity is important to an understanding of art.

DESIGN CHART	PRINCIPLES OF ART					
	Balance	Variety	Harmony	Emphasis	Proportion	Movement/ Rhythm
Line						
Color						
Shape						
Form						
Space						
Texture						

(ELEMENTS OF ART) — UNITY

Figure 2–15 Unity checklist.

Everyday Uses of Math

Are you a "math person?" Maybe you consider yourself a "word person" or a "computer person" instead. Do you sometimes wonder why you need to memorize multiplication tables or learn division? Whether you enjoy math or not, you will use math principles often in life—probably more often than you think.

If you have ever figured out the sales tax when you purchased a CD or school supplies, you used math. You need math skills to divide a square of chocolate cake into four equal pieces. Doubling or halving a muffin recipe is another everyday use of math.

Although you may not realize it, art also requires the use of math skills. Some of the principles of art, including balance and proportion, are based on math skills. You also use math to perform certain tasks in art. To make a grid for enlarging, for example, you need to measure, count, and divide. (See Technique Tip **5** on page **281**.)

In Charles Demuth's *The Figure 5 in Gold*, the most obvious reference to math is simply the number five. However, the artist also needed math skills to create the numeral in diminishing sizes.

Charles Demuth. *The Figure 5 in Gold*. Oil on composition board. 91.4 × 75.6 cm (36 × 29¾"). The Metropolitan Museum of Art, New York, New York. Alfred Stieglitz Collection, 1949.

MAKING THE CONNECTION

- ✔ Which principles of art did Charles Demuth use in *The Figure 5 in Gold*? Explain your answer.
- ✔ What math skills do you think Demuth needed to create this work? Explain your answer.
- ✔ Besides those mentioned, what are some other everyday uses of math?

INTERNET ACTIVITY

Visit Glencoe's Fine Arts Web Site for students at:

http://www.glencoe.com/sec/art/students

REVIEW

BUILDING VOCABULARY

Number a sheet of paper from 1 to 10. After each number, write the term from the box that matches each description below.

balance	principles of art
emphasis	proportion
harmony	rhythm
movement	unity
picture plane	variety

1. How parts of a work relate to each other and to the whole.
2. Combining one or more elements of art to create interest.
3. The arrangement of elements and principles of art to create a feeling of completeness or wholeness.
4. The principle of art that leads the viewer to sense action in a work, or it can be the path the viewer's eye follows through the work.
5. Making an element or an object in a work stand out.
6. A principle of art concerned with arranging the elements so that no one part of the work overpowers, or seems heavier than, any other part.
7. Guidelines that govern the way artists organize the elements of art.
8. The repetition of an element of art to make a work seem active.
9. The flat surface of a painting or drawing.
10. Combining the elements of art to accent their similarities.

REVIEWING ART FACTS

Number a sheet of paper from 11 to 15. Answer each question in a complete sentence.

11. What kind of balance does a hubcap have?
12. What happens when there is too much harmony in a work of art? What can be done to correct this problem?
13. What are some ways of achieving proportion in an artwork?
14. What principle might be used to organize a work of art that contains a motif?
15. What is a tessellation?

THINKING ABOUT ART

On a sheet of paper, answer each question in a sentence or two.

1. **Extend.** Suppose you were creating a painting of a crowd scene and wanted one figure to stand out. What art principles might you use to achieve this goal? Explain your answers.
2. **Compare and contrast.** How are the principles of movement and rhythm similar? In what ways are they different?

MAKING ART CONNECTIONS

1. **Language Arts.** Emphasis occurs in literature as well as art. In stories, for example, words are *italicized* to show they receive stress or emphasis. In plays, emphasis is achieved through stage directions—commands to the actor that appear after a part name. With a group of classmates, write a short story or play in which words or lines are emphasized. Read or perform your creation in front of the class.
2. **Community Connection.** Locate examples of formal and radial balance in your community. Search both for examples that are made by people and those arising in nature. Devote a page of your journal to your research. Share and compare your findings with classmates.

Figure 3–1 This is a lithograph, an artwork made by a printing method. Notice the colors and textures.

Napachie Pootoogook. *My New Accordion*. 1989. Lithograph on wove, rag paper. 112.4 × 79.9 cm (44¼ × 31⅞"). Dorset Fine Arts, Toronto, Ontario, Canada.

Art Media and Techniques

Every musical instrument has its own voice, or characteristic. You can identify a guitar by its twang, a tuba by its deep grumble.

Like musical instruments, art materials have different characteristics. Examine the artwork in Figure 3–1. Can you tell which technique was used to create the work?

In this chapter, you will learn about the tools and materials artists use. You will learn to appreciate the special characteristics of each.

OBJECTIVES

After completing this chapter, you will be able to:
- Define the term *medium of art*.
- Identify the different kinds of media used in drawing, painting, printmaking, and sculpture.
- Experiment with various art media.
- Use mixed media to create an original work of art.

WORDS YOU WILL LEARN

art medium
binder
gesture drawing
intaglio
perception
pigment
portrait
printmaking
sculpture
solvent

PORTFOLIO IDEAS

Each entry in your portfolio should be marked clearly for identification. Make sure each piece includes:
- Your name and the date of the artwork
- The assignment
- Your comments or self-reflection
- Any additional information requested by your teacher

Drawing

To most people, a pencil is a writing tool. To artists, it is a key. As an art medium, this familiar object opens the door to endless creative possibilities. An **art medium** is *a material used to create a work of art.* When we speak of more than one medium, we use the word *media.* Artists rely on a wide variety of media in their work, such as pencils, paints, charcoal, and pastels.

In this lesson, you will learn about media used in drawing. In later lessons, you will learn about media used to create other kinds of art.

Figure 3–2 What drawing medium was used for this sketch? How would you describe the characteristics of this art tool?

Gustav Klimpt. *Sleeping Boy.* 1905–07. Graphite pencil on cream wove paper. 55 × 35 cm (21¾ × 13¾") The Detroit Institute of Arts, Detroit, Michigan. Founders Society Purchase, John S. Newberry Fund.

WHY ARTISTS DRAW

In baseball, a pitcher takes warm-up throws before facing a batter. Musicians warm up before a performance. Artists follow a similar approach by drawing. Drawing "limbers" up the artist's eye. It helps develop visual **perception** (pur-**sep**-shun). This is *an awareness of the elements of an environment by means of the senses.* Perception is more than looking at an object. It is really "seeing" the object. It is studying how shapes, forms, lines, and colors blend to form the whole.

Some drawings are used to plan paintings or other large projects. Figure 3–2 shows this type of drawing, or "study." Other drawings are done as finished works of art. Such a drawing appears in Figure 3–3.

DRAWING MEDIA

Do you recall scribbling with a crayon when you were small? You didn't realize it at the time, but you were using a drawing medium. Crayons, colored markers, pencils, pens, and chalk are all drawing media.

Each drawing medium has its own characteristics. Chalk and crayon, for example, produce rough lines. Pens, by contrast, make smooth lines. Figure 3–4 shows lines made with three different drawing media. Notice the line quality of each.

SHADING TECHNIQUES

Look once more at the drawing in Figure 3–3. The scarf in this picture looks so real you can almost feel the texture in the fabric. The artist accomplishes this through shading. *Shading* is the use of light and shadow to give a feeling of depth and texture. There are four main shading techniques:

- **Hatching.** This is drawing thin lines all running in the same direction.
- **Crosshatching.** This is drawing crisscrossing lines.

Figure 3–3 Notice the attention to detail in this pencil drawing. What art principles have been used to organize the work?

Jeanette Leroy. *Scarf on a Coat Rack.* 1976. Pencil on paper. 55.9 × 38.1 cm (22 × 15″). The National Museum of Women in the Arts, Washington, D.C. Gift of Wallace and Wilhelmina Holladay.

- **Blending.** This is changing color value little by little.
- **Stippling.** This is creating dark values by means of a dot pattern.

Which of these shading techniques was used in Figure 3–3? Which was used in Figure 3–1 on page **40**?

✔ Check Your Understanding

1. What is *perception?* Why is developing perception important?
2. Name four drawing tools.
3. Demonstrate the four shading techniques.

Pencil

Oil pastel

Colored Marker

Figure 3–4   Drawing Media.

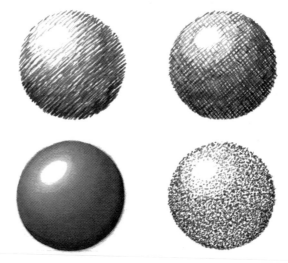

Figure 3–5   Shading Techniques.

LESSON 2

Gesture Drawing

Examine the drawing of the figures in Figure 3–6. From an art standpoint, the most important thing about the work is not *who* it shows, but *what* it shows. This drawing is of the human form. Capturing the human form has been a goal of artists through the ages. Notice the loose, scribbly quality of most of the lines. The artist used a technique called **gesture drawing.** This means *moving a drawing medium quickly and freely over a surface to capture the form and actions of a subject.* In gesture drawing you draw with your whole arm, not just your hand. Some gesture drawings are merely quick scribbles. Others are done with greater precision and care. How would you describe the lines the artist has used in

Figure 3–6? What parts of the subjects have been recorded with the most care?

WHAT YOU WILL LEARN

You will make several quick gesture drawings of a classmate using several different drawing media. Focus on the form and action of the subject, not on one part, like the foot or face. You will not be concerned with capturing the model's likeness, but rather the feeling of motion. You will then make a large, slower sketch of a seated figure. Emphasize one area of the figure using shading. (For more information on gesture drawing, see Technique Tip **1** on page **281**.)

Figure 3–6 Do you think the artist captured the appearance of the human forms? Where is line used to show details?

Honoré Daumier. *Family Scene.* c. 1867–70. Pen and black ink, and brush and gray wash, on ivory wove paper (discolored cream). 21.6 × 20.5 cm (8½ × 8"). Art Institute of Chicago, Chicago, Illinois. Helen Regenstein Collection, 1965.633

WHAT YOU WILL NEED

- Assorted drawing media, such as sticks of charcoal, soft graphite, unwrapped crayons, and markers
- Sheets of white paper, 12 x 18 inches (30 x 46 cm)
- Sharpened pencil

WHAT YOU WILL DO

1. You and your classmates will take turns modeling. Models should pretend to be frozen in the middle of an activity. This may be an everyday action, such as jogging, lifting, or dancing. Throwing a ball is another possibility.
2. Make at least four gesture drawings. Use a different medium for each drawing. Make your figures at least eight or ten inches tall. Begin by drawing the head. Sketch loose, free lines. Draw quickly to capture the overall form of the subject. Build up the shape of the figure little by little.

EXAMINING YOUR WORK

- **Describe.** Did you include all the body parts in each of your rapid gesture drawings? Identify the medium used for each drawing.
- **Analyze.** Point to and describe the different kinds of lines in your gesture drawings. Is the area you chose to emphasize clearly identified with shading?

3. Switching to the pencil, make a slower gesture drawing of a seated model. Fill an entire sheet of paper. Select one area of the figure to emphasize as the artist has done in Figure 3–6. You might select a hand, sleeve, or shoe. Emphasize this area with details and shading.
4. Display your finished pencil drawing along with those of classmates. Compare the detail emphasized in the different drawings.

Figure 3–7 **Student work. Gesture drawings.**

STUDIO OPTION

■ Have three volunteers pose, changing poses every 45 seconds. Do one gesture drawing of each person. Use rough, scribbly lines to capture the poses. Remember to draw quickly. Drawing quickly helps you warm up.

LESSON 3

Painting

Many people, when they hear the term *art*, think of paintings. This is not unreasonable when you consider that the first artists were painters. They produced their "artworks" on the walls of caves some 15,000 years ago. They made paint from crushed rocks mixed with animal fat or blood.

Since that time, many new painting media have appeared. In this lesson, you will learn about some of these.

PAINT

Although paints have changed over the centuries, the way of making them has not. Like paints used by early cave artists, those today contain three main parts:

- **Pigment.** Pigment is *a finely ground powder that gives paint its color.* The pigment that cave artists relied on came from minerals in rocks. Through the mid-1800s, artists continued to grind their own pigments.

Figure 3–8 Notice this artist's attention to detail. What shading technique did he use?

John Wilson. *My Brother.* 1942. Oil on panel. 30.5 × 27 cm (12 × 10⅝"). Smith College Museum of Art, Northhampton, Massachusetts. Purchased 1943.

Figure 3–9 When watercolors are applied to wet paper, the colors flow and blend.

Emil Nolde. *Self-Portrait*. 1917. Watercolor, reed pen, and black ink. 21 × 16.8 cm (8½ × 6½"). The Detroit Institute of Arts, Detroit, Michigan. Bequest of John S. Newberry.

- **Binder.** A binder is *a liquid that holds together the grains of pigment.* The binder allows the pigment to stick to the surface. The liquid parts of eggs have long been used as a paint binder.
- **Solvent.** A painter may also choose to use a **solvent** when working with paints. This is *a liquid used to control the thickness or thinness of the paint.* Solvents are also used to clean paintbrushes and other applicators.

PAINTING MEDIA

As with drawing media, there are many different kinds of paint. Each has its own personality. Some paints that artists use are oil-based. Others are made with plain water.

Oil-Based Paint

First used in the 1400s, oil paint remains a popular medium today. True to its name,

oil paint uses linseed oil as its binder. Its solvent is turpentine.

One advantage of oil paint is that it dries slowly. This allows the artist to blend colors right on the canvas. The work in Figure 3–8 is an oil painting. Notice how smoothly the colors blend together.

Water-Based Paint

The most popular of water-based painting media, watercolor takes its name from its solvent, water. The binder is gum arabic. Watercolors give a transparent quality to paintings. Compare the watercolor in Figure 3–9 with the oil painting in Figure 3–8. What differences do you see?

Tempera, another water-based paint, comes in both powder and liquid form. Because tempera is not oil-based, it dries more quickly than oil paint. It is also more opaque than watercolor.

Check Your Understanding

1. What are the three main parts of paint?
2. What is the difference between oil paint and tempera?

Creating a Portrait

Look once more at the paintings in Figures 3–8 and 3–9 on pages **46** and **47.** Both are examples of a type of artwork called *portrait.* A **portrait** is *a visual representation of a person at rest.* Compare these two portraits with the one in Figure 3–10. This artwork was done with oil pastels. This is a medium with properties of both drawing and painting media. Notice the delicate lines and soft tones in this work. See also how the artist used dark values to shade some areas of the subject and light values to highlight others.

WHAT YOU WILL LEARN

You and a partner will take turns serving as model and artist. As artist, you will create a portrait of the other person's face. You will make certain to place each feature of the face in its proper place. You will add shading and highlighting using oil pastels, as in Figure 3–10. Your portrait will express a mood or feeling, as do the portraits in Figures 3–8 and 3–9. To do this, you will have to capture the model's expression, which might be happy or sad, angry or bored.

Figure 3–10   What mood or feeling has the artist captured? What shading technique has she used to create depth?

Mary Cassatt. *Margot in Blue.* 1902. Pastel. 61 × 50 cm (24 × 19⅝"). The Walters Art Gallery, Baltimore, Maryland.

WHAT YOU WILL NEED

- Pencil and sketch paper
- Sheet of white paper, 9 x 12 inches (23 x 30 cm)
- Black colored marker
- Oil pastels

WHAT YOU WILL DO

1. Have your model sit facing you head-on. This means that you are looking squarely at the person's face. Ask the model to express a mood with his or her facial expression. Make several quick gesture drawings of the person's face. Add eyes, nose, mouth, ears, and hair, making certain each is in its proper place. Your goal is not to create an exact likeness. Rather, it is to capture the shape of the person's head and facial features. You are also to capture a mood or feeling as seen in your model's expression.
2. Transfer the best of your drawings to the sheet of paper.
3. Using the black marker, go over the outline of the head and facial features. Work quickly, as you did in the gesture drawings. The lines should have a sketchy quality, as in Figure 3–9 on page **47**.
4. Decide which areas of your portrait you will shade. Decide which you will highlight. Use a dark value of a single color of pastel for the shaded areas. Use a light value of the same color for highlighted areas.
5. Display your completed work along with those of classmates. Challenge students to identify the mood or feeling your portrait expresses.

EXAMINING YOUR WORK

- **Describe**   Identify the type of artwork you created. Did you include all of the facial features? Were these in the proper places on your portrait?
- **Analyze**   What value did you use to shade areas of the portrait? What value did you use to highlight areas?

Figure 3–11   **Student work. A portrait.**

STUDIO OPTIONS

■ Do a second portrait based on the same sketch. This time, substitute watercolors for the oil pastels. Moisten cakes of watercolor with a few drops of water. This will soften them. Use a fairly large brush to apply the paint. Compare the results of your two portraits.

■ Do a gesture drawing of a familiar object using oil pastels. Add shading as you did in your portrait. Reinforce some of the lines to add emphasis.

Printmaking

What comes to mind when you hear the word *printing?* You may think of writing in block letters. You may think of the process used to create books, newspapers, and magazines. To an artist, printing, or **printmaking,** is *transferring an image from an inked surface to create a work of art.* As in commercial printing, the artist uses a printing press of sorts. As in forming letters, the artist creates by hand the image to be printed.

PRINTMAKING BASICS

While prints may be made with many different media, all use the same basic tools. These are:

- **A printing plate.** This is a surface on which the print is made. The plate carries the mirror image of the finished print. Letters and numbers must be made backward on the plate.

- **Ink.** Ink is applied to the plate. It is responsible for the image appearing on the print.
- **Brayer.** The brayer is a roller with a handle. It is used to "ink"—or apply ink to—the plate.

Editions

Usually, more than one print is made from a single plate. Together, all the prints made from a plate form an *edition.* Each print in an edition is signed and numbered by the artist. The number is made up of two numerals with a slash (/) between them. The first number tells which print you are viewing. The second tells how many prints are in the edition. The number 4/50 means "the fourth print in an edition of fifty." How would you read 13/25?

Figure 3–12 What principle of art has been used to organize this work?

Shiko Munakata. *Floral Hunting Scene.* 1954. Woodcut, printed in black and dark grey. 131.8 × 159.7 cm (51⅞ × 62⅞"). The Museum of Modern Art, New York, New York. Gift of the Felix and Helen Juda Foundation.

Figure 3–13 **How does this intaglio print differ from the woodcut in Figure 3–12?**

Francisco de Goya. *Capricho n. 43: The Sleep of Reason Produces Monsters.* 1796–98, published 1799. Etching and aquatint. 21.5 × 15 cm (8½ × 6"). Courtesy of The Hispanic Society of America, New York, New York.

PRINTMAKING TECHNIQUES

Imagine touching your finger to a stamp pad and then pressing your finger on paper. In doing so, you would make a *relief* (ruh-**leef**) print. This is an image raised from a background that is inked and printed. The raised ridges on your finger would pick up the ink and then transfer your "fingerprint" to the paper. Relief printing is one of the oldest forms of printmaking. It dates back nearly 2,000 years.

A popular medium used in relief printing is wood. The artist cuts away the areas of the surface not meant to hold ink. Figure 3–12 shows a woodblock print, or *woodcut.*

Figure 3–13 shows the result of another printing process. This process is known as **intaglio** (in-**tahl**-yoh). It is *a printmaking technique in which the image to be printed is cut or scratched into a surface.* In a way, intaglio is the reverse of relief printing. The image on the plate is transferred when paper is forced into grooves that hold the ink. Study the intaglio print in Figure 3–13. Notice the many fine lines.

✔ Check Your Understanding

1. Define the term *printmaking.*
2. What are the three tools in printmaking?

LESSON 6

Sculpture

Have you ever built a house of cards? Maybe you have made a project out of modeling clay. Both activities borrow processes from the art of sculpture. **Sculpture** is *a three-dimensional work of art*. Artists who work in sculpture are called sculptors.

Figure 3–14 **What sculpting process and medium was used for this sculpture? What has the artist done to make this boxer look like a real person?**

The Pugalist. c. 50 B.C. Bronze. Museo Nazional Romano delle Ferme, Rome, Italy. Scala/Art Resource, NY

THE MEDIA OF SCULPTURE

Like other artists, sculptors use a wide variety of media in their work. One sculpting medium you may have worked with is modeling clay. Various woods and metals are other sculpting media. What medium was used for the sculpture in Figure 3–14?

No matter what medium is used, a work of sculpture will be one of two types:

- **Sculpture in the round.** This is a type of sculpture that is surrounded *on all sides* by space. Another name for sculpture in the round is *freestanding sculpture*. Like Figure 3–14, sculptures in the round can be statues of people. Not all freestanding sculptures have recognizable subjects, however. Examine the sculpture in Figure 1–16 on page **16.**
- **Relief sculpture.** This is a type of sculpture in which forms extend into space on *one* side only. Figure 3–15 shows an example of relief sculpture. If you could walk around to the back of this sculpture, you would find that it is flat.

SCULPTING TECHNIQUES

There are four basic sculpting processes. Each gives a different result. These are:

- **Carving.** In this process, the sculptor starts with a block of material. He or she cuts or chips away pieces of the block. The relief sculpture in Figure 3–15 was created by carving. What medium did the sculptor use?

- **Casting.** In this process, the sculptor starts by making a mold. He or she then pours in a melted-down metal or other liquid that later hardens. Bronze, the medium used in Figure 3–14, is a common metal used for casting. It is an alloy made of copper and tin. In recent years, sculptors have begun experimenting with different casting media. There is even a 9-foot statue completed in 1996 that is cast from chocolate!
- **Modeling.** Modeling is building up and shaping a soft material to create a sculpture. Fresh plaster can also be used for modeling.
- **Assembling.** Also known as *constructing*, assembling is a process in which pieces of material are glued or joined together. As in modeling, assembled sculptures are built up. A house of cards, for example, is made by assembling.

Check Your Understanding

1. Name three media used in sculpture.
2. What is the difference between sculpture in the round and relief sculpture?
3. Name four processes for making sculpture.

STUDIO ACTIVITY

Experimenting with Assembling

One way in which artists join the pieces of an assembled sculpture is through *slotting.* This is cutting slits in cardboard or similar media and then fitting the pieces together.

Gather sheets of scrap cardboard. These may come from a discarded carton or box. Cut the sheets into rectangles of varying sizes. Experiment with fitting together the pieces by slotting. Slot together at least ten rectangles. When you have created an interesting design, paint your sculpture. Use a large brush and school tempera. Title your work and display it along with those of classmates.

P O R T F O L I O

Take a photograph of your sculpture. In self-reflection, write what you learned about the slotting process and how it might be used in another project.

Figure 3–15   What kind of balance has the artist used? What sculpting medium was used?

King Prasenajit Visits the Buddha. Early second century B.C. Hard, reddish sandstone. 48 × 52.7 × 9 cm (19 × 20¾ × 3½″). Freer Gallery of Art, Smithsonian Institution, Washington, D.C.

LESSON 7
Making a Collage

Artists are always on the lookout for new ways of creating. One such way is shown in Figure 3–16. This work is a *collage* (kuh-**lahzh**). Based on a French word meaning "to glue," a *collage* is an artwork arranged from cut or torn materials that are pasted to a surface. The group of artists who came up with this idea lived and worked in the early 1900s.

Study Figure 3–16. The work contains a rich assortment of objects and materials. These include photographs of African masks and one of a cat. What other familiar images can you find? Notice how the artist used rectangular patches of colored paper to create a window.

WHAT YOU WILL LEARN

You will make a collage out of colored paper that exhibits a variety of shapes and hues. You will use images and, if you like, words clipped from magazines. Your collage will express a theme. The addition of original crayon drawings will help you carry out your theme.

WHAT YOU WILL NEED
- Discarded magazines
- Pencil and sketch paper
- Sheets of white paper, 9 x 12 inches (23 x 30 cm)
- Crayons or markers
- Scissors
- Sheets of construction paper in assorted colors
- Sheet of oaktag, 12 x 18 inches (30 x 46 cm)
- Glue

Figure 3–16 What kinds of shapes has the artist used? How many visual textures do you count? How has the artist introduced variety?

Romare Bearden. *Saturday Morning.* 1969. 111.8 × 142.2 cm (44 × 56"). Collage. © 1998 Romare Bearden Foundation/ Licensed by VAGA, New York, NY

WHAT YOU WILL DO

1. Decide on a theme for your collage. Some possibilities include sports, animals, nature, or cities. Browse through old magazines. Be on the alert for photos, illustrations, and words that go along with your theme. Carefully remove the pages containing these images.
2. Think of other words or images that support your theme. Make sketches of these images. Transfer your best sketches to white paper. Complete these drawings using crayon or marker.
3. Cut around the images you have selected or created. Arrange these on the oaktag in an interesting way. You may want to alternate your original drawings with your magazine clippings.
4. Next, cut shapes from construction paper. These are to fill the spaces between your images. They are also to serve as background. Add these around and under the images on the oaktag.

EXAMINING YOUR WORK

- **Describe**   Identify the images you chose or created for your collage. Explain how these images emphasize your theme.
- **Analyze**   Did you use a variety of shapes and hues in your collage? In what way is harmony demonstrated in your work?

5. When you are satisfied with your design, begin gluing the pieces. Start with the construction paper shapes. Work carefully so as not to disturb the unglued portions of your design. Use the glue *sparingly*. If any glue oozes out from under the pieces, carefully remove it with a slightly damp tissue.
6. When your collage is dry, display it along with those of your classmates. Challenge classmates to identify your theme.

Figure 3–17   **Student work. A collage.**

COMPUTER OPTION

Try This!

■ Find clip art that expresses the theme of your choice. Add original computer creations of your own that support your theme. With the Rectangle, Circle, or Polygon tool, create closed shapes of different sizes. From the Textures menu, choose different textures to fill these shapes. Choose designs such as brick and fabric for contrast. Fill the shapes. Arrange these under the images using the Order command. Save your work for your portfolio.

Computer Art

Throughout history, advances in technology have shaped the way artists create. The 1930s, for example, saw the arrival of paints made with plastic binders. These paints extended the media choices of painters. They were also less messy than oil paints because they used water as a solvent.

More recent advances have brought about other far-reaching changes in the way art can be created. In this lesson, you will learn about an advance that has touched off a new revolution in art. That advance is the digital computer.

THE MEDIA OF COMPUTER ART

Before the mid-1800s, painters had to grind pigments by hand. The appearance of paint in tubes changed all that. It made the painter's life easier.

In a very real sense, the same may be said of computers. They have made—and will continue to make—certain art tasks easier.

Computer Art Programs

Do you have a computer in your classroom? Maybe you have one at home. If you have

Figure 3–18 **What is happening in this picture? What statement might the artist be making about computer art?**

Rhoda Grossman. *Self-Portrait After Escher.* 1992. Electronic. Salzman International, San Francisco, California.

worked with computers—and even if you have not—you are probably aware that they do a number of different jobs. Each job is done by a separate program, or *application.* As is true of other computer applications, art images are stored as files in the computer's memory. Once saved, they may be opened and reworked.

Most computer art applications are one of two main types:

- **Paint programs.** In paint programs, images are stored as *bitmaps,* which are series of tiny dots. The advantage is the ability to edit pixel by pixel. In general, paint programs are capable of producing more lifelike pictures than those done in draw programs. Figures 3–18 and 3–19 were made using paint programs.

- **Draw programs.** In draw programs, images are stored as a series of lines and curves. Each line or curve results from a mathematical formula and is known as an *object.* An advantage of drawing programs over painting programs is that objects can be "resized"—shrunk or enlarged—without distortion. Figure 3–20 on the next page shows an image, or "group of objects," created in a drawing program.

In the last decade, the lines between paint and draw programs have begun blurring. Many paint programs nowadays do jobs that were once done only by a draw program, and vice versa.

Figure 3–19 **How does this self-portrait and the one on the facing page differ from the ones in Figures 3–8 and 3–9 on pages 46–47?**

Erol Otis. *Self-Portrait.* 1991. Electronic. Courtesy of the artist.

Lesson 8 *Computer Art* **57**

Figure 3–20 The image in the upper-left was made from the 298 separate "objects" shown in the lower-right. Do you recognize this familiar image?

Tools of the Computer Artist

In computer art, there are tools and there are *tools*. The physical tools that the computer artist actually handles are called *hardware*. Hardware includes the equipment, such as the monitor, keyboard, and printer, used in computer graphics.

The most important real tool of the computer artist is the mouse. This is the familiar pointing and clicking device. The mouse is used mainly to make selections from menus. These are lists of commands appearing in a bar at the top of the screen. The mouse may also be used as a drawing or painting device.

Tool	Description	Type of Program
Zoom tool	Magnifies a part of a painting or drawing.	Paint or Draw
or Brush tool	Paints lines of different thicknesses.	Paint
Pencil tool	Draws lines and curves.	Paint only
Eraser tool	Changes one color to another.	Paint
Fill tool	Adds color, gradients, patterns to closed objects or shapes.	Paint or Draw
Rectangle shape tool	Creates rectangles and squares.	Paint or Draw
Selection tool	Selects.	Draw
Selection tool	Selects a rectangular space around an object.	Paint
Lasso Selection tool	Selects only the object.	Paint
Ellipse or Round Shape tool	Draws ovals and circles.	Paint or Draw

Figure 3–21 Common on-screen tools.

Some other real tools used by professional computer artists include the following:

- **Stylus and graphics tablet.** In simplest terms, a stylus and graphics tablet are electronic answers to the pencil and paper. In recent years, these tools have been improved. The stylus now responds to pressure from the hand, much like a real pencil, pen, or brush. The woman in Figure 3–18 on page **56** is shown using a stylus and graphics tablet.
- **Scanner.** A scanner is a device that "reads" a printed image. It then translates the image into a language the computer—and the computer artist—can use. The work in Figure 3–19 began with a photograph that the artist scanned into his computer.

On-Screen Tools

A second category of tools computer artists work with is "on-screen" tools. These mimic the hand-held tools used by conventional artists. On-screen tools include pencils, pens, assorted brushes, and even erasers.

The set of on-screen tools varies from program to program. The table in Figure 3–21 shows some common tool icons and the type of program in which each is found. It also shows the icon, or picture symbol, commonly used to indicate each.

Check Your Understanding

1. What is the difference between a painting program and a drawing program?
2. Name three real tools and three on-screen tools.

STUDIO ACTIVITY

Experimenting with Art Software

There is an old saying that "experience is the best teacher." You are about to prove the truth of this saying, especially if you have never created computer art.

Begin by opening a new file. Do this by clicking "File" at the left of the menu bar and selecting "New." Using the Ellipse tool, draw an oval. Beginning at one edge, draw a second oval about twice the size of the first. Switch to the Rectangle tool. Create a tall, slender rectangle somewhere on the page. The rectangle should be about the same height as that of the large oval at its highest point. Switch to the Arrow Selection tool. Select or draw a "marquee" around the rectangle. A dotted line will appear around the shape. Click Edit, then Copy, then Paste. A second rectangle identical to the first will appear at the upper left corner of the screen. Drag the rectangle to a position under the left side of the large oval and just touching it. Re-select the original rectangle and move it to a corresponding position on the right side of the large oval. Perhaps now you will recognize the image you have created as an animal. Add details, such as a tail, using the Pencil or Brush tool. Complete your animal by adding color using the Fill tool.

PORTFOLIO

Save and print your animal. Put the printout in your portfolio with an evaluation of what you did to create the animal.

The Mass Production of Books

Gutenberg Bible. c. 1455. Vellum. The Huntington Library, San Marino, California/Superstock.

Look carefully at this page in your textbook. Now compare it with the same page in the textbook of the person sitting next to you. Do you notice any differences? Most likely, the two pages look identical. This textbook, like other modern books, was mass produced. This means that thousands were manufactured at the same time.

The mass production of books would not have been possible without the invention of movable type. Before 1450, every book was written by hand. To create a duplicate, a scribe copied the words using a brush or pen dipped in ink. Copying books took a great deal of time. Consequently, books were not widely available. Without books, the majority of people did not learn how to read.

All that changed, however, when Johannes Gutenberg invented movable type. This invention made it possible to print books efficiently and inexpensively. Books then became available to a larger number of people. With more affordable books, more people learned how to read.

The first book to be printed using movable type was the Gutenberg Bible. Although the illustrations were hand painted, the text was mass produced.

MAKING THE CONNECTION

- What do you think is the purpose of the illustrations on this page from the Gutenberg Bible? Explain your answer.
- Explain how books were created before the invention of movable type.
- How did the invention of movable type make it possible for more people to learn to read?

INTERNET ACTIVITY

Visit Glencoe's Fine Arts Web Site for students at:

http://www.glencoe.com/sec/art/students

CHAPTER 3
REVIEW

◆ BUILDING VOCABULARY

Number a sheet of paper from 1 to 10. After each number, write the term from the box that matches each description below.

art medium   pigment
binder   portrait
gesture drawing   printmaking
intaglio   sculpture
perception   solvent

1. Transferring an image from an inked surface to create a work of art.
2. A liquid that holds together the grains of pigment.
3. A printmaking technique in which the image to be printed is cut or scratched into a surface.
4. An awareness of the elements of an environment by means of the senses.
5. A visual representation of a person at rest.
6. A three-dimensional work of art.
7. A material used to create a work of art.
8. A finely ground powder that gives paint its color.
9. Moving a drawing medium quickly and freely over a surface to capture the form and actions of a subject.
10. A liquid used to control the thickness or thinness of the paint.

◆ REVIEWING ART FACTS

Number a sheet of paper from 11 to 20. Answer each question in a complete sentence.

11. What are three ways in which artists use the art of drawing?
12. Name and describe four shading techniques.
13. What is the binder in oil paint? What is one advantage of using this medium?
14. What is a water-soluble paint?
15. What are the three tools common to printmaking? Name two techniques of printmaking.
16. How does the use of space in sculpting differ from its use in other areas of art?
17. What is relief sculpture?
18. Name and describe four methods of sculpting.
19. Explain the difference between computer painting and drawing programs.
20. Identify three pieces of hardware used in computer art.

❓ THINKING ABOUT ART

1. **Analyze.** In this chapter, you learned how various art media have changed through the ages. What needs of the artist do you suppose brought about some of these changes? What role did changing technology play?
2. **Compare and contrast.** Imagine that you are planning a painting. What factors might lead you to select a water-soluble paint over an oil paint? What might prompt you to make the opposite choice?

── MAKING ART CONNECTIONS ──

1. **Music.** Preview and then bring to class a recording that reveals the characteristics of different musical instruments. Possibilities include Prokofiev's *Peter and the Wolf* and Britten's *The Young Person's Guide to the Orchestra*. Play the music for classmates. Identify the characteristics of each instrument's sound.

2. **Mathematics.** Computer drawing objects, as you learned in Lesson 8, are based on mathematical formulas. Interview a teacher in your school's computer science or math department about other advances in computer art that draw on mathematics. Share your findings with classmates in an oral report.

Figure 4–1   Look at this painting closely. If you see only a vase of flowers, move closer.

Jan Davidsz de Heem. *Vase of Flowers.* c. 1660. Oil on canvas. 69.6 × 56.5 cm (27⅜ × 22¼").
National Gallery of Art, Washington, D.C. Andrew W. Mellon Fund.

CHAPTER 4

Looking at Art

To understand some poems and stories, you need to look beyond the mere words on the page. You need to "read between the lines." Only by doing so are you able to see the true meaning.

The same may be said of art. Consider the painting at the left. On the surface, this simply looks like a vase of flowers. However, did you notice the lizard looking hungrily at a spider, the ants exploring an open pod, or the snail making its way across the shelf? What has the artist done to draw the viewer's attention to these details?

In this chapter, you will learn how to ask—and answer—questions like this one. You will learn how to "read" between the lines and make discoveries that will change the way you see and respond to art.

OBJECTIVES

After completing this chapter, you will be able to:

- Explain how subject, composition, and content relate to works of art.
- Define *aesthetics*.
- Identify the four steps of art criticism.
- Discuss the different ways in which critics judge works of art.

WORDS YOU WILL LEARN

abstract
aesthetics
aesthetic view
art critic
composition
content
credit line
non-objective
point of view
subject

PORTFOLIO IDEAS

Include some form of written self-reflection with your portfolio entry. In self-reflection, you have the opportunity to critique your own works. You tell what you learned from the assignment. You can also express feelings about the work by telling whether you think it succeeds, and what you liked or didn't like about doing the project.

Aesthetics

Taste is a personal matter. What is music to one person might be noise to another. In art, differences in taste may be traced to **aesthetics** (es-**thet**-iks). This is *the study of the nature of beauty and art.* Aesthetics raises the question "What makes a work of art successful?"

Over the centuries, thinkers seeking answers to this question have come up with different "aesthetic views" of art. An **aesthetic view** is *an idea or school of thought on what is most important in a work of art.* Historically, the debate among scholars has centered on three competing aesthetic views. These are the *subject view,* the *composition view,* and the *content view.*

SUBJECT VIEW

The subject view holds that a successful artwork is one whose subject looks convincing and lifelike. A work's **subject** is *an image viewers can easily identify.* The subject may be a person or people, as in Figure 4–2. It may be an object, such as a chair. It may even be an event, such as a holiday celebration. Look again at the painting in Figure 4–2. Notice how realistic the subject is. The work could almost be mistaken for a photograph. How do you think a scholar taking the subject view would evaluate this painting?

COMPOSITION VIEW

The second aesthetic view—the composition view—maintains that what counts most in an artwork is its **composition.** This is *the way the principles are used to organize the elements of art.* Supporters of the composition view attach the most importance to how the parts of a work fit together. They might look, for example, at the way balance is used to control shape or form. Such people would find much to applaud in the painting in Figure 4–3. Examine this work yourself.

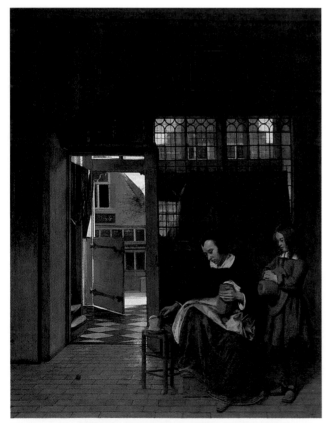

Figure 4–2 **What is the subject of this work? What elements and principles of art has the artist used? What mood or feeling does the work communicate?**

Pieter de Hooch. *A Woman Preparing Bread and Butter for a Boy.* 1660–63. Oil on canvas. 68.3 × 53 cm (26⅞ × 20⅞"). The J. Paul Getty Museum, Los Angeles, California.

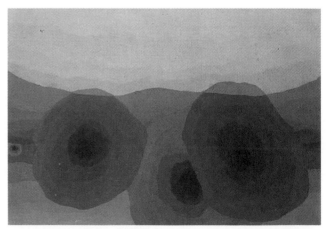

Figure 4–3 **Notice how this work communicates with the viewer even though it has no subject. What colors has the artist used? What shapes can you find?**

Arthur Dove. *Fog Horns.* 1929. Oil on canvas. 45.5 × 66 cm (18 × 26"). Colorado Springs Fine Arts Center, Colorado Springs, Colorado.

Figure 4–4 Examine the body language of the people in this painting. What mood is conveyed? What role does color play?

Pablo Picasso. *The Tragedy.* 1903. Oil on wood. 105 × 69 cm (41½ × 27⅛"). National Gallery of Art, Washington, D.C. Chester Dale Collection.

Notice that it lacks any recognizable subject matter. The artist has relied instead on the elements of color and shape to spark visual interest. What art principle has been used to organize these elements?

CONTENT VIEW

The third and final view states that the most important single ingredient of any artwork is its **content.** This is *the message, idea,*

or feeling expressed by a work of art. Scholars who hold the *content* view place the greatest value on a work's expressive qualities. A painting like the one in Figure 4–4 would earn high marks from people who hold this view. Notice the downward glances and forlorn expressions. Observe how the man's body language—his arms folded tightly about him—seems to shut out the world around him. You can almost feel this family's pain. Note the work's title. Do you find yourself wondering about the tragedy that befell them?

✔ Check Your Understanding

1. What is aesthetics?
2. What are the three commonly held aesthetic views?

LESSON 2

Art Criticism

Do you enjoy solving mysteries? Maybe you are a fan of brainteasers. In either case, having all the facts at hand is critical to finding a solution. So is arranging the facts in a logical fashion.

These statements apply not only to "whodunits" and puzzles. They also apply to artworks. In getting to the "bottom" of a work of art, you need to follow a series of ordered steps. In this lesson, you will learn about these steps and about the solutions they yield. You will also learn how to apply these steps to your own works of art.

THE ART CRITIC

As an amateur detective, you use evidence and clues to crack a case. In a sense, art critics do the same. An **art critic** is *a person whose job is studying, understanding, and judging works of art*. In getting this job done, critics will use all three aesthetic views.

When studying a work of art, the critic uses a four-step process. These steps are *describing, analyzing, interpreting,* and *judging.* The first three of these steps, as you will see, correspond to the three aesthetic views.

Figure 4–5 **Does this work succeed because it is lifelike, because of its composition, or because of the mood it expresses?**

Winslow Homer. *Crossing the Pasture.* c. 1872. Oil on canvas. 66.4 × 96.9 cm (26⅛ × 38⅛″). Amon Carter Museum, Fort Worth, Texas.

Figure 4–6a   What would you say is the subject of this painting?

Winslow Homer. *Crossing the Pasture*. Detail. c. 1872. Oil on canvas. 66.4 × 96.9 cm (26⅛ × 38⅛"). Amon Carter Museum, Fort Worth, Texas.

Describing

In describing a work, the critic asks the question "What do I see when I look at this work?" The work's *subject* is the focus of this step. Carefully list all the things you see in the work. Look at the credit line to find out what medium the artist has used and how large the artwork is.

Examine the work shown in Figure 4–5.

- How many figures do you see in the picture?
- What object are they both holding? What does the taller boy have over his shoulder?
- What animals do you see in the background?
- How would you describe the surroundings?

In answering these questions, you will be *describing* the subjects of this artwork.

Analyzing

In analyzing a work, the critic asks, "How is work of art organized? How are the elements and principles of art used?" The work's *composition* is the focus of this step.

Again, look at the detail of the painting in Figure 4–6a.

- What forms appear at the center of the composition? Why does the artist place the boys in the center, close to the viewer?
- Can you find any intense or bright colors in this picture?
- Where is the lightest value? What purpose does it serve?
- Notice the diagonal lines formed by the stick in the taller boy's hand and by the downward slope of the hill on the right. These lines converge on, and emphasize, the face of the taller boy. Can you find a third diagonal line that does the same?
- Can you find a more gently sloping diagonal that points to the face of the smaller boy?
- What colors has the artist used? What textures has he included?
- How has the artist used emphasis to make the subjects stand out?
- What role does proportion play in this artwork?

These questions and their answers are examples of the critic's analysis of the composition in the painting *Crossing the Pasture*.

Interpreting

In interpreting a work, the critic asks, "What is the artist saying to me? What moods, feelings, or ideas are expressed?" The work's *content* is the focus of this step. Look closely at Figure 4–6b.

- What emotion is communicated by the look and body language of the taller boy? Would you say that he stands tall and appears sure of himself?
- Contrast these observations with the facial expression and posture of the smaller boy.
- Why has the artist placed the boys against a darker, textured background?

Does this focus your attention on their faces and facial expressions? What do you think the artist has accomplished by drawing the viewer's eyes to the boys' expressions and body language?

- What visual clue can you find in the distance off to the left that might explain the boys' behavior?

Interpretation can be the most challenging step in art criticism. It is challenging because you must use your imagination. Do not be afraid to make an interpretation that is different from someone else's. Your interpretation will depend on what you have experienced in life.

Figure 4–6b   Notice the feelings conveyed by the boys' expressions. How does this information help you understand the story the painting tells?

Winslow Homer. *Crossing the Pasture*. Detail. c. 1872. Oil on canvas. 66.4 × 96.9 cm (26⅛ × 38⅛"). Amon Carter Museum, Fort Worth, Texas.

Judging

In judging a work, the critic asks, "Is the work successful?" This step depends on the answers to the questions asked during the first three steps. A work may be judged successful on the basis of its subject, composition, content, or some combination of the three. How do you think an art critic would judge the painting in Figure 4–5? Using what you have learned, how would you judge it?

If you have been an alert art sleuth up to this stage, you might have homed in on the story this painting tells. A part of it is revealed in the detail from the work in Figure 4–6b.

The slightly comical narrative centers on two boys, probably brothers. The two are seen crossing a field—taking a shortcut, maybe, after having just completed the morning's milking. Suddenly, each becomes aware of a real and present danger. Did you notice the bull in the background? The two boys certainly did! The younger boy's fear is obvious as he clings to his companion. The older boy, armed with a switch, proceeds fearlessly— or so he would like his younger brother to believe.

Once you have described, analyzed, and interpreted this painting, you will be able to decide for yourself whether or not it is successful. Do you find, now that you have gone through the three steps of art criticism, that you have made a judgment about whether Homer's *Crossing the Pasture* is a successful work of art? What is your opinion?

✔ Check Your Understanding

1. What is art criticism?
2. Name the four steps used by art critics. Explain what is done at each step.

STUDIO ACTIVITY

Reading a Credit Line

Look again at the painting in Figure 4–5 on page **66.** You can learn a lot about this work by examining the subject. You can also pick up an important clue by noting its title, *Crossing the Pasture.*

This information and much else appears in the painting's credit line. A **credit line** is *a listing of important facts about an artwork.* Appearing under or near a work, a credit line has six parts. It begins with the artist's name and the title of the artwork. The year the work was created and the art medium or media appear next. After that comes the size of the artwork. The last piece of information is the name of the museum, gallery, or other place in which the work is located. Referring to the credit line of Figure 4–5, you would learn that the work was painted by Winslow Homer in about 1872. The *"c."* before the date means "about." What medium did the artist use?

Every artwork in this book has a credit line. Use the credit lines in Figures 4–1, 4–2, and 4–3 to answer the following:

- Which of the works was painted by artist Pieter de Hooch?
- Which work was painted around 1600?
- What is the name of the artist who painted *Fog Horns?*
- Which of the works is housed in the National Gallery of Art?

P O R T F O L I O

Write a credit line for the next artwork you complete. Put it in your portfolio with your work.

Critiquing Non-Objective Art

Describing a work of art, you have learned, means identifying what you see. Sometimes this is easier said than done. Examine the artwork on this page. Compare it with the painting in Figure 4–3 on page **64**. How would you describe these works? What do you see when you look at each?

In this lesson, you will learn how to apply the steps of art criticism to works without recognizable subjects.

NON-OBJECTIVE ART

Artists do not work in isolation. Each generation builds on and refines the ideas of the one that came before. At times, throughout history, this process has led to startling changes. It has provided new answers to the question "What is art?"

One such major breakthrough came in the early 1900s. For several decades, artists had been experimenting with distorting shapes

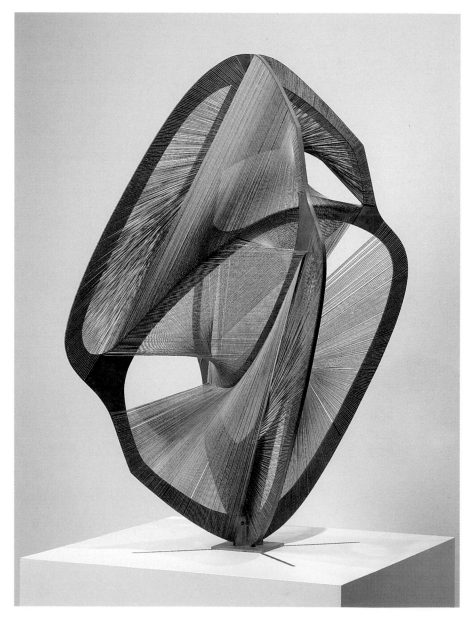

Figure 4–7 **What elements and principles of art would you point out during an analysis of this work. How is repetition used in this sculpture?**

Naum Gabo. *Linear Construction No. 4.* 1962. Bronze, stainless steel, piano wire. 128.3 × 63.5 × 63.5 cm (50½ × 25 × 25"). The Detroit Institute of Arts, Detroit, Michigan. Gift of W. Hawkins Ferry.

and forms. This new group took matters a step further. They abandoned subject matter altogether. They created non-objective works of art. **Non-objective** means *having no readily identifiable subjects or objects.*

Critiquing a Non-Objective Artwork

In studying non-objective works of art, critics apply the same four-step process outlined in the previous lesson. The main difference comes at the description step. To see this, look again at the sculpture in Figure 4–7. There is no identifiable subject. Even the title provides little help. In *describing* this work, a critic would, therefore, concentrate first on identifying the elements of art in it. He or she would take note of the different lines and forms that are used. Because the work is a sculpture that exists in three dimensions, the critic would pay special attention to the element of space. How would you describe the sculptor's use of space? How would you describe his use of negative space?

Now it is your turn to be a critic. Using the skills you have learned, try applying each of the following art-criticism steps to this artwork:

- **Describing.** How would you describe this sculpture? How many varieties of line have been used? What kinds of geometric or free-form shapes are visible? Is there any color used? Where are negative spaces apparent?
- **Analyzing.** How would you analyze this sculpture? What principle or principles of art have been used to organize the elements of art?
- **Interpreting.** What ideas, moods, and feelings are suggested by this work? Does the sculpture express an idea of some kind?
- **Judging.** Would you say that this work is successful? Does it have unity? What factors contribute to its success or lack of success?

STUDIO ACTIVITY

Experimenting with Non-Objective Art

Look once again at the painting in Figure 4–3 on page **64.** This time, notice the title. The artist has created the sensation of sound in this painting. He has done this by carefully arranging colors and shapes. As you gaze at this painting, listen for the deep, muffled song of distant fog horns.

Now try to achieve a similar effect yourself. First choose a familiar sound. It might be the sound of traffic on a busy street. It might be a barking dog or the hum of machinery. Select shapes, lines, and colors that express this sound. Create a visual version of this sound using colored markers and watercolors. Use the markers first. Then blend watercolor hues into your design.

P O R T F O L I O

For your portfolio, write an explanation of the sound you selected and describe how you created a visual version of this sound.

✓ Check Your Understanding

1. What is meant by non-objective art?
2. When examining a non-objective artwork, what is identified during the description step?

Creating a Realistic Painting

The emptiness and gloom of a nation fallen on hard times would seem like a strange theme for art. Yet, it is precisely this theme that runs through the works of American artist Edward Hopper. Hopper lived through a period called the Great Depression. This was a time when there was very little money. Many people in the United States and abroad were left without jobs or homes. Hopper's paintings accurately capture the mood of the era. They show lonely, often desperate people in shabby, rundown rooms.

Figure 4–8 shows one of Hopper's best-known paintings. Notice the **point of view.** This is *the angle from which the viewer sees the scene in an artwork.* Typical of Hopper's work, we do not see the people in this picture head-on. Instead, we are given a glimpse of them through a window.

WHAT YOU WILL LEARN

In this lesson you will use oil pastels to create your own Hopper "window." Like Figure 4–8, your painting will have a realistic subject. You point of view, like Hopper's, will be outside, looking into a lighted room through a window. It will be nighttime. The room will have no people. The furniture and other contents will overlap to indicate space. These objects will be drawn to show the mood or personality of the person living or working in this room.

WHAT YOU WILL NEED
- Pencil and sheets of sketch paper
- Oil pastels
- White drawing paper, 12 x 18 inches (30 x 46 cm)

Figure 4–8   Notice the title of the painting. What do you think it means? Why do you think these people sit idly around the counter of an all-night diner?

Edward Hopper. *Night Hawks.* 1942. Oil on canvas. 84.1 × 152.4 cm (33 × 60"). The Art Institute of Chicago, Chicago, Illinois. Friends of American Art Collection, 1942.51

WHAT YOU WILL DO

1. Begin by looking closely at the building across from the all-night diner in Figure 4–8. Study the row of dark windows on the second floor. Try to picture the kinds of rooms behind those windows. Decide whether they are fancy apartments, drab hotel rooms, offices, or something else. Think about the outside of the building. What material is it made of?

2. Imagine that the lights were turned on inside one of the rooms. Make several sketches of what your mind "sees." Draw a window frame like the one in Figure 4–8, only larger. As you sketch, continue to imagine the contents of the room. You might include wallpaper, carpeting, and other furniture. As you work, ask yourself, "What kind of person lives or works here?" Decide what clues you can provide in your drawing to tell viewers something about the mood or personality of this person.

3. Transfer your best drawing to the white drawing paper. Work lightly in pencil. Make the outside wall of the building look like brick, stone, or wood.

4. Color your picture using oil pastels. Select colors that will give your room a "personality" to match that of its imaginary occupant.

5. Like Hopper, avoid small, unnecessary details. Lay one color over another to create textures. Overlap shapes and forms to suggest space inside the room.

6. Display your finished drawing in a horizontal row along with those of classmates.

EXAMINING YOUR WORK

- **Describe** Are the objects inside the room easy to identify? What texture did you use for the outside of your building?
- **Analyze** Did you show the different values for objects inside the lighted room compared to those in the darkness outside? Did you overlap shapes and forms to suggest space?
- **Interpret** Does your drawing offer clues about the mood or personality of the person who might live or work in the room?
- **Judge** Do you think your drawing is successful? Does it present the subject matter in a realistic way?

Figure 4–9   Student work. Hopper windows.

STUDIO OPTION

Try This!

■ Create another version of your Hopper window. This scene is to be set during the day and is to reflect a mood opposite the one in your first drawing. This time the point of view will be looking through the window to the outside. Use pastels for the window frame and watercolors for the landscape out of doors.

Creating an Expressive Word Design

Have you ever had one of those days in which nothing seemed to go right? Maybe, like the young woman in Figure 4–10, you felt "blue." Study this fine-art print. Notice that the artist has not shown us much of the woman's face. We are still able to "read" her mood by observing her body language. What details of the woman's posture help us identify how she is feeling? What other moods can you identify from the way a person sits or stands?

WHAT YOU WILL LEARN

The artist has taken one approach to capturing a particular mood or feeling. In this lesson, you will take another approach. You will communicate the mood of your choice through a word, written in large block letters, rather than an image. You will use variety of shapes and colors to create a background that emphasizes the emotion suggested by this word.

Figure 4–10 **What does the subject's body language reveal about her mood?**

Albrecht Dürer. *Melencholia 1.* 1514. Engraving. 24.1 × 18.6 cm (9½ × 7⁵⁄₁₆″). The Metropolitan Museum of Art, New York, New York. Harris Brisbane Dick Fund, 1943.

WHAT YOU WILL NEED

- Pencil and sketch paper
- White drawing paper, 9 x 12 inches (23 x 30 cm)
- Tempera paint
- Mixing trays
- Brushes
- Water

WHAT YOU WILL DO

1. With classmates, brainstorm words naming moods and emotions. Possibilities include *happy, tired, worried, angry,* and *bored.*
2. Choose one of the words. On sketch paper, write the word out in large block letters. Experiment with different letter designs that communicate the mood you have chosen. You might, for example, use rounded, overlapping letters for an upbeat mood. Letters with straight edges and sharp points might communicate a negative mood, such as anger. Letters may be all capitals or upper and lower case but should fill the page.
3. Transfer your best design to the sheet of drawing paper. Still working in pencil, create a background design. This is to have the form of thick and thin bands extending horizontally or vertically from one edge of the paper to the other. As with the shape of the letters, the bands should reflect the word you are using. Zigzag lines might be used for the word tense. Curved lines signal a more peaceful mood.
4. Select a color scheme that emphasizes the emotion or feeling of your word. Again, think about the expressive nature of

EXAMINING YOUR WORK

- **Describe** Is the word you selected easily read? Did you use large block letters to write this word?
- **Analyze** Did you create a background made up of bands of color? Did these colors contrast with one another to create variety?
- **Interpret** Does your design reflect the mood or feeling of the word? Do the shapes and colors help emphasize that emotion?
- **Judge** Does your design communicate an emotion with letters, shapes, and colors? Is this a successful work of art?

color. Boldly contrasting hues, intensities, and values might be used to express tension. Hues, intensities, and values that are harmonious could express peace.
5. Paint the background bands in the colors you have selected. Do not paint the letters themselves.

Figure 4–11 Student work. An expressive word.

COMPUTER OPTION

Try This!

■ Choose a word related to a mood or feeling. Select the Text tool and type the word. From the Font menu, choose a typeface that reflects the mood of your choice. For example, use a playful font, such as Hobo, for an upbeat mood. Select the entire word, and drag the corner of the surrounding box to enlarge the word. Fill the entire screen. Fill your word with a color or preset pattern that helps communicate the mood you have chosen.

Creating an Abstract Figure

Non-objective art, as you learned in Lesson 3, began in the early 1900s. By avoiding subject matter, non-objective artists created a new means of self-expression. Since that time, other artists have taken a more middle-of-the-road approach to subject matter. They have produced art that is **abstract.** This means *having a recognizable subject that is shown in an unrealistic manner.*

The work in Figure 4–12 is an example of abstract art. Its subject is a character from Greek mythology. His name is Icarus. According to legend, Icarus tried to fly using wings held together with wax. Ignoring warnings, Icarus flew too close to the sun. The wax melted, and the youth fell to his death. Study this work of art. Can you recognize it as a falling figure?

Figure 4–12 How would you describe the use of negative space in this work? Why do you think the artist chose to make the figure abstract?

Henri Matisse. *Icarus.* Plate VIII from *Jazz.* 1947. Pochoir, printed in color. Each single page: 21.1 × 32.6 cm (8⅓ × 12⅝″). The Museum of Modern Art, New York, New York. The Louis E. Stern Collection.

WHAT YOU WILL LEARN

Using your imagination, you will create a simplified abstract shape. The shape will be of a falling figure. The image will be made with a single, continuous line. You will use a length of colored yarn to form the line. The same thickness of the line throughout will add harmony to your work.

WHAT YOU WILL NEED

- Pencil and sketch paper, 12 x 18 inches (30 x 46 cm)
- Waxed paper
- Transparent or masking tape
- Yarn, about 60 inches (152 cm) in length
- Large bowl
- White glue, thinned with water

WHAT YOU WILL DO

1. Study Figure 4–12. Notice the way the artist has captured the sense of a figure falling through space. Trace your finger around the outline of the abstract shape of this figure.
2. Complete several drawings of your own version of the falling Icarus. As in Figure 4–12, your work should be abstract. Use a single continuous pencil line to create your figures.
3. Transfer your best drawing to a sheet of sketch paper. Make a heavy line using pencil. Cover the drawing completely with a sheet of waxed paper that is smaller than the page. Secure the waxed paper in place with tape. The drawing should be clearly visible through the waxed paper.
4. Draw a line of white glue over the pencil line. Carefully lay the yarn on the line of glue. Allow time for the yarn to dry.

EXAMINING YOUR WORK

- **Describe**   Is your work easily recognized as an abstract figure?
- **Analyze**   Did you use one continuous line to create the abstract shape? Did the use of a line with the same thickness throughout add harmony to your design?
- **Interpret**   Does your figure appear to be falling through space?
- **Judge**   Using composition to measure accomplishment, is your work a success? Why or why not?

5. Once the glue is thoroughly dry, the yarn will be stiff and hold its shape. Carefully lift the shape off the waxed paper. Use thread to suspend your Icarus figure from a clothesline or the ceiling of the classroom.

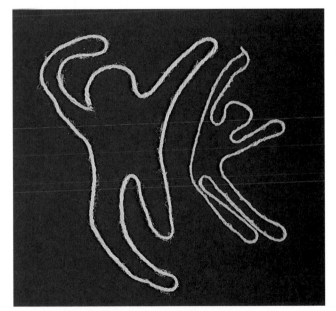

Figure 4–13   **Student work. Abstract figures.**

STUDIO OPTIONS

■ To add color to the shape of your figure, cut and glue on pieces of colored tissue paper.

■ To make a more three-dimensional form, create basic body shapes first. Cut out several of the same body shapes from analogous colors of construction paper. Overlap them to create a sense of movement. Glue them together using small "spacers" cut from cardboard. Arrange a display with the work of other students.

Lesson 6   *Creating an Abstract Figure*   **77**

Exploring Space

Jan Vermeer van Delft. *The Astronomer.* 1668. Oil on canvas. 51.5 × 45.5 cm (20¼ × 18"). The Louvre, Paris, France. Erich Lessing/Art Resource, NY.

Since the dawn of time, people have dreamed of exploring space. They looked to the heavens and questioned what was out there. Did other civilizations exist somewhere in the universe?

In the seventeenth century, when Jan Vermeer painted *The Astronomer,* major breakthroughs provided clues into the solar system. One important development was the telescope. Galileo, an Italian astronomer, developed a telescope that magnified objects by 20 times. Using this telescope, Galileo saw that the surface of the moon was made of mountains and craters.

It was 300 years later, however, before people were actually able to reach the moon. In the middle of the twentieth century, advances in technology finally provided the means necessary for space travel. In 1969, astronaut Neil Armstrong landed on the moon. He took "one small step for man, one giant leap for mankind."

Today, scientists send satellites into space to orbit the Earth. These satellites observe, measure, and record information that would be impossible to obtain from Earth. Weather satellites, for example, provide data that helps forecasters predict weather conditions around the world.

MAKING THE CONNECTION

- What clues tell you that the subject of Vermeer's painting is an astronomer?
- By studying this painting, what can you learn about astronomy in the seventeenth century?
- Find out more about astronomy. Besides the telescope, what other developments occurred during the 1600s?

INTERNET ACTIVITY

Visit Glencoe's Fine Arts Web Site for students at:

http://www.glencoe.com/sec/art/students

REVIEW

◆ BUILDING VOCABULARY

Number a sheet of paper from 1 to 10. After each number, write the term from the box that matches each description below.

abstract	content
aesthetics	credit line
aesthetic view	non-objective
art critic	point of view
composition	subject

1. The message, idea, or feeling expressed by a work of art.
2. A person whose job is studying, understanding, and judging works of art.
3. Art with a recognizable subject that is shown in an unrealistic manner.
4. Art with no readily identifiable subjects or objects.
5. An image viewers can easily identify.
6. The way the principles are used to organize the elements of art.
7. The study of the nature of beauty and art.
8. A listing of important facts about an artwork.
9. The angle from which the viewer sees the scene in an artwork.
10. An idea or school of thought on what is most important in a work of art.

◆ REVIEWING ART FACTS

Number a sheet of paper from 11 to 15. Answer each question in a complete sentence.

11. Why do students of art usually accept more than one aesthetic view?
12. What are the four steps of art criticism?
13. What kinds of art criticism questions join an art element with an art principle?
14. Why is it impossible to measure the success of a non-objective artwork in terms of subject?
15. When examining a non-objective artwork, what is identified during description?

THINKING ABOUT ART

1. **Interpretation.** Imagine that two critics are examining the same work of art. Each comes up with a different interpretation. What reasons can you think of that might explain this?
2. **Extend.** Do you think a critic could ever change his or her mind about an artwork's success or lack of success? Why or why not?
3. **Extend.** Which of the art-criticism questions do you find the most difficult to ask? Which is hardest to answer? Explain your answers.

MAKING ART CONNECTIONS

1. **Language Arts.** Review the artworks in this chapter. Select one that might be a good illustration for a short story or poem. Write the story or poem.
2. **Community Connection.** Find a work of art in your community. You might choose a public statue or other well-known work. Apply the four art-criticism steps to the work. Write your report on the work in a way that could be understood by readers who know nothing about art or art criticism. Use the classroom computer to publish your report. Share the report with family members and friends.

Figure 5–1 Notice the way in which the artist interacts with the viewer. What mood is expressed by this work?

Judith Leyster. *Self-portrait.* c. 1630. Oil on canvas. 74.6 × 65.7 cm (29⅜ × 25⅞"). National Gallery of Art, Washington, D.C. Gift of Mr. and Mrs. Robert Woods Bliss.

CHAPTER 5

Art Through the Ages

In art, background information is important. Look at the painting at the left. The work shows the artist turning from her self-portrait to look at the viewer. By looking at the credit line, you learn that it is a self-portrait. Take a closer look at the credit line, however. Notice not only the questions it answers—who painted the work and when—but also the ones it raises: Is this painting similar to others done around the same time? What other works did this artist produce?

In this chapter you will learn how to ask and answer such questions. You will learn how the time and place in which artists worked have a strong effect on the style and content of their artworks.

PORTFOLIO IDEAS

A strong art portfolio reflects what you learn about art history as well as art techniques. Make sure to include written entries that demonstrate your ability to describe an artwork from the art historian's point of view—by telling who created the work, and when and where it was created. Show that you understand how time and place influence an artist.

OBJECTIVES

After completing this chapter, you will be able to:
- Explain why art history is important.
- Recognize the changes and similarities among artworks through the ages.
- Understand the goals of different cultures and art movements.
- Create works of art of different cultures and times.

WORDS YOU WILL LEARN

applied art
architecture
art historians
art movement
bust
contours
diorama
fine art
hieroglyphic
painted screen
Renaissance
symbol

Art of Long Ago

No artist works completely alone. Artists of each age, rather, study and learn from works created in ages past. The same may be said of **art historians.** These are *people who study art of different ages and cultures.* Like art critics, art historians examine and analyze art. Unlike critics, art historians are not content to look only at artworks. Their job is to look *beyond* them. They record milestones in art and changes in the way artists work.

In this chapter, you will journey back through the ages. You will learn about some of these milestones and changes. Your journey will begin with a look at art of earlier times.

ART OF ANCIENT EGYPT

Have you ever followed a brook or stream to its source? If we follow the long, twisting "stream" of art history to its source, we end up on the banks of an actual river. That river is the Nile. The time is 5,000 years ago. The place is Egypt. There, in the cradle of Western civilization, powerful kings called *pharaohs* ruled. Farming and trade thrived. So did art.

Rules of the Egyptian Artist

The Egyptians built mighty temples and monuments. It was with an eye toward decorating these structures that much of their art was created. Study the relief carving in Figure 5–2. This work probably once graced a pharaoh's tomb. The subject is the Egyptian

Figure 5–2 Look at the subject of this sculpture. What does it reveal about the Egyptians' system of beliefs?

Egyptian. *Thoth, God of Learning and Patron of Scribes.* Egyptian. 26th Dynasty, 663–525 B.C. (Late period). Slate relief. 36.5 × 12 × 1 cm (14⅜ × 4¾ × ⁷⁄₁₆"). Dallas Museum of Art, Dallas, Texas. Gift of Elsa von Seggern.

god of learning. The figure has a human body and the head of a bird, specifically an ibis. This long-beaked creature was one of many animals the Egyptians worshiped. They believed the ibis possessed special powers.

Did you notice anything unusual about the way the figure is shown? Some body parts, including the head and arms, appear as they would if they were viewed from the side. Others, such as the shoulders, are shown as if they are seen from the front. This odd mix-and-match might seem at first to be a mistake. In fact, it is common to Egyptian art. It reflects certain strict rules Egyptian artists were forced to follow. The rules required that each body part be shown from its most familiar angle. What parts besides those mentioned above are shown as side views? Which are treated as views from the front?

ART OF ANCIENT GREECE

While Egypt was still at its peak, another great empire took root some 500 miles to the north. This was Greece. Greece reached its peak during the fourth and fifth centuries B.C. This was a time known as the Golden Age. It was called the Golden Age because it produced great writers and thinkers. It produced great political leaders. It also produced great artists.

Greek Vases

One of the most powerful leaders and influential thinkers of the Golden Age was a man named Pericles (**pehr**-ih-kleez). Pericles loved beauty and preached its importance. The aesthetic ideals Pericles held sacred may be seen in everything the Greeks created. Beauty can be found in the perfectly proportioned temples of the period. It is reflected in the idealized sculptures of gods and athletes. It also appears in carefully designed vases such as the one in Figure 5–3.

Examine this art object. Vases like this are examples of **applied art.** This is *art made to be useful as well as visually pleasing.* Applied art is usually seen in contrast with **fine art,** or *art made*

Figure 5–3 Notice how line has been used to suggest movement. What art principles have been used to organize this vase painting?

Greek. Exekias. *Quadriga Wheeling Right.* Slip-decorated earthenware. 46.2 cm (18¹⁄₁₆″). Toledo Museum of Art, Toledo, Ohio.

to be enjoyed visually, not used. In this program, you will see many examples of each type of art.

Like other Greek vases, this one is remarkable for the beauty of its form. It is equally noteworthy for the quality of the painting that decorates it. The painting was done by Exekias (ex-**zee**-kee-uhs), the most famous of Greek vase painters. It shows a chariot led by a team of four spirited horses. Notice the air of excitement in the work. What art elements contribute to this feeling? What principles of art are used to organize them?

ART OF ANCIENT ROME

Despite its greatness, Greece suffered from fighting within the empire. As a nation divided, it was doomed. After 1,300 years of almost continuous strife, Greece fell. The people who conquered it were the Romans.

Although Greek power came to an end as Rome grew in strength, Greek influence continued on. The Romans admired Greek art.

Following their conquest of Greece in 146 B.C., they shipped many Greek art treasures to their homeland. They also hired many Greek artists to work for them.

Roman Portrait Sculpture

Roman artists were skilled at creating life-like sculptures. Like the Greeks, they made statues of important people such as rulers.

Figure 5–4 **This face looks like one you might see on the street today. What quality of the work accounts for this?**

Roman. *Head of a Young Man.* A.D. 100–130. Marble. 22.5 × 16.5 cm (8⅞ × 6½″). Dallas Museum of Art, Dallas, Texas. Anonymous gift in memory of Edward Marcus.

Unlike the Greeks, who always showed the entire figure in their sculptures, Roman artists instead focused on heads and busts. A **bust** is *a sculpture that shows a person's head, shoulders, and upper chest.*

Many wealthy Romans had busts made of themselves and their families. These were placed in the subject's home. One such portrait sculpture appears in Figure 5–4. It is a marble head of a young man. Clearly, the artist made no effort to flatter the sitter. Rather, the sculpture captures in great detail the likeness of a real person, blemishes and all. Inspect this work. In what ways is it similar to other portrait sculptures you have seen? In what ways is it different? Would a critic taking the content view praise this work? Why or why not?

Check Your Understanding

1. What is the job of an art historian?
2. Why did Egyptian artists always show the human figure in the same unusual way?
3. When did ancient Greece reach its peak? When and by whom was it conquered?
4. How did Roman sculptures of people differ from Greek sculptures of people?
5. What is the difference between applied art and fine art?

STUDIO ACTIVITY

Making a Bottle Decoration

In its day, the vase in Figure 5–3 was admired not only for its beauty. It was also prized for the practical purpose it served—storing water.

Look again at Figure 5–3, specifically at the painting on the vase. This painting portrays a chariot race, a sporting event of the period. Think of a sporting event of your own time. Then select a familiar vase shape on which to record this event. One possibility would be the type of bottle in which commercial sports drinks are sold. Make a pencil drawing of your bottle shape. Your drawing should be large enough to fill a 9 x 12-inch (23 x 30-cm) sheet of white drawing paper. Decorate this shape with a picture of the present-day event you have chosen. Design your picture to fit the bottle shape. Complete your drawing with markers or oil pastels. Choose a color scheme similar to that used in the Greek vase painting.

PORTFOLIO

Imagine how your vase would have been used in ancient Greek history. Write a short paragraph telling why it was made and where it would have been kept. Keep your written description with your vase in your portfolio.

Egyptian Tomb Painting

Look back at the Egyptian relief sculpture in Figure 5–2 on page **82.** This work teaches us about the ancient Egyptian system of beliefs. The same may be said of the painting in Figure 5–5. The work is from the tomb of an Egyptian pharaoh named Sethi. He is the figure pictured on the right. With him is the goddess Hathor. According to Egyptian myth, Hathor was the goddess of the sky. She was also queen of heaven. It appears that Hathor is about to take the pharaoh's hand, as if to lead him somewhere. Where might she be preparing to lead the fallen pharaoh?

Look more closely at this painting. Did you notice the abstract shapes in the rounded boxes? They appear in the picture above the head of Sethi. These are examples of **hieroglyphic** (hy-ruh-**glif**-ik). This is *an early form of picture writing.* Perhaps these "words" identified the object that the goddess is handing to the pharaoh.

WHAT YOU WILL LEARN

In this lesson, you will design and create an Egyptian tomb painting. The subject will be a well-known figure from American or world history. In portraying this figure, you will try to show his or her character. You will also follow the rules of Egyptian art. You will use a repeating pattern for the figure's clothing, as in Figure 5–5. In the background, you will include hieroglyphics. These will be made up of objects that help define the person's identity. You will complete your tomb painting using tempera paints.

WHAT YOU WILL NEED

- Pencil and sheets of sketch paper
- White drawing paper, 12 x 18 inches (30 x 46 cm)
- Fine-tipped black marker
- Tempera paints
- Mixing tray
- Medium and fine brushes
- Paper towels

Figure 5–5   Notice the use of balance and texture in this work. What makes you think these figures are important?

Egyptian. *The Goddess Hathor Places the Magic Collar on Sethos I.* Thebes, 19th Dynasty. c. 1303–1290 B.C. Painted bas-relief. 226.5 cm (89⅛"). The Louvre, Paris, France.

WHAT YOU WILL DO

1. With a partner, brainstorm possible historical figures as subjects for your tomb painting. Choose a person you know a lot about. Think about objects and visual symbols that help define the person's identity. A **symbol** is *an image used to stand for a quality or idea.* If you chose George Washington, for example, your symbols might include an ax and a cherry tree. Jot down notes about your subject and symbols.

2. Study the figures in Figure 5–5. Notice the position of the head, shoulders, chest, arms, legs, and feet. Make pencil sketches of your subject. Follow the same formula the ancient Egyptian artist used.

3. Transfer your best sketch to the drawing paper. Make your figure large enough to fill the page. In the background, draw boxes with rounded corners. These are to contain your hieroglyphics. In the boxes, draw abstract visual symbols based on the notes you made.

4. Complete your painting by mixing tints and shades of tempera paint. Apply the colors to your figure and background objects. Carefully color the motifs in your pattern.

5. Switch to fine-tipped black marker. Lightly retrace the **contours,** or *outlines and surface ridges,* of important shapes, including body parts. Create a pattern on your subject's clothing.

6. When your painting is dry, display it alongside those of fellow students. Challenge classmates to identify the subject of your work.

Figure 5–6 **Student work. Egyptian tomb painting.**

EXAMINING YOUR WORK

- **Describe** Is your painting based on a figure from history? Did you include symbols that would help your viewer pinpoint the person's identity?
- **Analyze** Did you follow the rules of Egyptian art for representing human body parts? Did you use a repeating pattern to decorate the person's clothing?
- **Interpret** Did you capture the character of your figure? Were classmates able to identify your person?
- **Judge** Do you consider your painting successful? Why or why not?

STUDIO OPTION

■ Make a clay carving of your tomb design. Begin with a ball of modeling clay roughly the size of a grapefruit. Flatten the ball with your hand. Using a large wooden dowel or rolling pin, roll the lump into an oblong measuring approximately 6 x 8 inches. With a modeling tool or popsicle stick, carve the outline of your figure into the clay surface. Wipe the tool from time to time with a damp cloth to remove any excess clay. Add hieroglyphics and other background details. When the clay slab is dry, fire it with your teacher's help.

Eastern Art

No tour of the ancient art world would be complete without a swing through Asia. Here, halfway around the globe from the great temples and pyramids of Egypt, other mighty empires rose and fell. Each left behind an artistic tradition as rich as those of the Greeks and Romans.

In this lesson, you will read about two of those cultures. You will also view some of the art treasures they left behind.

ART OF ANCIENT INDIA

In the mid-1800s, railroad workers digging in the Indus River valley of present-day Pakistan made a remarkable discovery. They unearthed bits and pieces of a lost city. Archaeologists later pieced together this ancient puzzle. Their explorations revealed that the city was once the center of a river civilization that had existed some 4,500 years earlier. It had achieved a splendor at least as great as that of ancient Egypt.

Like the Egyptians, the people of the Indus River valley worshiped animals and the forces of nature. These beliefs were later combined with others to form the foundation of one of the world's great religions. That religion is Hinduism (**hin**-doo-iz-uhm). Today, this faith has 700 million followers.

Sculpture

Among the gifts passed down by the Indus River valley civilization was a knowledge of bronze casting. This sculpting method was used by later inhabitants of the region to create the work in Figure 5–7. The subject of this sculpture is Hanuman, king of the monkeys. According to Hindu myth, Hanuman helped the god Rama rescue Rama's wife from a demon's evil clutches.

Like other characters in Hindu legend, Hanuman represents a human virtue (**vur**-chew). A *virtue* is a positive quality, in this case loyalty.

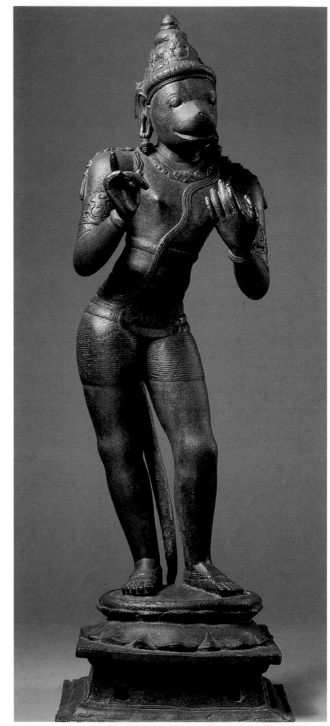

Figure 5–7 Notice that the creature has the body of a human but a monkey's head and tail. What does Hanuman's posture tell you about his character?

Indian, Tamil Nadu. *Standing Hanuman.* Chola Period. Eleventh century. Bronze. 64.5 cm (25⅜"). The Metropolitan Museum of Art, New York, New York. Purchase, funds and bequests from various donors.

ART OF ANCIENT JAPAN

The civilization of the Indus River valley is among the earliest on record. Evidence of an even older culture has been found on the island nation of Japan. This culture is believed to have sprung to life around 5000 B.C.

As with Indian art, the art of ancient Japan was inspired by religion. Interestingly, one of the religions that shaped much of early Japanese art began in India and then came to Japan through China in A.D. 552. That religion is Buddhism (**boo**-diz-uhm). Buddhism was an outgrowth of Hinduism. It emphasizes physical and spiritual discipline as the means for reaching a state of inner peace.

Screen Painting

One common form of Japanese artistic expression is shown in Figure 5–8. Each object is a **painted screen**. This is *an art object used as a wall or room divider.* Do you recall the name for art that is both useful and pleasing to the eye?

Look carefully at these screens. They show two creatures, one real and one mythical. Both have symbolic value. The tiger was believed to chase evil. The dragon was thought to bring luck.

STUDIO ACTIVITY

Creating a Japanese Drawing

Before creating artworks, Japanese artists would silently and carefully study their subject.

Bring an object of nature, such as a leaf, stone, or seed pod to class. Silently study the object from different angles. Examine its lines, form, texture, and color. Place the object out of sight. Using black or colored pencils, create the image of the object that remains in your mind.

P O R T F O L I O

For your portfolio, write a short paragraph explaining whether you were successful at creating an image of the object from your memory of it.

Check Your Understanding

1. How was the Indus River valley civilization discovered?
2. For what is this civilization most remembered?

Figure 5–8 The artist painted the subjects of these works realistically. What would defenders of each of the three aesthetic views have to say about these paintings?

Maruyama Okyo. *Tiger and Dragon Screens.* 1781. Edo Period. Ink and colors on paper. Each 168 × 188 cm (66¼ × 70″). Detroit Institute of Arts, Detroit, Michigan. Founders Society Purchase with funds from various contributors.

Making a Relief Sculpture

Examine the work in Figure 5–9. It is the product of another culture that has a long tradition. That culture is the Kota of central Africa. Unlike other peoples you have learned about, little is known about the Kota and other cultures of early Africa. In fact, much of the early art of these groups no longer exists. Many of their creations were crafted from wood. Often these were destroyed by the damp climate of the region.

The Kota sculpture in the picture is an abstract figure. Works like this were placed over a container. Inside the container were the remains of an honored ancestor. The original purpose of the sculptures remains a mystery. One popular view is that the works were meant to drive away evil spirits. What are some other possibilities?

WHAT YOU WILL LEARN

You will create an abstract sculpture modeled after the Kota figure in Figure 5–9. Like that sculpture, your work will have formal balance. It will be decorated with a pattern of lines made from glue. These will suggest facial features and add tactile texture.

WHAT YOU WILL NEED

- One large piece of cardboard, about 12 x 8 inches (30 x 20 cm), and several smaller pieces
- Pencil
- Scissors
- White glue
- Heavy twine
- Aluminum foil
- Transparent or masking tape

Figure 5–9 At one time the creations of African artists went unappreciated in the Western world. This is because they lacked realism. Have standards in art changed? If so, how?

African. Gabon, Kota. *Reliquary Figure.* Nineteenth-twentieth century. Wood, brass, copper, iron. 73.3 cm (28⅞"). The Metropolitan Museum of Art, New York, New York. Purchase 1983.

WHAT YOU WILL DO

1. Carefully study the Kota figure illustrated in Figure 5–8. Examine the tactile textures in the work. Notice the use of formal balance. On the large piece of cardboard, complete an outline drawing in pencil of a similar figure. Like the one pictured, your figure should be abstract.

2. Cut out your figure. With the pencil, add facial features and decorative lines. Squeeze white glue over the pencil lines. Lay twine over glue lines. Allow the glue to dry before proceeding to the next step.

3. Lay the prepared figure on a sheet of aluminum foil. Place a dull pencil point on the foil about one-half inch from the outer edge of the figure. Following the contour of the figure, make a light outline one-half inch larger.

4. Using the indented outline as a guide, cut out the foil copy of your figure. Beginning on one side, fold the foil over the edge of the cardboard. Gently smooth it down and press it into place.

5. Press the foil securely around the raised glue lines. Use the blunt end of a brush, dull pencil, or your fingers to make these lines stand out clearly. Be careful not to tear the foil.

6. When completed, the foil should be bent under all edges of the figure and smoothed flat everywhere except over the glue lines. Secure the foil to the cardboard with tape.

7. Use the same blunt tool to apply texture—dots and lines.

EXAMINING YOUR WORK

- **Describe** Does your figure include all the shapes identified in the original?
- **Analyze** Does your figure have formal balance? Does it show features of the face and decorations as patterns of line on the surface of the sculpture? Do these lines give your work an interesting texture?
- **Interpret** Do you think your figure looks as though it, too, could chase away evil spirits?
- **Judge** Suppose you were to make another Kota figure. What would you do differently to make it better?

Figure 5–10 **Student work. Relief sculpture.**

STUDIO OPTIONS

Try This!

■ Accent the decorations on the foil surface of your Kota figure. Do this by painting on a coat of black ink. You may have to apply several coats to penetrate all areas. When the ink has dried, lightly rub steel wool over the design. The raised areas will return to their original metallic finish. The other areas will remain black.

■ Use the steps outlined in this lesson to create an abstract figure of your own design. Before sketching a design for your figure, decide on its purpose. Ask yourself what mood the completed work will express.

Art of the Middle Ages and Renaissance

Empires, as you have learned, come and go. Rome was no exception. In the fifth century, this great empire suffered the fate that had earlier claimed Egypt, Greece, and the Indus River valley civilization.

The period following Rome's collapse was one of chaos. Today we know this time in history as the Middle Ages. It lasted some 1,000 years.

ART OF THE MIDDLE AGES

After Rome fell, some of its great temples and palaces were torn down. The stone was carried off and used to build fortresses. These were built to keep invaders out. In time, structures of this type led to a new form of architecture. **Architecture** is *the art of planning and creating buildings.*

Castle Building

You probably recognize the structure in Figure 5–11. It is a castle. This is a fortlike dwelling with high walls and towers. Many castles were further protected by moats and drawbridges.

Figure 5–12 The cathedral has graceful, upwardly soaring lines and large windows.

Beauvais Cathedral, West Facade. Beauvais, France.

Guards stationed in the towers would sound the alarm when enemies approached.

Study the castle in Figure 5–11. Do you think the architect's main concern was safety or comfort?

Cathedral Building

Just before Rome fell, Christianity spread throughout much of Europe. During the Middle Ages, the Church remained the single strongest force.

By around 1300, a new type of building began to appear. This type of structure is shown in Figure 5–12. It was a special type of church known as a *cathedral* (kuh-**thee**-druhl).

Compare the cathedral in this picture with the castle in Figure 5–11. The cathedral has graceful, upwardly soaring lines.

Figure 5–11 The architect of this castle avoided windows because the walls would not support them. What other factors might have led to a lack of windows?

View of castle, Alcazar, Segovia, Spain. Eleventh-fifteenth centuries. SEF/ Art Resource, N.Y.

ART OF THE RENAISSANCE

After ten centuries of slumber, Europe awoke in the 1400s to a period of unparalleled growth. Trade and knowledge spread. New discoveries were made in science. Artists and scholars developed an interest in the art and literature of ancient Greece and Rome. This period is known today as the **Renaissance** (**ren**-uh-sahns), which means *period of rebirth.*

Renaissance Painting

The Renaissance was a time of great discoveries in art as well. Painters achieved a level of realism never before imagined by using perspective to give depth and shading to provide three-dimensionality.

This realism is evident in the painting in Figure 5–13. The work was done sometime after the Renaissance. Notice the attention to detail. Every fold in the woman's clothing is faithfully recorded. So is the glint in her eye. Look at her expression. What do you suppose she is thinking about as she pauses from playing her violin?

✔ Check Your Understanding

1. What is meant by the term *Middle Ages?*
2. What was the main source of power in Europe during this era?
3. What changes occurred in art during the Renaissance?

STUDIO ACTIVITY

Making a Stained-Glass Window

Cathedrals like the one in Figure 5–12 were fitted with *stained-glass* windows. These were made of colored glass pieces held together with lead strips. Because of these windows, the insides of the cathedrals were bathed in softly tinted light.

Cut black butcher paper into a circle about 12 inches in diameter. Fold the circle in half three times until you have a cone shape. Cut out geometric and simple shapes from the two folded sides. Vary the sizes of the cuts. Open the circle. Cover each opening with a patch of colored cellophane. Cut the patches so that each slightly overlaps the shape it is meant to cover. Secure the cellophane patches with transparent tape. Place your finished work on a windowsill.

PORTFOLIO

When your stained-glass window is complete, write a short paragraph explaining how you made your choices of colors and shapes. Keep your description and your artwork together in your portfolio.

Figure 5–13 **Observe the striking use of value in this painting. How does it add to the lifelike quality of the work?**

Orazio Gentileschi. *Young Woman with a Violin.* c. 1612. Oil on canvas. 83.5 × 98 cm (32¾ × 38½″). Detroit Institute of Arts, Detroit, Michigan. Gift of Mrs. Edsel B. Ford.

Creating a Diorama

The Renaissance, you have learned, was a time of bold new discoveries. One of these was a technique called *linear perspective*. This technique aided painters in their quest for realism. In linear perspective, the horizontal lines of objects are slanted. This makes them appear to extend back into space. As Figure 5–14 shows, the lines meet at an imaginary point called the *vanishing point*.

The painting in Figure 5–15 uses linear perspective. Examine this lifelike work. Find the slanted lines in the vine-covered lattice-work above the dancers. Try extending these lines with your finger. At what point in the painting do they come together? Where else in the work has the artist used slanted lines? What other techniques has he relied upon to create a sense of depth?

WHAT YOU WILL LEARN

Linear perspective is used to lend a feeling of space to two-dimensional works. In this lesson, you will create a three-dimensional

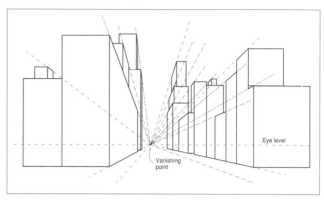

Figure 5–14   Diagram showing linear perspective.

work of art that uses both real and suggested space. You will use a variety of items to create a **diorama** (dy-uh-**ram**-uh). This is *a scenic representation in which miniature sculptures and other objects are displayed against a painted backdrop.* You will create a sense of deep space through changes in hue, intensity, and value.

WHAT YOU WILL NEED
- Pencil and sketch paper
- Cardboard box, lid discarded

Figure 5–15   This painting was done a generation after the Renaissance. It, nevertheless, owes a debt to the genius of that period.

Jan Steen. *The Dancing Couple.* 1663. Oil on canvas. 102.5 × 142.5 cm (40⅜ × 56⅛"). National Gallery of Art, Washington, D.C. Widener Collection.

- Construction paper in a variety of colors
- White glue
- Chalk or markers
- Tempera paints
- Mixing tray
- Brushes, paper towels
- A variety of found objects

WHAT YOU WILL DO

1. Complete several pencil sketches of an imaginary scene. Include buildings, trees, and other objects. Select a point of view that suggests depth. One possibility might be a view looking down a city street.
2. Turn the box on its side. On the outside of the box, use colored construction paper to decorate the bottom, sides, back, and top. Glue the paper in place. Allow time for the glue to dry.
3. Select your best sketch. Using chalk or markers, transfer the scene to the back wall of the box. Sketch the lines of buildings along the sides of the box. The lines of objects should mirror the natural lines of the box.
4. Choose hues of tempera paint that reflect the colors of objects in your scene. You might use brown for buildings, gray for pavements. Mix duller intensities and lighter values of these hues. These will be used to show objects in the distance. Use a fine brush to add details, such as doors and windows.
5. Use found materials to form free-standing houses, trees, and other objects in your sketch. Gravel might be used for a stone fence, for example. Bark might be used for tree trunks. To give a sense of deep space,

glue larger, more colorful objects in the foreground. Smaller, less colorful objects should be placed farther back.
6. Display your finished work.

EXAMINING YOUR WORK

- **Describe** What have you included in your diorama?
- **Analyze** Did you use changes in hue, intensity, and value to create the feeling of deep space? Did you use placement of objects to help carry out this feeling?
- **Interpret** Would anyone looking at your diorama think it is much deeper than it actually is?
- **Judge** Does your diorama succeed in using real and suggested space?

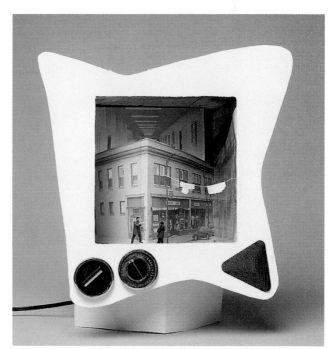

Figure 5–16 **Student work. A diorama.**

Try This! **STUDIO OPTION**

■ Do a realistic painting of the scene in your diorama. Your painting should use linear perspective to suggest depth.

Refer to Figure 5–14 to help you plan this project. Use size, overlapping, and values and intensities of hues to help create a feeling of space.

Lesson 6   *Creating a Diorama*   **95**

Art of the Nineteenth and Twentieth Centuries

Seen against the long tapestry of art history, the last hundred years is but a stitch. Yet, during this century, more changes have taken place in art than in all the centuries before.

In this lesson, you will learn about some of the changes that have occurred since the late 1800s.

Figure 5–17 Compare this painting with the one in Figure 5–15. In what way is this nature scene more "realistic" than the painting of the dancers?

Claude Monet. *Poplars on the Bank of the Epte River.* 1891. Oil on canvas. 100.3 × 65.2 cm (39½ × 25¹¹⁄₁₆″). Philadelphia Museum of Art, Philadelphia, Pennsylvania. Bequest of Anne Thomson in memory of her father, Frank Thomson, and her mother, Mary Elizabeth Clarke Thomson.

ART OF THE NINETEENTH CENTURY

In the centuries following the Renaissance, the pursuit of realism continued. Artists produced pictures that showed solid figures moving naturally in space. They created works in which sunlight poured through windows, glinting off glass goblets and other shiny surfaces. Their brushes captured the look and feel of warm skin, cold metal, and soft velvet.

Toward the end of the 1800s, the search for realism took a new direction. One group of French painters in particular "saw the light." They left their dark studios and went to paint outdoors. They worked feverishly, using all their energies to capture the fleeting effects of sunlight on objects. This group became known, at first jokingly, as the *Impressionists.*

Painting

The leader of this **art movement**—*a trend formed when a group of artists band together*—was an artist named Claude Monet (**klohd moh-nay**). Monet's goal was to record what the eye saw at any given moment. Have you ever noticed how, on a cloudy day, the sun "goes in" and "comes out" again without warning? It was this "reality" that Monet set out to capture.

The work in Figure 5–17 is one of his paintings. Viewed up close, it looks like a hastily done collection of paint dabs and dashes. When seen from a distance, however, the painting takes on an almost shimmering quality. The dabs and dashes are now brilliant flecks of color and blend together to form a stand of slender trees by the banks of a river. You can almost feel the gentle breeze rustling through the leaves on the trees and rippling the glassy surface of the water.

Figure 5–18 What statement might the artist be making about the passage of time? What clues are provided by the object in the hand of each figure?

Helen Lundeberg. *Double Portrait of the Artist in Time.* 1935. Oil on Masonite. 121.3 × 101.6 cm (47¾ × 40″). National Museum of American Art, Smithsonian Institution, Washington, D.C.

ART OF THE TWENTIETH CENTURY

You have learned that the Impressionists were seeking new ways to capture realistic appearances in their art. However, the search for realism was nothing new. Roman sculptors and Renaissance painters sought the same goal. Strands in the fabric of art history, it seems, loop back on themselves.

One strand that came full circle in the twentieth century is the use of symbolism in art. You learned about symbolism in the lessons on Egyptian art earlier in this chapter. A heavy reliance on symbols became a feature of a twentieth-century art movement known as *Surrealism.*

Painting

In their works, the Surrealists tapped into the mysterious world of dreams. In this nighttime "world," symbols often play important roles. Consider the curious painting

in Figure 5–18. Notice the work's title. You will probably have no trouble finding the two "portraits" of the artist. One—the artist as a child—appears in the lower half of the picture. The other—the adult artist—appears in the picture on the wall. The long, unnatural shadow cast upward by the child's image helps tie the two portraits together.

Yet, like most Surrealist paintings, this one asks more questions than it answers. What, for example, is the meaning of the clock? What are we to make of the empty container in the painting within a painting? Some critics have detected a sense of sadness or longing in this painting. What feeling does the work communicate to you?

✔ Check Your Understanding

1. What was the aim of the Impressionists? What was the goal of the Surrealists?
2. What is an art movement?

Using Abstraction in Art

While some artists today have borrowed ideas and techniques of the past, others have moved in new directions. One such ground-breaking direction is reflected in the painting in Figure 5–19. This work is an example of abstraction in art. As you read in Chapter 4, *abstract* means having a recognizable subject that is shown in an unrealistic or simplified manner. Abstract art straddles the fence between representational—or realistic—art and non-objective art.

Examine the painting in Figure 5–19. You will probably recognize the fragmented objects in this brightly colored work. The main one is a painter's palette. Protruding from it is an assortment of brushes. Why has the artist chosen to shatter these familiar images? What do the picture's content and title reveal about the changes you read about in the previous lesson?

WHAT YOU WILL LEARN

In this studio lesson, you will create your own abstract painting. Through abstraction, you will express your goals and hopes for the future. Your finished work will exhibit a variety of brilliantly colored, angular shapes. As in Figure 5–19, these will be joined together to make a visually pleasing whole.

WHAT YOU WILL NEED

- Pencil and sketch paper
- Two sheets of illustration board, one measuring 12 x 18 inches (30 x 46 cm) and the other 18 x 24 inches (46 x 61 cm)

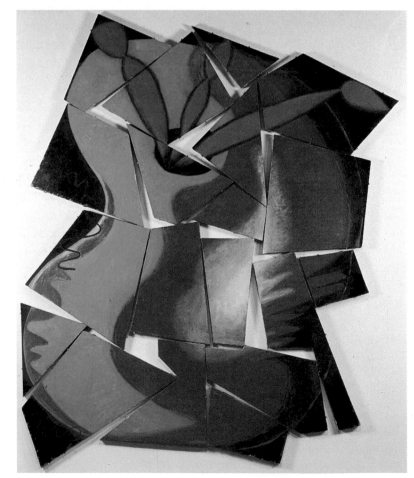

Figure 5–19 **Notice how the artist has used the art elements of shape and color. How are variety and harmony demonstrated in this painting?**

Elizabeth Murray. *Painter's Progress.* 1981. Oil on canvas in 19 parts. 294.5 × 236.2 cm (9'8" × 7'9"). Museum of Modern Art, New York, New York. Acquired through the Bernhill Fund and gift of Agnes Gund.

- Tempera or acrylic paints
- Brushes
- Mixing tray
- Paint cloth
- Ruler or other straight edge
- Scissors
- White glue

WHAT YOU WILL DO

1. Everyone has dreams and goals. Some people dream of becoming astronauts, others doctors or writers. What is your own life goal? Begin this studio lesson by answering that question. Think of symbols or objects connected with your goal. Draw several sketches of these images. Then abstract, or simplify, the images by eliminating all unnecessary details.
2. Transfer your best sketch to the sheet of illustration board. Fill the board completely with your drawing.
3. Using tempera or acrylic paints, paint your subject. Include a background area as the artist has done in Figure 5–19. Use bright hues.
4. When your work is dry, turn it over. With a ruler or other straight edge, draw straight lines at angles to one another. Include enough lines to divide the painting into at least 15 large and small angular shapes.
5. Use scissors to cut out your shapes. As you work, turn each piece over so its painted side is facing up. Carefully fit the cut-out pieces together so that you know where each one goes.
6. Center the rearranged shapes on the sheet of illustration board. Overlap some

EXAMINING YOUR WORK

- **Describe**   Did you select images that identify a particular dream or goal? Did you simplify the images?
- **Analyze**   Did you use a variety of brightly colored hues? Does your work contain large and small angular shapes?
- **Interpret**   Do you think other people could interpret the images in your picture? Would they be able to recognize the idea the images represent?
- **Judge**   Do you think the shapes in your composition are joined in a way so as to create a pleasing whole?

pieces. Leave narrow spaces between others. Move the shapes around until you are satisfied with the arrangement. Then glue the pieces in place. Title your work.

Figure 5–20   **Student work. Abstraction in art.**

COMPUTER OPTION

Try This!

■ Think of a familiar object, plant, or animal. Choose the Straight Line tool and draw the object using only straight lines. Vary the line thickness. Add color with the Bucket tool to some of the spaces. Give your work a title. Save and print.

Open a new page. Draw a second version with only the Straight line tool, but this time, rearrange

and move the lines farther apart. Add color to some of the spaces. Retitle, save, and print.

Open a new page. Draw a third edition. This time, look carefully at your second attempt. Create a pleasing design by rearranging the thick and thin straight lines, then add color. Retitle, save, and print. Display all three abstractions together.

Central Tibet. Temple Hanging. Detail. 1940. Appliqué with cut silk, brocade, and pearls. 1.2 × 13.1 m (4 × 43′). Los Angeles County Museum of Art, Los Angeles, California. Gift of Mr. and Mrs. James Coburn.

The Secret of Silk

Have you ever heard the expression "as smooth as silk?" Silk is a valuable fiber used to make fine fabrics. It is produced by the silkworm. Silk is sometimes also used in decorative textiles, such as the *Tibetan Temple Hanging* on this page.

The origin of silk dates back to the twenty-seventh century B.C. The silkworm moth was originally found only in China. For thousands of years, the people of China kept the silk-producing process a secret. Because silk was difficult to obtain, it became a valuable trade item.

Although silk fabric was traded to other countries, it was produced only in China. In about A.D. 300, however, a group of people from Japan smuggled silkworms out of China. They brought the silkworms and four young Chinese women back to Japan to teach them how to produce silk.

About 200 years later, a Roman emperor sent two monks to China to smuggle silkworm eggs. The monks hid the eggs in their hollow walking canes. With the secret revealed, silk production spread throughout Asia and the West.

MAKING THE CONNECTION

- ✔ How do you think silk fabric enhances this textile art?
- ✔ Explain why silk was a valuable trade item.
- ✔ How did the people of Japan learn the Chinese secret of silk production?

INTERNET ACTIVITY

Visit Glencoe's Fine Arts Web Site for students at:

http://www.glencoe.com/sec/art/students

REVIEW

BUILDING VOCABULARY

Number a sheet of paper from 1 to 12. After each number, write the term from the box that matches each description below.

applied art	diorama
architecture	fine art
art historians	hieroglyphic
art movement	painted screen
bust	Renaissance
contours	symbol

1. Art made to be enjoyed visually, not used.
2. People who study art of different ages and cultures.
3. An image used to stand for a quality or idea.
4. An early form of picture writing.
5. The art of planning and creating buildings.
6. A sculpture that shows a person's head, shoulders, and upper chest.
7. Period of rebirth.
8. Art made to be useful as well as visually pleasing.
9. Outlines and surface ridges.
10. An art object used as a wall or room divider.
11. A trend formed when a group of artists band together.
12. A scenic representation in which miniature sculptures and other objects are displayed against a painted backdrop.

REVIEWING ART FACTS

Number a sheet of paper from 13 to 17. Answer each question in a complete sentence or two.

13. What are the rules of Egyptian art for showing the human body?
14. Name a difference and a similarity between the way the Greeks and Romans showed the human figure.
15. What religious beliefs guided the art of the Indus River valley? What beliefs guided the art of ancient Japan?
16. What methods did Renaissance painters use to achieve realism in their works?
17. Compare and contrast the goals of the Impressionists and the goals of the Surrealists.

THINKING ABOUT ART

On a sheet of paper, answer each question in a sentence or two.

1. **Interpret.** Select any three artworks that you learned about in this chapter. Tell why each would appeal to an art critic taking the composition view.
2. **Compare and contrast.** The chapter covers two types of architecture from the Middle Ages. What are the most important differences between the two?

MAKING ART CONNECTIONS

1. **Music.** Like art, music has undergone changes over the centuries. Investigate this idea. Working with a group, research the following "movements" in the history of music: Romanticism, Expressionism, Neo-Classicism. For each, identify when the movement occurred and the names of the principal composers. Share your findings with classmates in an oral report. If possible, include short recorded passages of representative compositions.

2. **Community Connection.** Learn about the pointed arch. This was one of the architectural breakthroughs that permitted the building of cathedrals during the Middle Ages. Share your findings with family members and friends. If possible, include drawings, photos, or descriptions of churches or other structures in your community that use pointed arches.

Figure 6–1 Notice how the artist used warm colors to help the viewer feel the heat of a July day. What principles of art did he use to show the motion of the hay cutters?

Thomas Hart Benton. *July Hay.* 1943. Oil and egg tempera on composition board. 96.5 × 67.9 cm (38 × 26¾″). The Metropolitan Museum of Art, New York, New York. George A. Hearn Fund, 1943. © 1998 Thomas H. Benton & Rita P. Benton Testamentary Trusts/Licensed by VAGA, New York, NY

CHAPTER 6

Perceiving Nature

Nature has many faces. You see its fury in the lashing rains of a fierce thunderstorm. You feel its kiss on a gentle spring day. You sense its majesty in a night-time sky aglitter with a billion stars.

Because of its ever-changing personality, nature has long been a favorite art subject. Examine the painting at the left. Which of nature's faces has this artist captured?

In this chapter you will learn about the ways in which artists have celebrated nature. You will see recent tributes and some from the past.

PORTFOLIO IDEAS

A strong art portfolio contains samples of work created with a variety of media, techniques, and processes. Your entries might include preliminary sketches as well as finished works. By including self-reflections and written evaluations, you will learn more about yourself as an artist.

OBJECTIVES

After completing this chapter, you will be able to:
- Define the term *landscape.*
- Understand stylization.
- Explain what artists accomplish through nature studies.
- Experiment with two- and three-dimensional forms of self-expression.

WORDS YOU WILL LEARN

assemblage
landscape
monoprint
nature study
resist
study
stylized

LESSON 1

Landscape Art

How many products have you seen that carry the words *all natural* on their labels? This phrase has become commonplace in today's society. It represents people's desire to live in a healthy way and to appreciate nature. Artists have valued and represented nature throughout the years. Their works have long paid tribute to nature's beauty and its bounty.

LANDSCAPES

What do you see when you look out the nearest window? Do you see buildings, street-lights, and cars? Maybe you see plants, trees, and hills. If your answer leans more toward the second description, you are looking at a landscape. In art, the word **landscape** refers to *a drawing or painting of mountains, trees, or other natural scenery.* Artists have been creating land-scapes for more than one thousand years.

The possible subjects for a landscape are limitless. So are the ways in which artists have chosen to represent nature scenes. The landscapes in Figures 6–2 and 6–3 show two examples that have some similarities and some differences.

Perspective in a Landscape

Examine the painting in Figure 6–2. It shows a hilly Pennsylvania town in the early 1900s. What do you see first when you look at this painting? Is your eye attracted to the large building on the hill? What do you notice next? The train, the river, or the little build-ings in the foreground? Notice that the artist has made these buildings smaller than those in the distance. Why might the artist have cre-ated this visual puzzle? Perhaps he wanted to give more importance to the flag blowing proudly in the wind.

Figure 6–2 **Besides the perspective, what other unusual landscape features can you find in this picture? Can you identify the season of the year?**

Joseph Pickett. *Manchester Valley.* 1914–18. Oil with sand on canvas. 115.6 × 154 cm (45½ × 60⅜"). The Museum of Modern Art, New York, New York. Gift of Abby Aldrich Rockefeller.

Rhythm in a Landscape

Compare the painting in Figure 6–2 with the one in Figure 6–3. The two landscapes were painted about the same time. Like the work on the opposite page, this one shows a cheerful scene from nature. It even includes some of the same features, such as trees.

However, that is where the similarity ends. Whereas the landscape in Figure 6–2 portrays a city setting, the one in Figure 6–3 records a rural scene. The work, moreover, follows a careful design. Notice the row after row of evenly spaced seedlings in the bottom half of the picture. Notice how the artist overlapped the shapes to give depth to the scene.

✔ Check Your Understanding

1. What is a landscape?
2. What similarities can you find between this painting and the one on the facing page? What differences can you find?

STUDIO ACTIVITY

A Stylized Landscape

Look again at the plants, trees, and plowed fields in the landscape on this page. These objects have been represented in a highly **stylized** way. This means *simplified* or *exaggerated.* Some artists choose to stylize their works because it allows them to picture nature in a unique, personal way.

Select a park or other familiar nature scene in your community. On a sheet of drawing paper, sketch the trees, flowers, and other landscape features. Make your view stylized by simplifying or exaggerating the shapes of these objects. Complete your stylized landscape with markers.

PORTFOLIO

Write a description of how you stylized the objects in your landscape. Evaluate the success of your efforts and put this evaluation in your portfolio with your work.

Figure 6–3 Notice the use of repetition in this painting. What other principle of art has Miró used to give this artwork a lively feeling?

Joan Miró. *Vines and Olive Trees, Tarragona.* 1919. Oil on canvas. 72.5 × 90.5 cm (28½ × 35⅝"). The Metropolitan Museum of Art, New York, New York. The Jacque and Natasha Gelman Collection. © Artists Rights Society (ARS), New York/ ADAGP, Paris.

LESSON 2
Creating a Nature Scene

Have you ever taken a route so many times that you felt you could travel it with your eyes closed? Such a path appears in the work in Figure 6–4. It leads to a village in the artist's native Honduras. Notice how plants, trees, and the stone fence bordering the path are painted rhythmically as repeated shapes and textures. Despite being stylized, the work invites the viewer in for a stroll toward the town. Look carefully. The painting is organized so as to lead your eye to the center of interest. Can you identify that center of interest? What elements and principles of art are used to help draw your eye to it?

WHAT YOU WILL LEARN

You will make a nature scene of a familiar place that you know well or have recently visited. You will begin by collecting small natural objects to make an **assemblage** (ah-sem-**blahzh**). This means *a three-dimensional artwork consisting of many pieces assembled together.* You will also use markers and oil pastels to draw other objects and details. To do this, you will organize your work to create a center of interest. You will emphasize the most important part of the scene using lines, shapes, colors, and textures.

Figure 6–4 **Notice how the textures are created in this painting. What principle of art has the artist used to draw your eye to the center of interest?**

Jose Antonio Velasquez. *San Antonio de Oriente.* 1957. Oil on canvas. 66 × 94 cm (26 × 37″). Collection of the Art Museum of the Americas, Organization of American States, Washington, D.C.

WHAT YOU WILL NEED

- Pencil and sheets of sketch paper
- White construction paper or poster board, 12 x 18 inches
- Collection of small natural objects
- Oil pastels
- Markers
- White glue

WHAT YOU WILL DO

1. Visit a park or other local area that might make a good subject for a landscape. Carry a sketch pad with you. Make several sketches. Include important features such as plants, trees, houses, and hills. Show these as simple, flat shapes. Plan the picture to emphasize a particular object or area as the center of interest.
2. Before leaving the area, collect small objects in a plastic bag. Possibilities include small twigs, pebbles, sand, bark, leaves, or dried grass. Avoid objects that are likely to wilt or change in a few days, such as fresh flowers or insects.
3. Transfer your best sketch onto construction paper or poster board. Using oil pastels or markers, begin adding color. Apply hues that match the colors of the natural objects you plan to use.
4. Decide which areas of your composition you will decorate with the objects you collected. Choose objects whose natural textures suit the subject matter. You might use sand for a path. Attach the objects with white glue. Make sure all areas of the composition are covered.

EXAMINING YOUR WORK

- **Describe** Identify the objects and shapes in your landscape scene. Describe the setting.
- **Analyze** Explain how you organized your picture to create a center of interest. Which object or area did you emphasize? Where did you use tactile and visual textures?
- **Interpret** Decide what feeling or mood your work communicates to viewers. Find out if viewers can identify the place your picture describes.
- **Judge** Tell whether you feel your work succeeds. Explain your answer.

5. Step back and review the organization of your work. Make sure the elements of art emphasize one part of the picture. If you like, use drawing media to add buildings, animals, or human figures to the scene.
6. When the glue is dry, display your work.

Figure 6–5   **Student work. A nature scene.**

Try This!   STUDIO OPTIONS

■ Plan another assemblage. This time, create an imaginary landscape. Use a larger sheet of poster board or work with a small group to produce four separate panels that will fit together.

■ With a group, make a nature diorama. Combine found natural objects and drawings. Include forms of plant life and, if you prefer, animal life. These are to be sculpted to scale from materials such as modeling clay, wire, wood, and cotton.

Nature Close Up

Have you ever looked at a familiar object under a microscope or magnifying glass? Maybe you have seen the "rivers" that criss-cross the surface of human skin. Perhaps you discovered that grains of table salt, far from shapeless forms, are perfect cubes!

When seen up close, the world reveals many surprises. Artists have long known this. Many have recorded insect's-eye views of nature. In this lesson, you will see some of these.

NATURE STUDIES

As noted in Chapter 3, the art of drawing serves several purposes. One of these is to help artists improve perception—how they "see" objects. Another is to make studies. A **study** is *a drawing used to plan a painting or other large project.* The artwork in Figure 6–6 was created with both purposes in mind. The work is an example of a **nature study.** This is *a drawing used to help artists sharpen their perception of natural objects.*

Figure 6–6 Which of the works on these two pages is more realistic? What role do you think art materials played in this difference?

Leonardo da Vinci. *Oak Leafs and a Spray of Greenwood.* c. 1506–08. Red conte pencil. 18.8 × 15.4 cm (7½ × 6"). The Royal Collection © Her Majesty Queen Elizabeth II.

Figure 6–7 How many different plants do you count in this painting? How many of these forms do you recognize?

Albrecht Dürer. *The Great Piece of Turf.* c. 1503. Watercolor on paper. 41.3 × 31.8 cm (16¼ × 12½"). The Bridgeman Art Library, London. Albertina Graphic Collection, Vienna, Austria.

The artist who made this drawing is Leonardo da Vinci. Leonardo had many talents. He was an architect, a musician, and an inventor. As an artist, he filled many sketchbooks with drawings like the one on this page. He often included detailed written descriptions of what he saw. Study Figure 6–6. Do you recognize the objects hanging between the leaves of the branches? Leonardo called them "oak nuts." You probably know them better as *acorns.* Notice how the artist has created three dimensions working with pencil. How many different textures can you find in the work?

A Painting of Nature Up Close

Not all studies of nature are drawings. The work in Figure 6–7 is a painting. It was done around the same time as Leonardo's nature study. Like Figure 6–6, it shows a close-up view of plant life.

Study this painting. In it, the artist focuses mainly on the shapes and patterns of the leaves. He uses different values of green and yellow to capture lines and details. How does he create a sense of depth in this painting? What aesthetic view would you use to judge this work? (See Chapter 4, pages **64–65** for a review of the aesthetic views.)

✔ Check Your Understanding

1. What is a study? What is a nature study?
2. What were some of Leonardo da Vinci's talents besides art?
3. What is the point of view of the painting in Figure 6–7?

Drawing from a Bird's-Eye View

The painting in Figure 6–7 on page **109,** as you have learned, was done from an interesting point of view. So is the one in Figure 6–8. Look carefully at this work. Like those in the previous lesson, this one provides a close-up view of nature. In this case, the subject is a tree. The point of view is from high among the branches. There is much more to the work, however. Did you notice the lone human figure in the painting? He is easy to spot because of his red cap, which stands out vividly against the mostly brown earth tones. He is a hunter. You won't find his prey—a bird—in the picture. That is because the bird sits in the branches, gazing down at the hunter. You are seeing the scene through the bird's eyes!

WHAT YOU WILL LEARN

In this lesson, you will picture a familiar scene as a bird might view it. Depending on where you live, the scene may be in the country or city. You will include natural objects, such as mountains, fields, rivers, and streams, or objects made by people, such as buildings, streets, and trucks. After sketching the scene in chalk, you will add color by blending oil

Figure 6–8 Notice the attention to detail in this work. How many different visual textures can you find?

Andrew Wyeth. *The Hunter.* 1943. Tempera on Masonite. 83.8 × 86 cm (33 × 33⅞"). Toledo Museum of Art, Toledo, Ohio. Elizabeth C. Mau Bequest Fund.

pastels. Use colors that give your picture a certain mood or feeling. As in Figure 6–8, your work will make use of different textures to achieve variety.

WHAT YOU WILL NEED
- Pencil and sketch paper
- Any light color of construction paper, 12 x 18 inches (30 x 46 cm)
- Chalk
- Oil pastels

1. Select the place you will draw. Complete several sketches of this location from a bird's-eye view. Include natural or other objects found in the setting.
2. Decide which is your best sketch. Redraw it lightly in chalk on construction paper. Use a pencil eraser to remove any unwanted lines.
3. Choose hues of oil pastels that fit your subject. Blend some colors. Include

EXAMINING YOUR WORK

- **Describe** Tell what your work shows. Point to natural objects or those objects in the work that were made by people.
- **Analyze** Identify the hues in your work. Which hues were created by blending oil pastels? Explain how you added variety using different textures.
- **Interpret** Tell what mood your drawing captures. Did you record a stressful moment, as in Figure 6–8?
- **Judge** Tell whether you are satisfied with your drawing. Identify areas of the work that especially pleased you. Address what you would do differently next time.

different textures, as in Figure 6–8, to add variety to your work. Color in all of the areas of your picture.

Figure 6–9 Student work. A bird's eye view.

Try This! STUDIO OPTIONS

■ Draw a view of the same location as though you were a worm. Use a combination of media such as oil pastels and watercolors.

■ Using pencil, draw Figure 6–8 from the hunter's point of view. Decide what the hunter is looking at. Use crayons or markers to capture some of the same tones the artist did.

Art and the Seasons

The seasons showcase nature's many faces. Think of the changing leaves in autumn. Think of winter, with its icy chill. Imagine the beauty of spring with its new buds and shoots.

The seasons and their colors have appealed to artists throughout the ages. Many artists have used their art to share special views of one season or another.

A WORK SHOWING AUTUMN

From falling stars to rainbows to picture-perfect sunsets, nature stages many remarkable shows. One spectacular view is depicted in the painting in Figure 6–10. Study this work. It was done early in the twentieth century by a Canadian artist. The painting records the changing of the leaves in autumn. Have you ever heard autumn colors described as *fiery?* It is precisely this aspect of the leaves that the artist has captured. See how the sweeping brushstrokes and bright hues combine almost to suggest flames. As you study the painting, in which direction is your eye drawn? What principles have been used to organize the work?

A WORK SHOWING WINTER

Another seasonal event recorded by an artist is shown in Figure 6–11. The artist has offered a glimpse not only of an event but of

Figure 6–10   Where is this landscape set? What aspects of scenery has the artist included to define this setting?

Tom Thompson. *Autumn Foliage.* 1916. Oil on wood. 26.7 × 21.5 cm (10½ × 8½"). National Gallery of Canada, Ottawa.

a season. This winter scene has been preserved for over four centuries.

Examine the work. It shows a party of hunters and their dogs. They are returning home after a cold outing in the woods. A trio of birds huddle in the bare branches of the trees above the hunters. Still farther overhead is a bleak sky that promises more snow. Yet, the scene is not gloomy. In fact, it is almost cheerful. Down below the hunters, on a frozen lake, townspeople merrily skate.

Notice the suggestion of distance in the painting. The artist has used several of the techniques for capturing space covered on page **16** in Chapter 1. Two of these are *size* and *placement*. Observe how the trees in the background are smaller and placed higher up in the picture plane than the hunters are. What other techniques for suggesting space can you find?

✔ Check Your Understanding

1. What images and colors are linked with different seasons?
2. Which of these colors and images appear in the two works in this lesson?

STUDIO ACTIVITY

Creating Seasonal Colors

Look once more at Figure 6–10. The objects in the work—leaves and branches, a lake, and the sky—are clearly recognizable. The work also captures the mood of autumn. Imagine that the artist had painted the same landscape in the dead of winter. What colors do you suppose he would have chosen?

Here is your chance to find out. Do a rough pencil sketch of a similar scene on a sheet of white construction paper. Your landscape does not have to be identical to the one in Figure 6–10. Complete your drawing using colored chalk. Select hues to emphasize the season and the mood.

PORTFOLIO

Share your work with classmates. Take turns critiquing each other's work. Take notes on the comments made about your landscape and put them in your portfolio with the work.

Figure 6–11 This work by Pieter Bruegel shows winter activities in the 1500s. How has the artist used color to portray a winter landscape?

Pieter Bruegel. *Return of the Hunters.* 1565. Oil on wood. 117 × 162 cm (46 × 63¾″). Kunsthistorisches Museum, Vienna, Austria. Erich Lessing/ Art Resource, NY

Painting a Seasonal Event

Examine the painting in Figure 6–12. The subject of this work is a family sharing dessert after dark. Look closely at the scene. It shows a front porch where brothers and sisters, parents, and grandparents are enjoying cold watermelon on a hot summer night. Flowers are blooming, a quarter moon shines high in the sky, and the family has gathered at the end of the day. How has the artist used color to show it is nighttime? How has she used value? Do you think her recollection of summer nights is a pleasant one?

WHAT YOU WILL LEARN

You will create a visual record of where you live right now. Your record will depict your home at a season of the year that holds special meaning for you. You will include objects, details, and colors that provide clues as to the time of year. Choose a point of view for your picture, perhaps a view like the one in Figure 6–12. Plan the composition of your work to communicate your feelings. Use repeated lines, shapes, and colors to create harmony.

Figure 6–12 **Notice how the artist has used color and shape in this scene. What principles of art has she used?**

Carmen Lomas Garza. *Sandia/Watermelon*. 1986. Gouache. 50.8 × 71.1 cm (20 × 28″).
© 1986 Carmen Lomas Garza. Private collection.

WHAT YOU WILL NEED

- Pencil and sketch paper
- White drawing or construction paper, 12 x 18 inches (30 x 46 cm)
- Markers
- Oil pastels, watercolors
- Brushes, water
- Paper towels

WHAT YOU WILL DO

1. Complete several sketches showing your home and surrounding area at a particular time of year. Include details and objects that provide clues as to the season. Organize the composition to emphasize a mood or feeling.
2. Transfer your sketch to drawing or construction paper. Outline important objects—animals, people, houses, and so on—with a fine-tipped black marker. Repeat lines and shapes to create a sense of harmony.
3. Choose hues of oil pastels that communicate the season and mood of the picture. Use these to color the outlined objects. Repeat colors to increase a sense of harmony.
4. Switch to watercolors. Using a medium brush, paint over the oil pastels and blank areas to cover the remaining spaces. Work freely over the entire surface. The oil pastels, which are oily, will act as a **resist**. This is *an art medium, such as crayon, that serves as a protective coating.* The pastels will prevent the watercolors from reaching the paper.

Figure 6–13   **Student work. Winter holiday season.**

EXAMINING YOUR WORK

- **Describe**   Identify the objects in your picture. Point out your home and other interesting features of your neighborhood. Describe the point of view you used.
- **Analyze**   Explain how your work is organized. Identify how you used the elements of line, shape, and color to create harmony.
- **Interpret**   Explain the mood of your work. Can classmates correctly identify the season you have captured?
- **Judge**   Decide if your work succeeds in communicating a special seasonal event. What would you change if you were to do it again?

STUDIO OPTIONS

■ Working with several classmates, plan and make a mural. The work should detail a special historical event in your school or community, such as Founder's Day. Research the history of the event. Complete the mural on a sheet of wrapping or butcher's paper using the media of your choice.

■ Make a memory collage of a favorite seasonal event. Think of images that bring to mind the sounds, smells, and tastes of that event. Include photographs and pictures from magazines and newspapers. Add original drawings that help convey this memory.

The Power of Nature

"March comes in like a lion and goes out like a lamb." You have probably heard this saying. It describes two of nature's personalities. The second of them is nature's gentle side. This can be seen on a mild spring day when there is sunshine, a soft breeze, and the season's first flowers.

The first—nature's rough and sometimes frightening side—is another personality. With floods, earthquakes, and tornadoes, we experience the power of nature. In the lesson, you will see and learn about artworks that relate to nature's power.

CAPTURING A STORM IN A PAINTING

Sometimes nature's fury makes the headlines. The threat of a hurricane sends coastal residents packing. A blizzard dumping three feet of snow closes schools for days.

Weather conditions command the attention of the news media and artists. The painting in Figure 6–14 shows the raw power of nature. Look closely at this work. You can almost feel the force of the wind that tears at the struggling tree in the foreground. You can almost hear the sound of the foaming waves crashing against the rocks.

Figure 6–14 **In what direction is the wind blowing in this picture? How do you know this?**

Frederick Varley. *Stormy Weather, Georgian Bay.* 1920. Oil on canvas. 132.6 × 162.8 cm (52⅛ × 64"). National Gallery of Canada, Ottawa.

Expressive Color Schemes

The creator of the painting in Figure 6–14 achieved this powerful effect using a cool color scheme. The limited use of color in this painting emphasizes the idea that the wind is everywhere. There is no escape or shelter from it. Its fierce gusts overpower the trees, land, the water, and even the sky. What basic hues are used in this painting? Where do you find light values of those hues? Where are darker values used?

CAPTURING A STORM IN A PRINT

You will find a similar theme running through Figure 6–15. This work is a wood-block print. Notice the work's title. Ejiri is a place in the artist's homeland of Japan. Examine the use of line and color in the work. In what ways is this "view" of the wind similar to the one in Figure 6–14? What differences can you find between the two works?

 ## Check Your Understanding

1. What type of color schemes show nature's seasons?
2. What is a monoprint? Why can only a single image be created using this printmaking technique?

Making a Monoprint

You are about to make a **monoprint.** This is *a print made by applying ink or paint to a plate and then transferring the image by hand-rubbing.*

Begin by drawing a simple landscape in crayon on a sheet of gray or pale blue construction paper. Use mostly dark values of the colors you choose.

Place a drop of liquid starch the size of half a dollar on a table top. Sprinkle a small amount of white powdered tempera onto the starch. With one bare hand, mix the starch and paint. Spread the mixture out until it is the size of your drawing. Make diagonal lines and swirls in the paint with your hand. Wash and dry your hands. Carefully lay your drawing face-down on the "plate" you have created. Press all over the surface with your other hand. Lift your print by pulling it up from one side. Lay it on newspapers to dry.

 P O R T F O L I O

Examine your monoprint. Evaluate the success of your technique on a sheet of paper and put it in your portfolio with the print.

Figure 6–15 How would you have been able to identify a gust of wind as the subject of this painting without the aid of the title?

Katsushika Hokusai. *A Gust of Wind at Ejiri,* from the series *The Thirty-Six Views of Fuji.* 1831–33. Wood block print. 24.5 × 37.5 cm (9⅝ × 14¾"). The Metropolitan Museum of Art, New York, New York. Rogers Fund, 1936.

LESSON 8
Painting a Storm

Have you ever had days when things just didn't seem to go right? So, it seems, does nature. Such a day is the subject of Figure 6–16. The work pictures a bleak, rainy afternoon. Unlike the works you studied in the previous lesson, there is no fury in the storm depicted here—just gloom. Notice the churning gray clouds overhead. See the rippling puddles underfoot of anyone unlucky enough to be out on such a day. The monochromatic tones of clouds and buildings make you glad to be inside, where it is safe and dry. That is, in fact, where you are as you look at this scene. Did you notice the blurred lines on the window at the left? The distortion is caused by the rain on your own window—the one you are gazing through. Can you find the single raindrop that has beaded on the glass?

WHAT YOU WILL LEARN

You will paint an expressive bad-weather scene. You will begin by selecting a season,

Figure 6–16 The artist uses slanted lines to represent the falling rain. What type of line does he use to capture the clouds? What type of color scheme does he use?

Charles Burchfield. *Night of the Equinox.* 1917–55. Watercolor, brush, and ink, gouache and charcoal on paper. 102 × 132.5 cm (40⅛ × 52³⁄₁₆″). National Museum of American Art, Washington, D.C. Gift of the Sara Roby Foundation/Art Resource, NY

time of day, and place. You will include trees, plants, and objects that help to describe the setting and the weather conditions. You will use tints and shades of a single hue of tempera paint. Various tints and shades of blue, for example, might be used to suggest a landscape with falling snow. You will use a variety of lines to help express movement.

WHAT YOU WILL NEED
- Pencil and sketch paper
- Poster board or heavy construction paper, 12 x 18 inches (30 x 46 cm)
- Tempera paint
- Paper plate
- Brushes
- Water container
- Paper towels

WHAT YOU WILL DO
1. With classmates, brainstorm examples of bad weather. Jot down specific images that come to mind. Choose a particular image. Decide on the time of year and place.
2. Working by yourself, complete several sketches of your foul-weather scene. Sketch plants, trees, and other objects quickly. Use a variety of lines that suggest movement, as in Figure 6–16. Repeat some of the lines to create rhythm.
3. Transfer your scene onto poster board or construction paper. Choose a color of tempera that best fits your scene. On the paper plate, mix white and black tempera with the color you selected to create different tints and shades. Paint your scene. As you work, keep mood and color uppermost in your mind.

EXAMINING YOUR WORK

- **Describe** Identify the season in your painting. Identify the time of day and place.
- **Analyze** Explain how you organized your work. Identify the different tints and shades you used. Where did you repeat lines or shapes to show movement?
- **Interpret** Tell what mood or feeling your work communicates. What is the title of your painting? Does it capture this mood or feeling?
- **Judge** State whether your artwork is successful. What details help make your painting expressive?

4. Paint all of the spaces. Switch to a small brush with fine bristles to paint small shapes and details. Use black or white tempera to outline any important areas.
5. Choose a title for your work that reflects the mood and weather. See if other students can identify the season, time of day, and place in your painting.

Figure 6–17 Student work. Rain in spring.

COMPUTER OPTION

■ Use your program's Shape and Fill tools to create a simple landscape. Shapes should be flat. Choose dark shades of colors. If the software you are using has a Blend or Smear brush, select and use it. Paint objects with diagonal lines. Make some lines longer than others. Describe the effect you have achieved.

Frank Johnston. *Fire-Swept Algoma*. 1920. Oil on canvas. 127.5 × 167.5 cm (50⅛ × 66"). National Gallery of Canada, Ottawa.

Why Do We Need to Preserve Forests?

Have you ever been camping in the woods? Do you enjoy eating a picnic lunch in a park? Have you ever been hiking or biking on wooded trails? Forests are an important part of our natural environment.

Not only do forests provide recreational areas, but they are also essential to human life. Trees and other plants absorb carbon dioxide in the air. In turn, they give off the oxygen we need to breathe. In addition, forests prevent soil erosion and provide a place for animals to live.

In pioneer times, American settlers thought that the Earth's natural resources were unlimited. They cut down many of the huge forests that once covered the eastern United States. They used the wood for lumber and cleared the land in order to build homes and create farmlands. Many forests have also been destroyed by fire. The majority of forest fires are started by carelessness. In Frank Johnston's painting, we see the tragic effects of a forest fire.

Today, we realize the importance of forests and other natural resources. Many conservation efforts have been made, including the establishment of national parks and forests.

MAKING THE CONNECTION

- ✔ Why are forests so important?
- ✔ What message do you think Frank Johnston was trying to convey in *Fire-Swept Algoma*?
- ✔ What techniques did the artist use to convey his message?

INTERNET ACTIVITY

Visit Glencoe's Fine Arts Web Site for students at:

http://www.glencoe.com/sec/art/students

REVIEW

◆ BUILDING VOCABULARY

Number a sheet of paper from 1 to 7. After each number, write the term from the box that matches each description below.

assemblage   resist
landscape   study
monoprint   stylized
nature study

1. A drawing or painting of mountains, trees, or other natural scenery.
2. An art medium, such as crayon, that serves as a protective coating.
3. A three-dimensional artwork consisting of many pieces assembled together.
4. Simplified or exaggerated.
5. A drawing used to plan a painting or other large project.
6. A drawing used to help artists sharpen their perception of natural objects.
7. A print made by applying ink or paint to a plate and then transferring the image by hand-rubbing.

◆ REVIEWING ART FACTS

Number a sheet of paper from 8 to 12. Answer each question in a complete sentence.

8. Give two reasons why artists might stylize works of art.
9. What were Leonardo da Vinci's two purposes in creating the drawing in Figure 6–6?
10. What is point of view?
11. What are some hues associated with spring? What colors are associated with winter?
12. What season is shown in Figure 6–12? How did the artist convey this time of year?

❓ THINKING ABOUT ART

On a sheet of paper, answer each question in a sentence or two.

1. **Analyze.** How did the artist of Figure 6–11 on page **113** prevent the scene from appearing lonely and gloomy?
2. **Compare and contrast.** The paintings in Figures 6–14 and 6–16 both make use of limited colors. Yet, the two works communicate different moods. How do you explain this?

⎯ MAKING ART CONNECTIONS ⎯

1. **Music.** Storms have been the subject not only of works of art. They have also been depicted in numerous musical compositions. Speak with a music teacher in your school or community to learn about musical works that "describe" storms. Two such works are Moussorgsky's *Night on Bald Mountain* and the "Cloudburst" movement of Grofe's *Grand Canyon Suite.* If you can, listen to one or more of these compositions. Share them with classmates, explaining how the works capture some of the images shown in the works in Lesson 7.

Figure 7–1 How many different animals can you find in this picture? Would you expect to see these animals together? What message might the artist be sending by grouping the creatures in this manner?

Bev Doolittle. *The Sacred Circle*. 1991. Watercolor. 58.4 × 58.4 cm (23 × 23″) Courtesy of The Greenwich Workshop, Inc., Shelton, Connecticut.

Observing Animals

Animal shapes are part of our earliest experiences as children. Our first toys include stuffed animals. Picture books of animals help us learn to read. Is it any wonder animals have long fascinated artists?

The painting on the facing page is made up of a group of nine artworks that Bev Doolittle did on the subject of animals and their environments. Notice how the art is placed so that the white areas in each artwork join to form the "sacred circle."

In this chapter, you will see the many different ways in which artists have shown animals in their work.

PORTFOLIO IDEAS

Make sure each entry remains separate and protected in your portfolio. You may want to separate artworks with a piece of tissue paper or newsprint. Mount and label photographs for clear identification. All entries should be easy to identify and see or read.

OBJECTIVES

After completing this chapter, you will be able to:

- Identify the way in which artists use the environment for subject matter.
- Explain the effects of culture and beliefs on art.
- Define the term *symbol,* and tell how symbols are used in art.
- Create art featuring real and imaginary animals.

WORDS YOU WILL LEARN

appliqué
calligraphy
environment
folk art
illumination
mascot
Old Stone Age
porcelain
symbol
tapestry
totem
trait

Animals in Earliest Art

Does your family have a cat or dog? Maybe you own a bird or horse. Perhaps you know someone else who does. Animals, whether they are pets or roam wild, share our **environment,** or *surroundings*. Like other objects in the environment, animals have also long been a favorite subject of artists.

In the lessons to come, you will learn about different ways artists have portrayed animals. This lesson will focus on the role of animals in earliest art.

ANIMALS AS SUBJECTS

Using animals as art subjects is as old as art itself. For proof, look at the painting of a horse in Figure 7–2. This picture is on the wall of a cave in the Dordogne region of France. Two boys came upon the cave while playing ball. The boys made their discovery in 1941. The picture, however, is tens of thousands of years old. It dates back to the **Old Stone Age.** This is *the historical period that occurred between 30,000 and 10,000* B.C.

Experts regard this painting as one of the earliest artworks on record. Why did the first artists make pictures of animals? The experts have come up with likely answers to this question by looking closely at the role animals played in the environment of people long ago.

To people of the Old Stone Age, animals meant life. Their main source of food was the animals around them. They wore the animals' pelts, or furs, to protect them from the cold. For these reasons, a successful hunt was important and the paintings may have been used in a *ritual,* or ceremony, to bring luck.

Tools of the Early Painter

The environment of early artists not only answers the question of *why* they made cave paintings. It also answers the question of how. Like artists today, they started with pigment, which often came from clay. Iron deposits in the clay may account for the heavy presence of red, yellow, and brown. The pigment was then mixed with animal fat,

Figure 7–2 This prehistoric cave painting is sometimes called *The Chinese Horse.* Animals shaped like this one appear in later Chinese art.

Cave Painting. Lascaux, Dordogne, France. *Chinese Horse* (The Yellow Horse). c. 15,000–10,000 B.C.

vegetable juice, or egg white as binders. The paint may have been brushed on with fingers, leaves, or animal hide. It may also have been blown onto the wall through a hollow reed.

EARLY ANIMAL SCULPTURES

After the Old Stone Age, animal art was not limited to painting. Some early artists worked in three dimensions. The miniature hippopotamus shown in Figure 7–3 comes from ancient Egypt. This sculpture is nearly 4,000 years old. It was found in the tomb of an important member of Egyptian society. The hippo was meant to protect the body after death. It is believed that this hippo was placed in the tomb as a good luck charm to protect the tomb from intruders.

There is another way in which the hippo in this artwork relates to its environment. The creature's head, back, and sides are decorated with features of the lotus plant. This plant grows in the marshes where hippos live. The sculptor painted a "record" of the hippo's environment on its body.

✔ Check Your Understanding

1. Why may early cave dwellers have made pictures of the animals in their environment?
2. What clue to the environment of the hippopotamus is included in the Egyptian sculpture?

STUDIO ACTIVITY

Inventing a Mascot

Look again at the hippo in Figure 7–3. Its form is so appealing that it has become the mascot of Metropolitan Museum of Art in New York City. A **mascot** is *an animal or person used by a group as a sign of luck.* Your school sports teams may have mascots.

Make a mascot for your class or for yourself. Begin by thinking about popular animal sayings. *Sly as a fox* and *strong as a bull* are two such sayings. Decide on the **trait,** or *personal characteristic*, your mascot will show. Write the trait down on a sheet of paper. Next, study the shapes of animals in pictures found in books or magazines. Select an animal to draw. If possible, your choice should relate to the trait you wrote down. Notice the outline of the animal's body. Practice by making some rough sketches. Then, using markers, draw the shape of the animal on white paper. Add the head, legs, tail, and other details. Your mascot may be cartoon-like or realistic.

P O R T F O L I O

Write a short paragraph telling how you used the elements of art to draw your animal. Put it in your portfolio with your artwork.

Figure 7–3   The artist has given clues to the hippo's environment by decorating its body with lotus plants. These grow in the marshes where hippos live.

Egyptian. Meir, Tomb of Senbi. *Figure of Hippopotamus.* Twelfth Dynasty (1991–1786 B.C.). Ceramics-Faience. 11 × 20 cm (4⅓ × 7⅚″). The Metropolitan Museum of Art, New York, New York. Gift of Edward S. Harkness, 1917.

LESSON 2
Creating a Totem

Study the painting in Figure 7–4. It shows a long-necked tortoise. It is the work of an Australian Aborigine (ab-uh-**rij**-ih-nee). The term *Aborigine* comes from two word parts. The first part, *ab*, means "from." The main part, *origine*, means "the beginning." Aborigines are so called because their ancestors were the first humans to settle a given area. The traditions of Australian Aboriginal art go back 50,000 years. This fact was proven by researchers who discovered and dated rock engravings and paintings similar to those being done today.

The tortoise in this picture was the artist's totem. The word **totem** means *an object that serves as an emblem or respected symbol.* This totem may have been used to protect the artist's family from harm.

WHAT YOU WILL LEARN

You will design and create a totem of your own. As in Figure 7–4, your totem will be an animal. Select as your totem an animal that you believe symbolizes the kind of person you think you are. Begin by drawing the outline of the animal of your choice. Then fill in the outline with a pattern. Next, color the lines of the pattern with oil pastels or crayons. Finally, use a contrasting color of watercolor paint to fill in the animal shape and complete your totem.

WHAT YOU WILL NEED

- Sketch paper and pencil
- White drawing paper, 12 x 18 inches (30 x 46 cm)
- Oil pastels or crayons
- Watercolor paints
- Large, soft brushes

WHAT YOU WILL DO

1. With a partner, brainstorm a list of animals that would make good subjects for a totem. Share your ideas with the class.
2. From all the ideas presented, choose an animal as the subject of your own totem. Select an animal that you believe symbolizes the kind of person you think you are. Study photographs of that animal and make several sketches. Focus mainly on the animal's outline. Choose your best drawing. Decide on a name for your totem. Write this name on the sketch you have chosen.

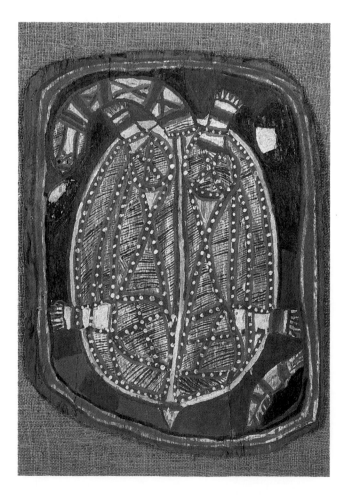

Figure 7–4 Notice the artist's use of line in this picture. What has he done to give the work variety?

Spider Nabunu. *Long-Necked Tortoise.* 1956–1960. Bark painting. 57.2 × 43.2 cm (22½ × 17"). The Art Gallery of New South Wales, Sydney, Australia. Aboriginal and Torres Strait Islander Collection. Gift of Stuart Scougall.

3. Using a light pencil line, transfer your line drawing to a sheet of white paper. Fill the page, as the Aboriginal artist has done in Figure 7–4. Letter a name for your totem somewhere in your design.
4. Next, study the pattern of lines and dots the Aboriginal artist has used. Notice how this pattern adds texture to the painting. Think of a pattern that would go well with the animal you have selected. Practice making this pattern. Then fill in the animal's body using this pattern.

Figure 7–5   Student work. A totem.

EXAMINING YOUR WORK

- **Describe**   Explain what animal appears in your totem. Tell what name you chose for your totem and where it appears in the design.
- **Analyze**   Identify the pattern you used to fill the shape of your animal. Tell what colors of oil pastel you used and which colors of water-color you selected. Explain whether the colors emphasize your pattern.
- **Interpret**   Write a brief paragraph explaining what this animal symbolizes. Explain why it makes a good totem.
- **Judge**   Tell whether you think your work is successful. Explain what you would do differently if you had a chance to do the project over again.

5. With oil pastels or crayons, go over all the lines in your picture. This includes the lines that make up your pattern. Use pressure to make the lines bold so the oil pastels will resist the watercolor.
6. Finally, select contrasting colors of water-color paint. Choose colors that will make your design stand out and emphasize your pattern. Using a large brush, apply these colors to the entire surface of your paper. Do not worry about painting over the lines you made. The natural oils in the oil pastels or crayons will resist the paint.

Try This!   ## COMPUTER OPTION

■ Select the Pencil tool, Brush tool, or Shape tool of your program. Using the tool you chose, create several unfilled animal shapes. Select textures from the pattern menu to fill each shape, using a different pattern for each one. If your software has a Blend command, blend the textures. Identify which shapes and blends look like fur, feathers, or scales. Title and save your picture.

LESSON 3
Sea Creatures

The word *earth* has two meanings. It is the name of the planet we live on and also another word for "land." Yet, land accounts for only 30 percent of Earth's surface. The rest is given over to a mysterious world with its own special population, the world of water— the rivers, lakes, and oceans.

Like creatures of the land, the animals of this special environment have long held a fascination for artists.

EARLY ART OF SEA ANIMALS

Ancient Egypt, which you learned about in Lesson 1, was one of the first great civilizations to create many kinds of art. Another early people who invented numerous art forms were the Chinese.

The jar shown in Figure 7–6 is described as "blue-and-white ware." It is made of **porcelain** (**por**-suh-lihn), a *fine-grained, high-quality form of pottery.* Porcelain is very hard to work with because it is a very stiff clay. The Chinese perfected work in this medium during the 1300s. It was around that time that this jar was made.

The jar is notable not only for its craft. It is also important because of the design on its surface. The design shows a fish in its natural environment.

Notice the attention to detail shown in this jar. You can easily find the fish's mouth, eye, gills, and other body features. The fish is shown surrounded by water lilies and other water plants. The artist appears to have been quite familiar with these fresh-water plants.

Figure 7–6 Notice how the shape of the flower petals has been repeated to create the full blossom. Where have lines been repeated to create other forms?

China. Yuan Dynasty. *Blue and White Jar with a Design of Fishes and Water Plants.* Early 1300s. Porcelain with underglaze decoration. 29.8 × 34.9 cm (11¾ × 13¾"). The Brooklyn Museum, Brooklyn, New York. Gift of the Executors of Augustus S. Hutchins.

Figure 7–7 Where has the artist used line in this work? Where has she used repetition to create harmony?

Ayako Miyawaki. *Various Fish.* 1967. Cotton collage on burlap. 33 × 29.9 cm (13 × 11¾"). National Museum of Women in the Arts, Washington, D.C. Gift of the artist.

PRESENT-DAY ART OF SEA ANIMALS

Ancient Chinese ways of making art were shared with China's neighbors. One of those neighbors is the island nation of Japan. The artwork in Figure 7–7 was done by a Japanese artist not long ago. Her name is Ayako Miyawaki.

Many people, when they think of art, think of paintings. Artists, as you have learned, are forever looking for new ways of creating. The work of art in Figure 7–7 was created with fabrics and fibers. It is an example of a technique called **appliqué** (ap-lih-**kay**). This is *an art form in which cutout shapes are attached to a larger surface.* They can be stitched or glued in place.

Miyawaki cuts her fabrics freehand. In this artwork, she has carefully cut out fabrics to represent various kinds of fish. Observe how

the shapes of the fish differ, and how their mouths, fins, and tails vary in shape. Look at the striped and plaid fabrics the artist has used. Can you tell where she has overlapped fabrics to add gills and eyes? The symbol in the lower right corner is the artist's signature. It appears in every one of her works.

✔ Check Your Understanding

1. In what century and by whom was the technique for blue-and-white ware invented?
2. Explain the term *appliqué.*

Making a Glue-Line Print

What do you think of when you hear the word *tuna*? If you are like most people, you think of flakes of fish that come packed in a can. There is more to tuna than this, however. The print in Figure 7–8 shows a whole tuna. This sea creature is a member of the yellow-fin family. It swims in both the Atlantic and Pacific oceans.

WHAT YOU WILL LEARN

Look again at Figure 7–8. This work is an example of the type of print called an *etching*. The artist has added extra color to this print by painting the finished work.

In this studio lesson, you will create another type of print. This type, a glue-line print, uses ordinary white glue. Like Figure 7–8, your print will be of a fish. It will make heavy use of the element of line. You will add an undersea environment such as seaweed to your design.

WHAT YOU WILL NEED

- White glue
- Scrap paper
- Toothpick
- Pencil and sketch paper
- Sheet of medium-weight cardboard, 8½ x 11 inches (22 x 28 cm)
- Water-based printing inks
- Inking plate and soft brayer
- Sheets of kraft paper, 9 x 12 inches (23 x 30 cm)
- Oil pastels or colored pencils

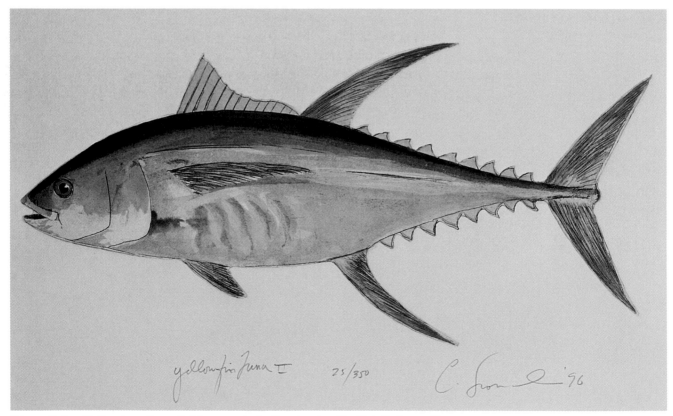

yellowfin tuna I   25/350   C. Leonard '96

Figure 7–8   Notice how the artist has used shading to give the fish its form. How has he used line?

Charles Leonard. *Yellow Fin Tuna.* 1996. Hand-colored etching. 38 × 56 cm (15 × 22″). Private collection.

WHAT YOU WILL DO

1. Squeezing the white glue directly from its container, practice drawing lines on scrap paper. Use a large amount of glue to make a thick line. If it forms dots, use a toothpick to pull them together.
2. Refer to the saved fish sketches you made in the Studio Activity on page **129.** Using pencil, transfer one of the sketches onto the cardboard. This is to be your printing plate.
3. Sketch and then transfer an undersea environment to your plate.
4. Using the glue as in Step 1, "draw" over the lines on your printing plate with glue.
5. When the glue looks clear, it is completely dry and the plate is ready to print. Squeeze a small amount of ink onto the inking plate. Roll your brayer into the ink, first in one direction, then in the other. Be sure that the brayer is well coated and sticky with ink. Transfer the ink to your printing plate by rolling the brayer across your fish design in all directions.
6. Lay a piece of kraft paper on top of the printing plate. Using the palm of

your hand, gently press the paper onto the plate.
7. Pull the kraft paper carefully off the plate. Put it in a place where it can dry without being disturbed. Make two more prints with fresh paper, re-inking the plate each time.
8. When the prints are dry, add color with oil pastels or colored pencils.

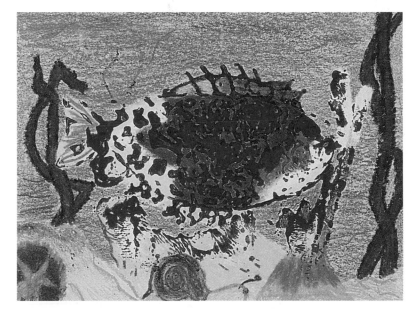

Figure 7–9   Student work. A glue-line print.

STUDIO OPTION

Try This!

■ Draw an underwater creature using a glue line on dark construction paper. Let the glue dry. Use chalk to add color. Do a crayon rubbing for another version of your creature and its environment.

Birds in Art

Have you ever wondered what it would be like to soar like a bird? If you have, you are not alone. Since earliest times, humans have dreamed of flying. This dream became a reality in 1903. That year the Wright Brothers conquered the air in the first "flying machine."

The desire to capture the grace and majesty of birds has not been limited to inventors. Artists, too, have long been inspired by the beauty of flight and of creatures that fly.

Figure 7–10 Notice that some birds appear higher in the picture. This was the artist's way of adding depth. What are some other ways of suggesting space?

Habib Allah. *Concourse of the Birds* from the Mantiq at-Tayr (Language of the Birds), by Attar. c. 1600. Colors, gold and some silver on paper. 25.4 × 11.4 cm (10 × 4½"). The Metropolitan Museum of Art, New York, New York. The Fletcher fund.

EARLY BIRD ILLUMINATION

You have probably heard the saying "A picture is worth a thousand words." Artists have understood the truth of this saying for more than eleven centuries. Since about A.D. 850, artists have been making pictures to illustrate books. The picture in Figure 7–10 is from ancient Persia. It is a type of *hand-painted book illustration* known as an **illumination.** The word *illuminate* means "to light up." These miniature paintings were so named because they "shed light on" the words, or made them easier to understand. Imagine that the book you are reading right now contained no pictures. Think how hard it would be to "see" the artworks from descriptions of them alone.

The illumination in Figure 7–10 tells a story. It is about thirty birds that set out on a long journey. Their goal is to find the king of birds.

Notice the many different types of birds in this picture. How many can you identify? What other animals are in the scene?

Illuminations and the Element of Line

Like most Persian paintings, this one makes strong use of the element of line. With your finger, trace the flowing curves that make up the birds, tree, and landscape. These lines suggest graceful movement. The tree is made to look as if it is growing beyond the picture's frame.

You may have noticed the curves in the two corner boxes. These are more than just decoration. They are an example of **calligraphy** (kuh-**lig**-ruh-fee). This word is from two Greek words meaning "beautiful" and "writing." Calligraphy is *the art of beautiful writing.* These curves are letters of the Persian alphabet. Notice that the thickness of these lines varies from curve to curve.

RECENT BIRD ART

Although we think of birds as creatures of flight, the sky is only one environment in which birds live. The nature study in Figure 7–11 shows another. This is the Brazilian rain forest in South America. The brightly colored winged creatures in the work are hummingbirds. Hummingbirds are special because of their ability to fly backward and their great speed. They are also the smallest of all birds. Some are less than 3 inches (8 cm) long!

Here the artist has provided a close-up of three of these unusual birds in their natural environment. They hover near an orchid, a type of flower. The birds may have fed moments earlier on the flower's nectar. What principle of art has the artist used to draw the viewer's attention to the birds and flower?

✔ Check Your Understanding

1. What is an illumination? For what were illuminations used?
2. In what way is a line of calligraphy different from lines of other kinds?
3. What is the environment of the birds in Figure 7–11?

STUDIO ACTIVITY

Practicing Calligraphy

Look again at the calligraphy in Figure 7–10. With practice, you can learn to make lines like these.

Select a round watercolor brush and dip the bristles in black watercolor paint. Move the brush slowly in the paint while twirling the handle. This will form the brush into a point. Grasp the brush near the metal part, above the bristles. Holding the brush straight up and down, touch the tip lightly to a sheet of sketch paper. Begin drawing a line slowly. The line should be thin. Press down slightly as you go. This will make the line thicker. Continue practicing, reloading the brush with paint as needed.

Once you feel comfortable making lines of different thickness, draw an outline of a bird on white paper. Work from a picture or from memory. Start at the beak. Make a single line that gets thicker as it rounds the curve of the body. Your finished bird should look graceful.

 P O R T F O L I O

Evaluate your calligraphy in a short paragraph. Put this in your portfolio with your artwork.

Figure 7–11 How many different textures and shapes can you find in this rich painting?

Martin Johnson Heade. *Cattleya Orchid and Three Brazilian Hummingbirds.* 1871. Oil on wood. 34.8 × 45.6 cm (13¾ × 18"). National Gallery of Art, Washington, D.C. Gift of Morris and Gwendolyn Cafritz Foundation.

Making an Animal Sculpture

Around the time the Wright Brothers were experimenting with flight, a Romanian artist was doing the same. His name was Constantin Brancusi (**kon**-stan-teen bran-**koos**-ee). The sculpture shown in Figure 7–12 is the result of one of Brancusi's more successful experiments. Study the work. In it, the artist has captured the essence of a soaring bird. What elements of art contribute to this feeling? What principle has been used to arrange the elements of art?

WHAT YOU WILL LEARN

Notice how Brancusi has simplified the bird into a solid form. Using the method of modeling, you will create an abstract sculpture of a real or imaginary creature at rest. You will begin by molding the basic form of this creature with clay. When the clay has turned leather hard, you will create a texture or polish the animal to give harmony to your sculpture.

WHAT YOU WILL NEED

- Pencil and sketch paper
- Wooden board
- Ball of clay (about the size of an orange)
- Clay modeling tools

WHAT YOU WILL DO

1. Look at Figure 7–12. Observe how the artist has simplified the shape of the bird. Draw several sketches of an animal at rest. Simplify the shape of your animal, keeping the legs, tail, and head close to the body. Choose your best sketch.

Figure 7–12 How would you describe the artist's use of line? What idea or feeling does this sculpture communicate?

Constantin Brancusi. *Bird in Space.* 1928. Bronze (unique cast). 137.2 × 21.6 × 16.5 cm (54 × 8½ × 6½″). Museum of Modern Art, New York, New York. Given anonymously.

2. Knead your ball of clay on the board to rid it of air bubbles. Begin to form the ball into the general shape of the animal in your sketch. Use your fingers or clay modeling tools to make shallow indentations that indicate the position of the head, legs, and tail. Keep turning your sculpture as you work to make sure it looks good from all angles.

3. If you intend to fire the piece in a kiln, use a pencil to push holes into the bottom, when the clay is firm but not dry, to keep it from exploding in the kiln.

4. Finish your sculpture by using clay modeling tools to add texture to part or all of the surface. A comb or toothbrush pulled across the surface will create the look of fur. You can use the back of a spoon to polish the surface for a shiny look. This is called burnishing.

5. Display your finished work with that of your classmates to make an abstract zoo.

EXAMINING YOUR WORK

- **Describe** What kind of a creature did you create? What surface texture did you use?
- **Analyze** Name the most important element and principle of art you used in creating your animal. Tell how you used them to give your animal harmony.
- **Interpret** Were you able to create the impression that your animal was at rest? Describe how you created this feeling.
- **Judge** Which aesthetic view would you use to judge this work? Tell whether you think your work is successful.

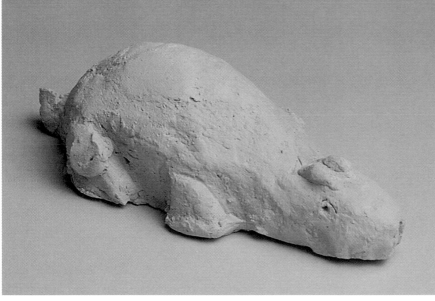

Figure 7–13   **Student work. A creature at rest.**

Try This! STUDIO OPTION

■ Do a second clay sculpture, this time creating an imaginary creature. Exaggerate the features of this animal, making it look fierce and active. Use many textures to provide a varied surface. Give your creature a name that fits its personality. Photograph this sculpture for your portfolio.

Fantasy Animals

Land, sea, and air are the only true environments of animals. Yet, artists sometimes turn to another special environment when creating animal art. This is the environment of the imagination.

Some imaginary animals in art are inspired by myths, legends, or beliefs. Others reflect an artist's personal style or tastes. Still others are made up of the body parts of many animals. You may have read Dr. Seuss books when you were small. If you did, you are probably familiar with such animals.

Figure 7–14 **What techniques has the artist used to give a feeling of depth in this tapestry?**

The Unicorn Tapestries,VII: The Unicorn in Captivity. c. 1500. Silk, wool, silver and silver-gilt threads. 3.7 × 2.5 m (12' 1" × 8'3"). The Metropolitan Museum of Art, New York, New York. Gift of John D. Rockefeller, Jr., The Cloisters Collection.

FANTASY ANIMALS FROM MYTH

The ancient Egyptians, you may recall, viewed animals as symbols. A **symbol** is *an image used to stand for a quality or an idea.* The hippopotamus was a symbol of strength.

Another animal symbol from long ago appears in Figure 7–14. You may recognize this fantasy animal as a unicorn. The name blends the word parts *uni*, meaning "one," and *corn*, meaning "horn." It comes from the single twisted horn on the creature's forehead. White in color, the unicorn was a symbol of purity. Its horn was thought to have many magical powers. One power was the ability to restore health to someone who has been poisoned.

Fantasy Animals in Applied Art

The artwork in which the unicorn appears is a **tapestry.** This is *a woven wall hanging with decorative designs or colorful scenes.* This tapestry was made during the Middle Ages. It was one of a series of seven. Together they recorded the legend of the hunt for the unicorn. In this tapestry, the unicorn has been captured. It rests on a bed of flowers deep in the forest.

The artist has placed the unicorn in the center of the scene. This emphasizes its importance in the story. The light color value of the animal makes it stand out from the colorful background of plants and flowers. Notice how the artist has used the fence to create a sense of depth. This technique is called *overlapping*. The front half of the fence overlaps, or covers, the unicorn's back legs. Where else is overlapping used in the work? What other techniques has the artist used to suggest depth?

FANTASY ANIMALS THAT REFLECT STYLE

In art and the surrounding world, colors are sometimes used as symbols. A person who is scared is called "yellow." Someone who is sad is said to feel "blue." During the early 1900s, a group of artists in Europe developed a new way of making art, called *Expressionism*. It was called this because it expressed inner feelings. Color was very important to the Expressionists. It was especially important to one of their leaders, Franz Marc.

An Expressionist Fantasy Painting

Yellow Cow, the painting in Figure 7–15, is one of Marc's most famous. To Franz Marc, *yellow* meant "gentle" and "cheerful." This leaping cow is so cheerful it seems as though it is about to jump off the canvas. Trace the sweeping curve that starts at the cow's tail. It pulls your eye through the painting.

Check Your Understanding

1. What is a symbol?
2. What was the unicorn's color? What did that color symbolize?

Figure 7–15 What kinds of color has the artist used to communicate a message about the animal in this picture?

Franz Marc. *Yellow Cow.* 1911. Oil on canvas. 141 × 189 cm (55⅜ × 74½"). Solomon R. Guggenheim Museum, New York, New York.

Lesson 7 *Fantasy Animals* **137**

Creating a Fantasy Creature

Look at the artwork in Figure 7–16. This is an example of folk art. **Folk art** is *art made by artists who have had no formal training.* The painting by Edward Hicks on page **140** is another example of folk art. In some cases, the name of the folk artist is not known.

The main medium in this example of folk art is bottle caps. The type used, called a crown cap, was first produced in 1891. Some bottlers today still use crown caps. These metal caps add an unusual surface texture to the giraffe. The work contains many other found objects as well. These include tree branches and a fur tail. All are attached to a metal body. How many different found media can you see?

Notice how the giraffe seems as though it is about to move. The diagonal slant of its legs and its neck help create that feeling.

WHAT YOU WILL LEARN

You will create a three-dimensional fantasy animal using recyclable materials and other found objects. Your creature will have a head, a body, legs, and a tail. Depending on the materials you collect, you may create other parts. These might include wings, ears, horns, spikes, hair, or fur. To add color, you will finish your creature by painting it or covering it with interesting buttons, fabric scraps, papers, foils, and so on. Give your creature a name. You will also write a story about its life and environment. Finally, present your creature to the class by telling your story.

Figure 7–16 **What unusual material has the artist used to create this giraffe? What is the main principle of art in this sculpture?**

Unknown American Artist. *Bottlecap Giraffe*. c. 1966. Carved and painted wood, bottlecaps, rubber, glass, animal hair and fur. 184.2 × 137.2 × 44.5 cm (72½ × 54 × 17½"). National Museum of American Art, Smithsonian Institution, Washington, D.C. Gift of Herbert Waide Hemphill, Jr. and museum purchase made possible by Ralph Cross Johnson.

WHAT YOU WILL NEED

- Assorted recyclable packing materials (yogurt cups, tubes, or other containers)
- White glue or masking tape
- Masking or transparent tape
- Newsprint for papier-mâché
- Cellulose wallpaper paste and water
- School tempera paints
- Assorted brushes
- Buttons, fabric scraps, pieces of broken toys, and other found materials
- Sheets of corrugated cardboard, poster board, or colored construction paper

Figure 7–17 Student work. Fantasy creatures.

EXAMINING YOUR WORK

- **Describe** List the materials used to create your animal. Describe the materials used for ears, eyes, and so on.
- **Analyze** Describe the form you created. What surface texture did you use? What colors did you select?
- **Interpret** What kind of mood or feeling does your creature express? Was your story funny or serious?
- **Judge** Which aesthetic view would you use to describe your work? If you were to do this project again, what, if anything, would you change?

WHAT YOU WILL DO

1. Collect a variety of recyclable packing materials. You might gather boxes, plastic containers, or tubes. Study these items. Practice placing them together to create the form of an imaginary creature. The form should include a head, a body, and legs.
2. When you have decided on an arrangement, attach the objects with masking tape. Apply papier-mâché strips to strengthen the joints and cover the body.

3. Choose colors of tempera paint. Decide whether your creature will have a smooth or rough surface texture. Apply the paint using brushes that will give the desired texture. Use large-bristled brushes for a rough texture. Use fine-bristled brushes for a smooth texture.
4. Add a tail, ears, eyes, and other parts. Use buttons, felt, trims, fabric, and other found objects. If you prefer, substitute pieces of cardboard, poster board, or colored construction paper.
5. Give your creature a name. Write a brief story about the creature and its environment. Present your fantasy creature to the class by reading your story aloud.

Try This! ## COMPUTER OPTION 🖥

■ If your classroom computer has a 3-D modeling program, experiment with combining basic three-dimensional forms to make a fantasy animal. You might use a cube for the body and a cone for the neck. A sphere or ellipse might be the head. Use smaller versions of these shapes to make eyes, a nose, and so on. Adjust the lights to cast interesting shadows. Use the Render command to complete your creature.

Edward Hicks. *The Peaceable Kingdom.* c. 1837. Oil on canvas. 73.7 × 90.8 cm (29 × 35¾"). The Carnegie Museum of Art, Pittsburgh, Pennsylvania. Bequest of Charles J. Rosenbloom.

The Founding of Pennsylvania

The Liberty Bell. Independence Hall. Gettysburg Battlefield. What do these things have in common? They are all located in the state of Pennsylvania.

Pennsylvania was founded by William Penn, an English Quaker. The Quakers are a religious group. In 1681, King Charles II of England gave William Penn a territory in North America. The territory was a payment for a debt that the king owed to Penn's father. In 1682, William Penn sailed to America. The land that Penn owned was located between New Jersey and Maryland. The king named it Pennsylvania, which means Penn's Woods.

About 15,000 Native Americans were living in the area that became Pennsylvania. In October 1682, William Penn met with the Native Americans and made a treaty of friendship with them. This meeting is shown in *The Peaceable Kingdom.* Penn also founded the city of Philadelphia.

The Peaceable Kingdom was painted by Edward Hicks, who lived in Pennsylvania. Hicks was a pacifist, which means that he did not believe in violence. He believed that people could get what they wanted through peaceful means.

MAKING THE CONNECTION

 What is the overall theme of this painting?

 Identify the animals shown in this work. Why do you think Hicks grouped these particular animals together?

 Look for information about Edward Hicks. What influenced him to be a pacifist?

INTERNET ACTIVITY

Visit Glencoe's Fine Arts Web Site for students at:

http://www.glencoe.com/sec/art/students

REVIEW

BUILDING VOCABULARY

Number a sheet of paper from 1 to 12. After each number, write the term from the box that matches each description below.

appliqué	Old Stone Age
calligraphy	porcelain
environment	symbol
folk art	tapestry
illumination	totem
mascot	trait

1. The historical period that occurred between 30,000 and 10,000 B.C.
2. Surroundings.
3. A fine-grained, high-quality form of pottery.
4. A woven wall hanging with decorative designs or colorful scenes.
5. An art form in which cutout shapes are attached to a larger surface.
6. Art made by artists who have had no formal training.
7. The art of beautiful writing.
8. An image used to stand for a quality or an idea.
9. A hand-painted book illustration.
10. An animal or person used by a group as a sign of luck.
11. Personal characteristic.
12. An object that serves as an emblem or respected symbol.

REVIEWING ART FACTS

Number a sheet of paper from 13 to 22. Answer each question in a complete sentence.

13. What do experts believe was the purpose of the cave paintings?
14. Explain why experts believe a sculpture of a hippo was placed in the tomb of Soneb.
15. Name two ways in which an appliqué can be fastened to a background surface.
16. What type of print is *Yellowfin Tuna?* How are such prints made?
17. What art element was emphasized most in Persian painting?
18. What effects are achieved through the use of this element in the illumination in Figure 7–10?
19. What did the color yellow symbolize for Franz Marc?
20. What did the artist symbolize in the painting *The Peaceable Kingdom?*

THINKING ABOUT ART

On a sheet of paper, answer each question in a sentence or two.

1. **Extend.** Lesson 1 mentions one source of pigment available to cave dwellers. What other sources do you think these early artists used? What colors do you suppose these sources produced? What kinds of containers do you think the artists used to mix their paints? Explain your answers.
2. **Interpret.** Choose one artwork from the chapter with symbolic meaning. Explain the symbol. Tell how it adds to your appreciation of the work.

MAKING ART CONNECTIONS

1. **Science.** Learn about carbon-14 dating. This is a technique scientists have used to prove that cave paintings were really done thousands of years ago. Use an encyclopedia or on-line resource. Share your findings in a report.
2. **Technology.** Use a still camera or video camera to record actions of a pet or other animal. Your video might show birds or fish. Share your photographs or video with your classmates. Discuss which images make the best art subjects and why.

Figure 8–1 Notice the torn posters and handbills in the background of this painting. What do these objects seem to reveal about the subject in the foreground?

William M. Harnett. *Attention, Company!* 1878. Oil on canvas. 91 × 71 cm (36 × 28″). Amon Center Museum, Fort Worth, Texas.

142

Portraying People

Like snowflakes, no two people are exactly alike. Each has his or her own likes, dislikes, thoughts, feelings, and dreams. It is this one-of-a-kind quality that has made people a favorite subject of artists.

Study the painting on the facing page. The subject of this work is a child playing soldier. Notice the youth's "rifle" and "military hat." What do these props suggest about the power of the child's imagination?

In this chapter, you will learn how to "read" works of art that depict people.

OBJECTIVES

After completing this chapter, you will be able to:

- Explain what is meant by having a *style* in art.
- Identify differences in the way people have been portrayed in different ages and cultures.
- Complete artworks with people as subjects.

WORDS YOU WILL LEARN

ancestor figure
figure study
murals
portraiture
public art
self-portrait
style
trompe-l'oeil

PORTFOLIO IDEAS

There are different ways to choose what to put into your portfolio. For example, you might select an artwork because

- it represents your best example of composition
- it demonstrates your growth in using a specific medium, or
- it shows the skill you exhibited in making an artwork.

Portraits

Ever since the first cave dwellers roamed the earth, the world's population has been steadily growing. So has the number of ways of portraying people in art. Each age has given rise to new art styles. A **style** is *an artist's personal way of using the elements and principles of art to express feelings and ideas.*

In this chapter, you will see examples of different styles artists have used to depict people through the ages.

PORTRAITS AS HISTORICAL RECORDS

Today, we know what our leaders and other celebrities look like. It wasn't always so.

Imagine for a moment that you live in an age before television, newspapers, and magazines. Such a time existed in the not-too-distant past. As recently as the early 1800s, people who wanted to see important figures had to rely largely on painted *portraits* of them.

Portrait from the 1500s

Figure 8–2 shows a portrait from the 1500s. As the credit line reveals, the subjects are a woman and her son. Look again at the credit line. The artist, you will notice, did not work alone. Like other successful portrait painters of the era, he had a "workshop" of assistants. The need for such helpers was prompted by two factors. One was a demand

Figure 8–2   Compare this work with the Roman portrait sculpture on page 84 (Figure 5–4). Which of the works do you think is truer to life? Why?

Agnolo Bronzino. *Eleonora of Toledo and Her Son.* c. 1550. Oil on panel. 1.2 × 1 m (48 × 39⅜"). Detroit Institute of Arts, Detroit, Michigan. Gift of Mrs. Ralph Harmon Booth in memory of her husband Ralph Harmon Booth.

Figure 8–3 Compare the use of light and shadow in this portrait and the one in Figure 8–2. Which painting uses light more effectively? Why do you feel as you do?

Franz Hals. *Portrait of an Elderly Lady*. 1633. Oil on canvas. 103 × 86.4 cm (40¼ × 34″). © 1997 Board of Trustees, National Gallery of Art, Washington, D.C. Andrew W. Mellon Collection.

for copies of portraits, which were often given as gifts. Another was a lack of technology for reproducing images. The full potential of the printing press, still in its infancy, had not yet been realized.

Turn your attention to the portrait itself. Look at the way the figures are dressed. What does this tell you about their social standing? Do you think they were rich or poor? Do you think the artist's main goal was to show these people as they really looked or as they preferred to be shown?

EXPRESSIVE PORTRAITS

The portrait in Figure 8–2 represents a style of art known as *Mannerism*. In its day, this term was used scornfully. It was applied to works that seemed overly stiff and formal.

Compare this painting with the one in Figure 8–3. This second work was done in the 1600s, almost a one hundred years after the

first. Notice the expression on the subject's face. Her eyes, which reflect the wisdom of her years, are boldly fixed on the viewer. Deep lines are etched in the woman's face. Even the firm grip of her hand on the arm of the chair seems to signal an inner strength and energy. What words would you use to describe this sitter's personality? What kinds of behavior would you expect from her?

✔ Check Your Understanding

1. What is style?
2. How did portrait painting change from the 1500s to the 1600s?

Creating an Expressive Face

Have you ever heard the expression "whistling in the dark?" It refers to efforts to look and sound brave in the face of danger. The iron mask in Figure 8–4 was created for much the same purpose. It was worn by a fifteenth-century Japanese warrior—making him look fierce and frightening to enemies—while adding to his own confidence in battle. Take a closer look at this art object. Notice the furrowed brow, the wide-open eyes, and the angry scowl. Does the expression on this mask succeed in frightening you?

WHAT YOU WILL LEARN

In this lesson, you will create a masklike, expressive face. You will use a variety of large and small shapes in contrasting colors torn from colored construction paper. These will be assembled and glued to a sheet of black construction paper. To make the face as expressive as possible, you will exaggerate and distort the features and use contrasting colors. Then arrange the shapes in layers to give your picture a bold, expressive look.

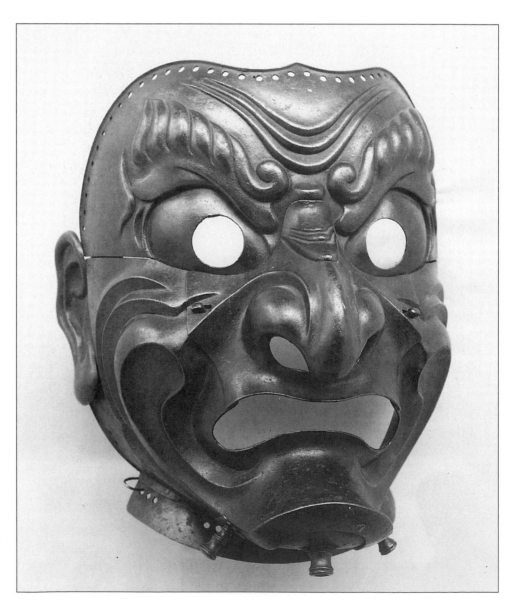

Figure 8–4   What expression do you "read" on this mask? What features give it such an expression?

Japan. *Mask.* 1716. Iron repoussè. 19.7 × 17.1 cm (7¾ × 6¾"). The Metropolitan Museum of Art, New York, New York. Rogers Fund, 1913.

WHAT YOU WILL NEED

- Pencil and sheets of sketch paper
- Colored construction paper 9 x 12 inches (23 x 30 cm)
- White glue or glue sticks
- Cardboard cut into ½-inch(1.3-cm) squares
- Scissors

WHAT YOU WILL DO

1. Begin by studying the Japanese mask in Figure 8–4. Note the way the artist distorted the features and expression of the face to make it appear more frightening.
2. Complete several sketches of faces, focusing on expressions. Experiment with different ways of exaggerating and distorting the facial features. Notice the different moods and feelings suggested by the sketches.
3. Using your best sketch as a guide, tear a wide oval or round shape from a piece of construction paper. *Do not use scissors for this task.* Glue the shape to a sheet of construction paper.
4. Tear other shapes from the construction paper to form the eyes, eyebrows, nose, and mouth. For each feature, tear out *six or more* shapes. Layer them from large to small. Keep in mind that the more shapes you use for a single feature, the more sculpted it will look. To make your work more expressive, distort the shapes. Be sure to use bright, contrasting colors.
5. Assemble the various features on the face shape. For each feature, glue the largest piece in place first. Continue stacking smaller shapes in this fashion. The result will be a layered effect.

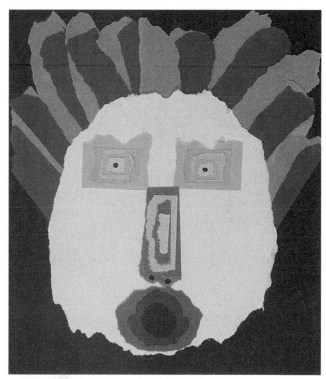

Figure 8–5   **Student work. Expressive face.**

EXAMINING YOUR WORK

- **Describe**   Are all the features of the face included in your mask? Are these features distorted?
- **Analyze**   Did you use a variety of large and small shapes? Point out places on your mask where contrasting colors are used.
- **Interpret**   Would viewers agree that your mask is expressive? If asked to describe your mask with a single word, what word would you choose?
- **Judge**   Do you think you succeeded in creating an expressive face? If you were to do another, what would you change to make the work more effective?

STUDIO OPTION

■ Cut and tear a number of different large and small geometric shapes from a sheet of white drawing paper. Using fine-tipped markers in complementary or analogous colors, create a variety of patterns on each of these shapes. Assemble these shapes on a sheet of colored construction paper to create a different kind of expressive face.

Lesson 2   *Creating an Expressive Face*   **147**

Figures in Action

One of the hardest parts of a barber's or hairstylist's job is working on a customer who won't sit still. Even the slightest movement presents a real challenge to the stylist's sure hand.

This observation holds true not only for haircutters but also for artists. For the artist, however, the challenge provided by the human body in motion is a *welcome* one. It is an opportunity to present people as they often appear—in the midst of one activity or another.

In this lesson, you will learn about artworks that show figures in action.

FIGURE STUDIES

As emphasized in Chapter 6, the Renaissance artist Leonardo da Vinci filled many sketchbooks with drawings. Among the sketches he made were hundreds upon hundreds of figure studies. A **figure study** is *a drawing that focuses on the human form.* Leonardo observed and faithfully recorded in great detail the workings of the arms and legs in motion.

The studies Leonardo made set the stage for generations of artists to follow. Take a moment to study the drawing in Figure 8–6. Notice the way in which this artist captures a messenger in flight.

Figure 8–6 Do you detect a sense of urgency? What kinds of lines has the artist used to convey this feeling?

Honoré Daumier. *The Young Courier.* Black chalk and gray wash on laid paper. 15.5 × 23.2 cm (6⅛ × 9⅛"). © 1997 Board of Trustees, National Gallery of Art, Washington D.C. The Rosenwald Collection.

ACTION PAINTING

The recording of figures in action is not limited to drawing. Neither is it confined to works with highly representational subjects. For proof, look at the abstract painting in Figure 8–7.

The work shows the fluid movement of dancers. Notice how the dancing figures seem to blend into one another. The bright hues give the work a joyous quality. The work is so lively that some viewers have claimed they can hear the music.

✔ Check Your Understanding

1. What is a figure study?
2. Describe the body language of the figures in motion on these two pages.

Figure 8–7   **Notice the simple shapes the artist has used. What principle of art has he used to suggest movement?**

Arthur B. Davies. *Dances.* 1914–15. Oil on canvas. 2.1 × 3.51 m (7′ × 11′ 6″). Detroit Institute of Arts, Detroit, Michigan. Gift of Ralph Harmon Booth.

STUDIO ACTIVITY

Creating a Figure Study

You and a partner are to take turns serving as model and artist. Each of you is to concentrate on capturing the other in action. Begin by posing your model as if he or she were frozen in an act of some kind. Possibilities include throwing a ball, sweeping the floor, or lifting an object off the floor. Moisten a 9 x l2-inch (23 x 30-cm) sheet of white drawing paper with water. Tint the paper with one or more colors of watercolor. While the paint is still wet, quickly draw the model using a black marker. Concentrate on capturing the major action lines of the body. Do not worry that the ink spreads and blurs.

Complete several such drawings. Arrange the works in order.

P O R T F O L I O

On a piece of paper, note whether your efforts at capturing action improved with practice.

Drawing a Figure in Action

The action painting in Figure 8–7, as you saw, has an energetic quality. Its mood is achieved, moreover, through a union of free-flowing abstract shapes.

Both those comments apply equally to the work in Figure 8–8. Take a moment to examine this painting closely. Do the playful shapes in it remind you of the interlocking pieces of a jigsaw puzzle? If so, your thinking is in line with the artist's. All of his art was meant to be playful. Notice the work's title. The word *reveler* means merrymaker. Can you find the head, arms, and legs of this merrymaker?

WHAT YOU WILL LEARN

In this studio lesson, you will paint an abstract figure in action. You will not worry about making your subject look real. Instead, you will concentrate on using a variety of lines, shapes, bright colors, and textures to suggest a moving figure. These art elements will add up to a cheerful design.

WHAT YOU WILL NEED

- Pencil and sheets of sketch paper
- White drawing paper, 12 x 18 inches (30 x 45 cm)

Figure 8–8 **Notice the variety of lines and shapes in this painting. How has the artist tied these elements together to form a human figure?**

Jean Dubuffet. *The Reveler.* 1964. Oil on canvas. 195 × 130.2 cm (76¾ × 51¼"). Dallas Museum of Art, Dallas, Texas. Gift of Mr. and Mrs. James H. Clark.

- Black marker with a medium point
- Several brushes
- Tempera paints, mixing tray
- Scissors
- White glue
- Black construction paper

WHAT YOU WILL DO

1. Begin by looking again at Figure 8–8. Concentrate on the lines of the figure. Observe how the artist has used a variety of lines, shapes, colors, and textures, within the overall shape. See how these add action to the work's composition.

2. Complete several pencil sketches of a student model in an action pose. In your sketches, focus on capturing the lines of action in the figure. Draw only the outline of the figure.

3. Working lightly with a continuous pencil line, transfer your best sketch to the sheet of white drawing paper. Make your drawing large enough to fill most of the paper. Go over the pencil line with a black marker.

4. Still working with the marker, divide your figure into a variety of large and small shapes.

5. Switching to tempera and brush, paint the smaller shapes within the large figure shape. Select bright, cheerful colors that contrast with one another. You do not have to paint all the shapes. You may also want to add painted lines or lines made with the marker to some of the shapes. Notice that the artist has done this in Figure 8–8 to create different textures.

6. With scissors, cut out your drawing. Use white glue to mount the drawing on a sheet of black construction paper.

EXAMINING YOUR WORK

- **Describe**   Can you easily identify the head, arms, and legs in your figure? Does the figure appear to be moving?
- **Analyze**   Did you break up your figure with a variety of large and small shapes? Did you also use a variety of colors and textures?
- **Interpret**   Do you think most viewers will recognize your work as an abstract figure in action?
- **Judge**   What do you consider to be the best part of your composition?

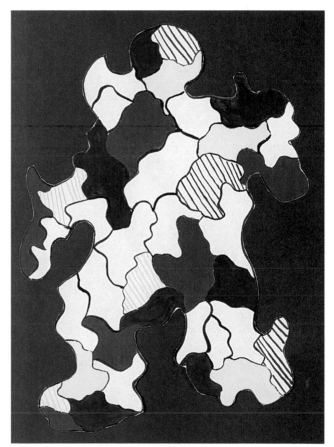

Figure 8–9 **Student work. Abstract figure in action.**

STUDIO OPTION

■ Complete another abstract figure in action. This time, use dark, somber colors. Mount your finished composition on a sheet of brightly colored construction paper. Compare it to your first painting. Which is more successful?

Portraits in the Round

Are you familiar with the phrase *in the flesh?* It is a colorful way of saying "in person." This phrase also calls to mind a property of people that can never be fully captured in two-dimensional paintings or drawings. That is the three-dimensionality of the human form. What better way to show this property than in art that has three dimensions?

In this lesson and the next, you will explore another approach to **portraiture (pohr-tray-chur)**—*the art of making portraits*—that highlights this property. You will learn about and see examples of portraits "in the round."

SCULPTURE

Many artists through the ages have strived for realism in their works. Look back at the painting that opened this chapter on page **142**. The work, completed toward the end of the 1800s, exhibits an art style known as **trompe-l'oeil** (trohmp-**loy**). This is *a style of painting in which objects are depicted with photographically realistic detail.* The term is French for "trick the eye."

Renaissance Portrait Sculpture

The groundwork for this pursuit of realism was laid during the Renaissance. One of

Figure 8–10 **Does this figure appear calm and relaxed? If not, how would you describe him?**

Michelangelo. *Moses.* c. 1513–15. Marble. Approx. 244 cm (8′) high. San Pietro in Vincoli, Rome. Scala/Art Resource, NY

the giants of this period was the artist who produced the work in Figure 8–10. You probably know his name. It is Michelangelo. Although Michelangelo made many great paintings, he thought of himself first as a sculptor. His paintings and sculptures reflect an interest in realism that is similar to that of trompe-l'oil.

Study Figure 8–10. The subject is the Bible figure Moses. Michelangelo has brought the figure to rousing life through his careful attention to detail. Examine the left arm, for example. See how each muscle and vein stands out in vivid relief.

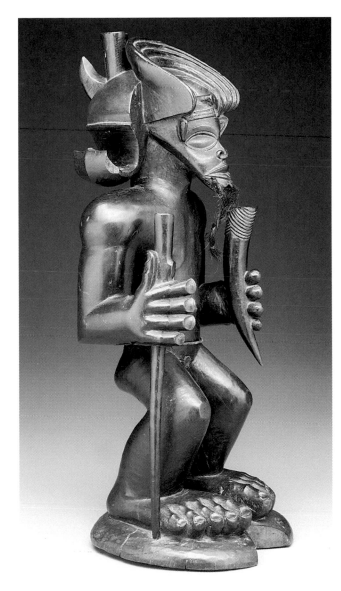

Figure 8–11 **What clues can you find that this figure was a great leader and hunter?**

Africa. Angola. Chokwe. *Chibinda (The Hunter), Ilunga Katele.* Mid-nineteenth century. Wood, hair, hide. Height: 40.6 cm (16″). Kimbell Art Museum, Fort Worth, Texas.

STUDIO ACTIVITY

Experimenting with Abstract Designs

Like most artists of early Africa, the Chokwe people relied heavily on abstraction. Notice the free-form curves that make up the headdress of the subject in Figure 8–11.

Make an abstract design for a wall in your room at home. Use shapes and lines that reflect your hobbies and interests.

P O R T F O L I O

Ask two or three classmates to evaluate your abstract design. Were they able to identify the images you wanted to show with shapes and lines? Write down what, if anything, you might do differently if you were to repeat the activity. Put this critique in your portfolio with the artwork.

African Ancestor Figure

As with two-dimensional art, styles of portrait sculpture vary from culture to culture. The work in Figure 8–11 is typical of the style of art of the Chokwe (**choh**-kway) people of Africa. The work is an example of an **ancestor figure.** This is *an image carved in wood that was used as the resting place of a spirit.* This particular ancestor figure is based on an actual person—a great leader and hunter.

Examine this carving. Like most African figures, it was created for two reasons. One of these was respect for the dead. The other reason was a fear of angry spirits of the dead. Notice that each body part is carved with great care. What words would you use to describe the look and posture of this figure?

Check Your Understanding

1. Which of the sculptures in this lesson served as an example for artists who created realistic art later on? Explain your answer.
2. What is an ancestor figure?

Creating a Clay Portrait

Style in art, as you have learned, can differ from place to place. As you are about to see, it can also change over *time*. Compare the portrait sculpture in Figure 8–12 with the one in Figure 5–4 on page **84**. Both works are portraits. Both were done in ancient Rome. Yet, the differences between the two are easy to see. The work on this page is more blocklike and less natural than the earlier sculpture on page **84**. What factors might explain these changes? What might they reveal about the changing goals of artists in ancient Rome?

WHAT YOU WILL LEARN

In this lesson, you will create a carved portrait. Your work, which will be made from clay, will be a relief sculpture. Your work need not look like any subject in particular, although you should try to make it lifelike. The features in your work will be in correct proportion to the face. Where possible, you will use tactile texture to make your portrait interesting to the eye and to the touch.

WHAT YOU WILL NEED

- Two wood strips to use as guides, each about ½ inch (1.3 cm) thick
- Board
- Clay
- Rolling pin
- Modeling tools
- Newspaper
- Sheet of plastic

Figure 8–12 The subject was a great emperor of Rome. How would you describe the expression on the face of this figure?

Roman. *Portrait of the Emperor Constantine I.* c. A.D. 325. Marble. 95.3 cm (37½"). The Metropolitan Museum of Art, New York, New York. Bequest of Mark Clark Thompson, 1923.

WHAT YOU WILL DO

1. Wedge the clay. Place the wood strip guides on the board about 8 inches (20 cm) apart. Flatten the clay between the guide sticks with the palm of your hand. Use the rolling pin to roll out the clay.

2. With a modeling tool, lightly draw an oval shape in the clay. This is to represent your subject's face.

3. Add lightly etched guidelines to help you locate the position for each feature of the face. Form the nose by cutting its contour in the clay, then carefully pulling the form outward. Support the feature with a small ball of clay until it hardens enough to support itself. Cut and shape small pieces of clay to serve as pupils, eyelids, eyebrows, and lips. Attach each by crosshatching, adding slip to each piece to be joined.

4. Use modeling tools to add texture to hair and eyebrows.

5. Hold your relief with one hand, and with the other gently push the facial area out to form a more three-dimensional look.

6. Roll up a thick layer of newspaper pages. Cover this with a sheet of plastic. Gently lay your relief on top of this rolled-up bundle to give it a rounded appearance.

7. When your relief is completely dry, have your teacher help you fire it. Display the finished portrait.

EXAMINING YOUR WORK

- **Describe** Are all the features of your relief in correct proportion to the face? Have they been placed in the right locations?
- **Analyze** Did you make use of tactile texture in your relief?
- **Interpret** Do you feel that your portrait is lifelike?
- **Judge** How do you feel about your portrait? Are you satisfied with its appearance? What is its best feature?

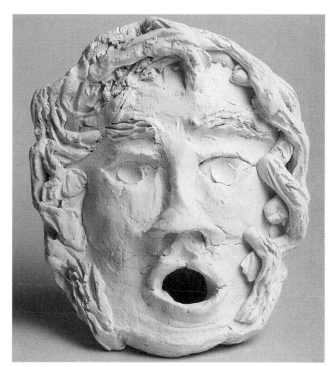

Figure 8–13   Student work. Clay portrait.

Try This! COMPUTER OPTION

■ Create an *embossed*, or relief, design. Using a drawing program, begin by selecting the Rectangle tool and draw a rectangle 4 inches wide by 1 inch tall. Fill the rectangle with a medium shade of gray. Switch to the Text tool and set the type size to around 35 points and the color to black. Placing the cursor over the box you have drawn, type your name. Make two copies of your name, using the Duplicate or Copy and Paste commands. Fill one copy with the same shade of gray you used for your rectangle. The third should have a white fill. Use the Arrange command to layer the white and black copies behind the gray one. Move the white and black copies until only a small amount of each shows below and above the gray copy. Does your name look like a relief design?

Heroes in Art

Every culture and generation has its heroes. Some heroes are living, breathing people. Firefighters, law enforcement officers, and doctors are but a few of these. Other heroes are lasting symbols of values we hold dear. The larger-than-life Paul Bunyan and his faithful companion, Babe the blue ox, are a pair of such folk heroes.

In this lesson, you will meet examples of each type of hero. You will also see ways in which these heroes have been celebrated and remembered in art.

PUBLIC ART

Are there statues in your city or community? Perhaps there is a statue of your city's founder in a local park or square. Such works are examples of **public art.** This is *art to be displayed in and enjoyed by a community.* Usually, public art is found outdoors. It may be in the form of statues, fountains, or murals. **Murals** are *large two-dimensional works painted on walls.*

Memorial Art

The work displayed in Figure 8–14 is a special type of public art. Called *memorial art,* its purpose is to help people remember the singular achievement or dedication of a group or individual. The group commemorated in this work were United States Marines. Some 6,000 of these brave fighters gave their lives in a single battle while fighting for democracy during World War II.

Figure 8–14 This artwork is displayed, appropriately, in Arlington National Cemetery outside Washington, D.C. Heroes of World War II and other campaigns are buried here.

Raising the Flag on Iwo Jima. Arlington Cemetery, Arlington, Virginia.

HUMAN LEGENDS IN ART

Figure 8–15 shows a hero of a different sort. He is the folk legend John Henry. A mythical railroad worker of the 1800s, he has been the subject of countless songs and poems. John Henry symbolizes the "sweat and tears" of hardworking people during our nation's time of growth. In this painting, he raises two hammers above his head as he gazes out on future generations of settlers heading west. How has the artist captured the inner—and outer—strength of this hero? What meaning can you attach to the rainbow that appears in the distance? Notice how the muscles of the figure's forearms glisten. What sculpture from this chapter does this attention to detail call to mind?

 **Check Your Understanding**

1. What is public art? What are murals?
2. What folk hero appears in Figure 8–15?

 **STUDIO ACTIVITY**

Making a Hero Exhibit

With several classmates, plan a "Heroes in the News" exhibition. Search newspapers and magazines for illustrations of heroes of the moment. Cut out the images. Work together to think of words that help convey the heroism of the people in the pictures. Write these words in decorative fashion on strips of colored construction paper. With white glue, paste the images and words to a sheet of poster board.

 P O R T F O L I O

Take photographs of the poster so that each member of your work-group has a copy. Attach your photo to a self-reflection and put them into your portfolio.

Figure 8–15 **Notice that the artist has chosen not to show John Henry's face. Why do you suppose this is so?**

Jerry Pinkney. *John Henry.* 1994. Pencil, colored pencils, and watercolor on paper. 32.4 × 40.6 cm (12¾ × 16"). From *John Henry* by Julius Lester, published by Dial Books, 1994.

Creating a Mixed-Media Banner

In the previous lesson, you viewed art based on several heroes. Figure 8–16 contains yet another such work. Do you recognize the hero in this painting? It is Joan of Arc. Joan of Arc lived in France in the 1400s. She was not much older than you when she bravely led an army of French troops against the English.

Look closely at Figure 8–16. The picture is filled with figures and action. Even so, Joan is easily identified. She is mounted on a white charger and carries a huge banner.

WHAT YOU WILL LEARN

In this lesson, you will create your own banner honoring a hero. Your banner, which will use mixed media, may focus on a real-life or made-up hero. The work will be divided into three sections. In each section you will use different media to create images and symbols associated with your hero. Using different media will allow you to create a variety of visual textures. These in turn will add interest to your banner.

WHAT YOU WILL NEED

- Pencil and sheets of sketch paper
- Ruler or other straight edge
- Butcher paper, 18 x 24 inches (46 x 61 cm)
- Scissors
- Tissue paper in assorted colors
- White glue
- Pen
- Magazines
- Colored markers

Figure 8–16 Do you sense movement when you look at this artwork? What element of art contributes to this strong feeling?

Franck Craig. *"La Pucelle": Jeanne d'Arc Leads Her Army*. 1907. Oil on canvas. 190 × 341.5 cm (74¾ × 134⅜"). Musee d'Orsay, Paris, France. Erich Lessing/Art Resource, NY

WHAT YOU WILL DO

1. Select a hero. Sketch several designs for banners to honor your hero. Use straight or curved lines to divide each banner design into three sections.

2. In each of the three sections, create images or symbols that tell something about your hero. For example, a banner honoring Paul Bunyan might include trees, an ax, and a blue ox. Make your drawings large. Avoid small details.

3. Using a ruler or other straight edge, transfer your best banner design to a sheet of butcher paper. Fill the paper with your design. With scissors, trim away the portions of the paper beyond the banner's outline. Divide the banner into three sections with straight or curved pencil lines. Using your sketch as a model, lightly draw the images and symbols for each section.

4. Cut or tear shapes from sheets of colored tissue paper. Overlap and glue these down to complete one section. Define shapes and details with pen. Cut or tear pictures and words cut from magazines to complete another section. Complete the third section using colored markers. Make certain to fill each section of your banner with color. Take care not to cross the lines between sections.

5. Place your banner on display. Ask classmates if they can identify your hero.

EXAMINING YOUR WORK

- **Describe**   Identify the images and symbols in each of the three sections of your banner.
- **Analyze**   Does your banner show a variety of visual textures? In which section of your banner do you think texture is best demonstrated?
- **Interpret**   Could classmates identify the hero your banner honors? What image or symbol was most helpful to them in making this identification?
- **Judge**   What is the best feature of your design? If you were to make another banner, what would you do to change it?

Figure 8–17   Student work. Mixed-media banner.

Try This! STUDIO OPTION

■ Make a small drawing of a banner with a different shape, and divide it into three sections. Lay a sheet of waxed paper over the drawing. Use the edge of a scissors to scrape crayon shavings onto the banner image, which can be seen appearing through the waxed paper. Use a different color for each of the three sections. Lay another sheet of waxed paper on top. With an adult's help, use a warm iron to melt the crayon shavings. Cut your banner shape out, and add loops for hanging.

Lesson 8   *Creating a Mixed-Media Banner*   **159**

The Family Unit

Henry Moore. *Family Group.* 1948–49. Bronze (cast 1950). 150.5 × 118 × 75.9 cm (59¼ × 46½ × 29⅞"). The Museum of Modern Art, New York, New York. A. Conger Goodyear Fund.

What kind of family do you have? Perhaps you live with your mother, father, and a brother or sister. Maybe you live with just one parent. You might live with a parent, stepparent, and stepbrothers or stepsisters. Families come in all shapes and sizes. They are the most common type of group in our society.

Although family structures vary, many similarities exist among families. Throughout history, the functions of families have remained the same. The most basic function is to provide for family members' physical needs. These needs include food, clothing, and shelter. Families also provide for members' emotional needs. They offer love, support, and security. Families have other important functions as well. They teach values, offer guidance, and encourage independence.

The family has always been a popular theme in art. Henry Moore explored this subject in *Family Group.* In his sculpture, Moore depicts a common family group— mother, father, and child.

MAKING THE CONNECTION

✔ Notice the position of the child in Henry Moore's sculpture. What message do you think the sculptor was trying to convey about this family group?

✔ What are some of the functions of families?

✔ Find other examples of artwork that depicts families. Compare the artists' messages. Do the families seem realistic or idealistic?

INTERNET ACTIVITY

Visit Glencoe's Fine Arts Web Site for students at:

http://www.glencoe.com/ sec/art/students

CHAPTER 8
REVIEW

BUILDING VOCABULARY

Number a sheet of paper from 1 to 8. After each number, write the term from the box that best matches each description below.

ancestor figure	public art
figure study	self-portrait
murals	style
portraiture	trompe-l'oeil

1. Art to be displayed in and enjoyed by a community.
2. A drawing that focuses on the human form.
3. A style of painting in which objects are depicted with photographically realistic detail.
4. A painting or drawing of an artist's own image.
5. The art of making portraits.
6. An image carved in wood that was used as the resting place of a spirit.
7. Large two-dimensional works painted on walls.
8. An artist's personal way of using the elements and principles of art to express feelings and ideas.

REVIEWING ART FACTS

Number a sheet of paper from 9 to 13. Answer each question in a complete sentence.

9. Why did portrait painters in the 1500s need assistants?
10. What features gave the Japanese mask a fierce look?
11. What types of lines are emphasized in the action figure drawings in this chapter? Why are they emphasized?
12. What are some of the ways in which Michelangelo made his figures lifelike?
13. What are two reasons why the Chokwe of Africa made figure carvings?

THINKING ABOUT ART

On a sheet of paper, answer each question in a sentence or two.

1. **Synthesize.** Explain the following statement: Art styles change over time and from place to place. Restate this in your own words. Use examples from the chapter that illustrate the truth of this statement.
2. **Extend.** In what ways has technology changed the way in which artists show people in their works?
3. **Compare and contrast.** What are some similarities and differences among the two types of "hero art" discussed in the chapter?

MAKING ART CONNECTIONS

1. **Language Arts.** With the help of the school librarian, locate a book of poems that includes "The Ballad of John Henry." Practice reading the poem aloud. Share it with classmates as they look at Figure 8–15. Follow up with a discussion of the qualities of this fictional character that the artist pinpoints in his work.
2. **Community Connection.** With a group, brainstorm examples of public art in your own community. You might take a walking tour to look for examples. Keep on the alert not only for statues but also for decorations on buildings. Use the four steps of art criticism to write a short explanation of why each example you find is important. Print out copies of your comments on the classroom computer. Share these with family and community members.

Figure 9–1 What art element has the artist used to lead your eye into and around this nighttime street scene? What principle of art is used to organize this work?

Vincent van Gogh. *Cafe Terrace at Night*. 1888. Oil on canvas. 81 × 65.5 cm (31⅞ × 25¾"). Rijksmuseum Kroller-Muller, Otterlo, the Netherlands.

Visiting Places

Do you have a favorite place? Many people do. Maybe it is an afterschool hangout, a park, or a shopping mall. Your favorite place might even be—or be in—another city or a country you have visited.

Artists, like the rest of us, have favorite places. One of these is recorded in the artwork on the facing page. What can you tell about this place by looking at the picture? How does the artist communicate his feelings for this place?

In this chapter, you will journey to some new places. You will also visit some familiar ones. You won't need a ticket or passport—just a good imagination and a knowledge of the elements and principles of art.

PORTFOLIO IDEAS

Find an artwork in this chapter that has a dramatic feeling. What elements of art did the artist use to create the artwork's expressive qualities? What principles of art were used? Create your own portfolio entry. Include your preliminary sketches and any notes you made to explain the techniques you used.

OBJECTIVES

After completing this chapter, you will be able to:
- Understand approaches artists have taken in using places as subjects for their work.
- Recognize how the idea of *home* has changed over time.
- Define *cityscape* and *seascape*.
- Create two- and three-dimensional works that show space.

WORDS YOU WILL LEARN

architects
cityscape
columns
The Eight
elevation
façade
panorama
Rococo
seascape
staged photograph

LESSON 1

Personal Places

Rooms come in all sizes and shapes. Some are large and airy. Others are small and cramped. How would you describe your room at home? Regardless of your answer to that question, this much is clear: your room, whether or not it is shared, is one of a kind. It contains your personal things, and there is no other place exactly like it.

Perhaps it is this unique quality that has made rooms a popular subject for art.

PAINTING OF A ROOM

Possibly the first artist ever to make a picture of his room was Vincent van Gogh (van **goh**). You may have heard of him. Books, movies, and even a song have been devoted to his dark, troubled life. Before van Gogh, few artists thought a room without people could be a subject worthy of art. Yet, the artist found peace and safety in his simple room that he could find nowhere else. He wanted to express his personal feelings in his art.

Look closely at van Gogh's painting of his room in Figure 9–2. What do you think he was trying to say about this safe haven in a stormy world? What objects did he emphasize? Did you notice that the window shutters are closed? What meaning, if any, do you attach to this? Carefully study each of the items in the room. Do these items tell you anything about the artist's feelings or mood?

STAGED PHOTOGRAPH OF A ROOM

A room of a very different kind appears in Figure 9–3. This room is different from van Gogh's not only in its content but also in the medium the artist chose. This work is a

Figure 9–2 What personal "stamp" has the artist placed on his room? In what ways is this room similar to yours? How is it different?

Vincent van Gogh. *Bedroom at Arles.* 1888. Oil on canvas. 73.6 × 92.3 cm (29 × 36³⁄₁₀″). The Art Institute of Chicago, Chicago, Illinois. Helen Birch Bartlett Memorial Collection.

staged photograph. Far from an ordinary snapshot, this is *a photographic composition that makes use of artificial images or processes.* In this case, Sandy Skoglund sculpted each of the goldfish from clay. She also painted the room to look like an underwater environment. Then she used models to pose while she photographed the room.

Examine the strange world the artist has created. Notice the title. Can you think of other creatures who, like goldfish, live in a "controlled environment"? Maybe you keep such creatures as pets. Imagine waking up in a room like this one!

Check Your Understanding

1. Why did van Gogh choose to paint a picture of his room? What did he hope to communicate through his painting?
2. How did Sandy Skoglund create her staged photograph?

STUDIO ACTIVITY

Drawing Your Room

Look again at the painting in Figure 9–2. Notice that the artist was not concerned with realism. Here, as in other paintings, he used vivid colors to communicate how he felt about his subject.

Using markers or oil pastels, draw your room at home. Personalize your work, as van Gogh has done, by selecting colors that create a mood. Feel free to add "new" furniture and other details that reflect your personality. Does your finished drawing express your feelings about your room?

PORTFOLIO

Write a self-reflection on a piece of paper telling what techniques you used to picture your personality and whether you feel the technique was successful. Put this paper in your portfolio with the artwork.

Figure 9–3 How is the room in this staged photograph different from the painting in Figure 9–2? What kind of color scheme did the artist use?

Sandy Skoglund. *Revenge of the Goldfish.* 1981. Staged photograph. Lorence Monk Gallery, New York, New York.

Lesson 1 *Personal Places* **165**

Furniture Design

What word comes to mind when you look at the room in Figure 9–4? The title, *Spring Cleaning,* may help you answer that question. The artist has recorded a room cluttered with toys, books, appliances, and other belongings. The subject is about to begin the task of throwing out possessions and other objects she no longer wants. Which choices would you make if this were your room? Which items would you throw out?

WHAT YOU WILL LEARN

The floor of the room in Figure 9–4 is already crowded. Nevertheless, in this lesson you will create a piece of furniture or "knick-knack" for this room that fits in with all the others. You will use tempera paints for this purpose. Your design will exhibit intense colors and patterns featuring bold lines and shapes. Your completed object will match the style of those in the painting.

Figure 9–4   Does your room at home look anything like this one? What feeling toward this room and its contents is suggested by the title?

Fred Assa. *Spring Cleaning.* 1979. Oil on canvas. 122 × 91.4 cm (48 × 36″). Collection of the artist.

WHAT YOU WILL NEED

- Pencils and sketch paper
- White drawing paper, 9 x 12 inches (23 x 30 cm) or larger
- Tempera paints
- Brushes
- Mixing tray or paper plate
- Paint cloth
- Black marker

WHAT YOU WILL DO

1. Begin by inspecting the contents of the room in Figure 9–4. Notice the assortment of items the person living in this room has collected. What are the person's interests—her likes and dislikes? With a group, brainstorm other objects the occupant of this room might add to the collection shown.

2. Choose an object mentioned during the brainstorming session. Complete several sketches of it. Imitate as well as you can the style of the objects shown in the picture. Use a bold pattern of lines and shapes in each of your sketches.

3. Select your best sketch and transfer it to the white drawing paper. Fill the entire sheet with your drawing. Choose bright colors of tempera. Again, the intensity of the colors you select should be in keeping with the artist's. Paint your design. When it has dried, add textures and patterns with a black marker.

4. With classmates, plan a "furniture exhibit" that includes your newly designed piece. Place your completed paintings on a bulletin board, or arrange a display elsewhere in the classroom.

EXAMINING YOUR WORK

- **Describe** Is your design easily recognizable as a piece of furniture or other room object?
- **Analyze** Did you use bright colors to decorate your object? Did you add a pattern of bold lines and shapes?
- **Interpret** Would your object blend in with those in the painting? Where in the picture do you think it would be best placed?
- **Judge** Do you think your work is successful? On what grounds do you base this judgment?

Figure 9–5 Student work. An invented lamp.

COMPUTER OPTION

Try This!

■ Using the Pen, Pencil, or Shape tool, create an object that would fit in with those in Figure 9–4. Make sure you have completed a closed figure. Fill your object with a pre-programmed pattern or other interesting fill. Title and save your work to a disk.

Architectural Design

Home. Think about that word. Where do you head when you "go home"? For some people, "home" is a cozy apartment. For others, it is a sprawling mansion. For still others, it is a shelter made of straw or fabric. These are just some of the forms that dwellings have taken since the earliest people set up house-keeping in caves.

In this lesson, you will expand your understanding of the place called *home.* You will also learn about some of the challenges of home design facing **architects**—*artists who plan and create buildings.*

A HOME OF THE PAST

Imagine that you are going to design a house for yourself, and money is no object. What sort of dwelling would you build? What kinds of features would you include inside? It was precisely these questions that faced a king who ruled France in the 1700s. This king, Louis XIV, had very lavish tastes. His answers to these questions, or at least part of them, appear in the photograph in Figure 9–6.

This is a single room in the house Louis had built for him. The building, the Palace at

Figure 9–6   Notice the detail of the painted ceilings. What feeling do you think you would get standing in this room?

Louis Le Vau and Jules Hardouin-Mansart. The Hall of Mirrors at the Palace at Versailles, France. 1646–1708. Erich Lessing/Art Resource, NY

Versailles (vuhr-**sye**), was named for the Paris suburb where it was built. Study the room. It is interesting not only for what it reveals about the king. It is also interesting for the new art style it launched. That style was called **Rococo** (roh-**koh**-koh). This is *an art style of the 1700s that emphasized graceful movement, curving lines, and delicate colors.* Rococo architecture relied on the heavy use—sometimes overuse—of pattern. Notice how every surface is covered in one kind of rich decoration or another. What words would you use to describe this room?

A HOME OF THE TWENTIETH-CENTURY

It is hard for most people to imagine living in a place like the Palace at Versailles.

Figure 9–7 Notice the use of vertical and horizontal lines on the exterior of this building. What would you expect the inside of this house to look like?

Frank Lloyd Wright. *Falling Water House,* Bear Run, Pennsylvania. 1936. Copyright © 1997, The Frank Lloyd Wright Foundation, Scottsdale, Arizona.

Compare the two buildings in Figures 9–6 and 9–7. What differences do you detect? Obviously, the house on this page has much simpler and cleaner lines. The most striking thing about it, though, is its location. It was built on a rocky ledge directly above a small waterfall. The house, designed by twentieth-century architect Frank Lloyd Wright, even earned a nickname based on its unusual setting: "Fallingwater."

Notice the way in which the house blends into its natural surroundings. Its horizontal lines echo the natural rock formations, its vertical ones the cascading water. Wright once commented, "A house should not be *on* a hill, it should be *of* a hill." What do you think the architect meant by these words? How is this idea reflected in the work of architecture on this page?

✔ Check Your Understanding

1. How is Rococo style captured in the Palace at Versailles?
2. How did the architect of "Fallingwater" make this structure feel like part of nature?

Creating a Fanciful Exterior

If you thought gingerbread houses were the stuff of fairy tales, think again. The buildings in Figures 9–8 and 9–9 both look as though they might be made of gingerbread. Yet, both are real structures, made of hard materials. The house in Figure 9–8 represents a style of architecture popular in the 1800s. The building with the onion-shaped domes is even older. It was built in the city of Moscow in Russia during the 1500s. The structure was a cathedral and has now been made into a museum.

Figure 9–9 This is a cathedral in Russia. What art elements have been used to decorate this structure?

St. Basil's Cathedral, Moscow. 1551–60.

Figure 9–8 What kinds of shapes have been used to decorate this house?

Victorian "Painted Lady" (gingerbread house).

WHAT YOU WILL LEARN

You will make an elevation of a house like the one in Figure 9–8. An **elevation** is *a drawing of an outside view of a building*. Your elevation will show the **façade** (fuh-**sahd**). This is *the front of a building*. In your design, you will include a porch and other features of the house. You will use a combination of lines and shapes to decorate the surfaces. Finally, you will make a decorative border for your drawing with cut geometric shapes. These will follow a regular rhythm, which is explained in Chapter 2, page **33**.

WHAT YOU WILL NEED

- Pencil and sketch paper
- Assorted colors of construction paper, 12 x 18 inches (30 x 46 cm)
- Oil pastels or crayons
- Small sheet of paper or paper towel
- Scraps of construction paper
- White glue

WHAT YOU WILL DO

1. Study the house in the picture. Complete several quick sketches of a similar house. Begin with simple shapes such as squares, triangles, rectangles, and half circles. Use these to build arches, towers, and **columns.** These are *vertical posts that rise to support another structure.* Add a porch and a variety of window and door shapes.

2. Choose your best sketch. Using oil pastels, transfer your design to a sheet of construction paper. Begin with a light color of pastel. Use this to draw the lines and shapes of the house, doors, and windows. While you work, place a small sheet of paper or a paper towel under your hand. This will prevent the colors from smearing.

3. Add railings and decorative touches like the ones in Figure 9–8. Use different combinations of repeated lines—straight, zigzag, curved—and shapes to invent patterns, natural rhythms, and textures. Decorate every surface of the house.

4. After your drawing is complete, make a border for the picture. Use small squares of construction paper for this. Choose colors that complement your house

EXAMINING YOUR WORK

- **Describe** Does your house have features and decorations like those in Figure 9–8?
- **Analyze** Did you use a variety of patterns, textures, and details to decorate all the spaces of the house?
- **Interpret** What part of the house looks the most important? What details contribute to this feeling?
- **Judge** Compare your house with the one in Figure 9–8. Explain how they are alike and how they are different. Is your design successful?

design. For variety, you may want to cut some of the squares into triangles, circles, diamonds, or other shapes. Layer the shapes and colors to make a regular or alternating rhythm around the picture. Glue them down.

Figure 9–10 **Student work. A fanciful exterior.**

STUDIO OPTIONS

■ Paint a tempera "gingerbread" house elevation on newspaper. Use the lines of the text to guide your vertical and horizontal lines. Begin by sketching the outside lines and shapes of the house with a light color of tempera paint. Then mix a variety of tints and shades. Fill all the spaces with color and a variety of lines and shapes to make patterns, textures, and decorations.

■ Take photos of local homes. Make a display for the bulletin board. Your local historical society may have community resources such as a photo file of historic buildings in your community.

Lesson 4 *Creating a Fanciful Exterior* **171**

Cityscapes

Cities have been around in one form or another for more than 7,000 years. Like rooms, however, they have begun to appear as subjects of art only recently. In this lesson, you will learn about various ways in which artists have viewed and portrayed cities. You will also learn about the contributions of architects to the changing face of cities.

THE CITY IN ART

Factories, traffic jams, and high-rise apartment buildings are all part of modern city life. They are also a theme in some cityscapes. A **cityscape** is *a drawing or painting focusing on large buildings and other objects found in cities.* As an art form, the cityscape dates back to the early 1700s.

At the beginning of the twentieth century, the focus of the cityscape began to shift. Many artists began concentrating on the less glamorous aspects of the inner city. Such a painting appears in Figure 9–11. On its surface, the painting is a realistic picture of an industrial scene. Included are plant buildings, loading docks, girders, pipes, and assorted heavy machinery. The painting does not stop there, however. Notice its organization. Observe the use of geometric forms and shapes. Count the many horizontals, verticals, and diagonals. Note the careful combination of light and dark values of a single hue. In what way can this painting be said to be greater than the sum of its parts?

Figure 9–11 **Find the pipe running across the center of this carefully composed work. What other object follows a straight path, then veers off at the last instant? What other "echoes" of lines and shapes can you find?**

Charles Sheeler. *City Interior.* 1936. Aqueous adhesive and oil on composition board. 56.2 × 68.4 cm (22 × 27"). Worcester Art Museum, Worcester, Massachusetts. Elizabeth M. Sawyer Fund in memory of Jonathan and Elizabeth M. Sawyer.

THE ART OF THE SKYSCRAPER

Ancient cities were located in spacious river valleys such as along the Nile in Egypt. They had plenty of room to spread out. This is not true of modern urban centers such as New York, London, and Tokyo. In the last hundred years, these overcrowded cities have had only one direction in which to go. That direction is up.

The solution to the problem of limited space was solved toward the close of the 1800s. The person credited with the solution was a pioneering Chicago architect. His name was Louis H. Sullivan. Sullivan hit upon the idea of a steel frame made of criss-crossing beams. To this day, Sullivan's steel "skeleton" is at the heart of every skyscraper. An example of this modern architectural wonder appears in Figure 9–12. What steps has the architect taken to make this structure less boxlike than other skyscrapers you may have seen?

STUDIO ACTIVITY

Drawing a Building Detail

With sketchbook in hand, walk through your community. Be on the lookout for buildings with interesting or unusual designs. Once you find such a building, make a detailed sketch of a section of it. You might concentrate on a single floor, a corner, or even a window or door. Capture as many different types of lines and textures as you can.

PORTFOLIO

Take a photograph of the detail you selected to draw. Put it in your portfolio with your drawing. Use the photo to refresh your memory if you decide to redraw your artwork at a later time.

✔ Check Your Understanding

1. What is a cityscape?
2. What was Louis H. Sullivan's contribution to modern-day architecture?

Figure 9–12 The top of this skyscraper borrows its design from a style of Rococo furniture. Do you recall what Rococo means?

Philip Johnson and Associates. AT&T Building, New York, New York.

Creating a Mixed-Media Cityscape

There is something magical about the sights and sounds of the big city. Some cities, even at night, seem to give off energy and electricity. One such place is the focus of Figure 9–13. Do you recognize this city? It is New York. One artist who fell under its spell was a painter named John Sloan. Sloan belonged to *a group of American realists who worked at the beginning of the twentieth century.* Because there were eight in the group, they referred to themselves simply as **The Eight.**

In their paintings, The Eight realistically recorded the images of everyday life in the big city. Look closely at the cityscape in Figure 9–13. At its center, an elevated commuter train roars around a curve partially hidden by a low-rise building. You can almost hear the screech of metal and clatter of wood as the train rushes toward you.

WHAT YOU WILL LEARN

You will create a city skyline. Your work will be made up of buildings cut from construction paper in a variety of hues. These will be set against a watercolor background suggesting day or night. To create a sense of space, you will place darker-colored buildings in the bottom foreground. These will overlap lighter-colored buildings placed higher in the picture plane.

Figure 9–13 Critics, scornful of the subject matter of The Eight's work, dubbed the group the *Ashcan School.* What other art movements have you learned about with similar stories?

John Sloan. *The City from Greenwich Village.* 1922. Oil on canvas. 66 × 85.7 cm (26 × 33¾"). National Gallery of Art, Washington, D.C. Gift of Helen Farr Sloan.

WHAT YOU WILL NEED

- Pencil and sketch paper
- White drawing paper, 12 x 18 inches (30 x 46 cm)
- Water container
- Watercolor paints
- Large brush
- Paint cloth
- Sheets of thin paper, such as newsprint
- Crayons or oil pastels
- Ruler or other straight edge
- Scissors, white glue

WHAT YOU WILL DO

1. Complete several sketches of city skylines. Include overlapping buildings of different sizes and shapes. Add details such as windows and signs.
2. With the brush, cover the sheet of white drawing paper evenly with water. Decide whether your scene will take place at night or during the day. Depending on your choice, load a brush with a dark (for night) or light hue of watercolor paint. Add color to the wet paper. Do not worry that the color "bleeds," or runs. In fact, you may wish to use two or more colors, allowing them to mix together.
3. Set your watercolor painting aside to dry.
4. Referring to your sketches, cut out different building shapes from colored construction paper. Use a straight edge and scissors for this task. Cut larger buildings from the darker paper and smaller buildings from the lighter ones.

EXAMINING YOUR WORK

- **Describe** Does your picture look like a city skyline?
- **Analyze** Do the sizes, colors, and placement of your buildings create the feeling of space?
- **Interpret** Does the sky suggest a particular time of day?
- **Judge** Are you pleased with your picture? What do you like best about it?

5. Arrange your cut-out buildings on the dry watercolored sheet. About a third of the way down from the top of the sheet, start arranging the smaller, lighter-colored buildings. Place the darker buildings closer to the bottom of the sheet—in the "foreground." Do these last, so that they overlap the lighter buildings. When you are satisfied with the placement of your buildings, glue them down.
6. Draw windows, signs, and other details with oil pastels or crayons.

Figure 9–14   Student work. A mixed-media cityscape.

STUDIO OPTION

■ Make a skyline *relief*. Do this by gluing building shapes in place so they project outward from the painted background. Use stacks of small pieces of cardboard to place building shapes at different levels.

The Outdoors

The invention of the airplane in 1903 by the Wright Brothers changed the way people viewed their world. From the air, nothing on earth seemed as powerful or important as it did at eye level. Cars, buildings, and even entire cities looked like toys. Roads and rivers looked like small ribbons. Plowed fields became so many squares on an endless patchwork quilt.

As you will see, this new view of our world was to have a lasting impact on another world. That was the world of art.

LANDSCAPES

As noted in Chapter 6, successful *landscapes*—representations of scenes from nature—invite the viewer in. They tempt you with their shapes and colors.

A very different approach to landscape painting was taken by the artist responsible for Figure 9–15. This landscape, completed in 1980, does not invite you *into* it. Rather, it begs your eye to move *across* it. The painting will seem immediately familiar to players of certain "highway" video games. In this artwork, as in some of those games, you follow the line of a road that winds through the countryside. On your journey, you pass clumps of trees, tennis courts, and houses. What sets this painting apart is the ever-shifting point of view and brilliant analogous colors—purples, reds, oranges. The subject is a well-known stretch of road in southern California. The artist has attempted to capture not only how the scenery looks to him but also how it *feels.* Notice that you may start your trip at either the left edge or right edge of the painting. What differences do you detect when you view the work beginning from one side or the other?

SEASCAPES

Even before the invention of the airplane, artists were recording broad vistas and panoramas. A **panorama** is *a complete view of an area in all directions.* One popular panoramic subject is exhibited in Figure 9–16. This work is a **seascape,** *a drawing or painting of the ocean and objects found on or around it.*

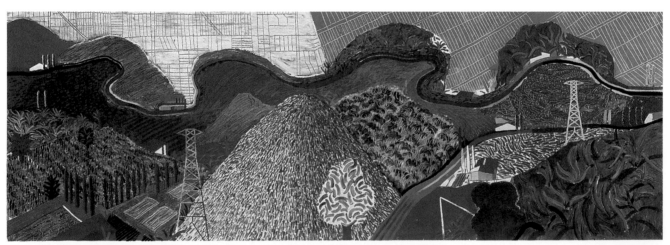

Figure 9–15 **Which images demand that you "slow down"? Which require that you "speed up"? What art elements or principles control your speed?**

David Hockney. *Mulholland Drive: The Road to the Studio.* 1980. Acrylic on canvas. 218.4 × 617.2 cm (86 × 243"). Los Angeles County Museum of Art, Los Angeles, California. Purchased with the funds provided by the F. Patrick Burnes Bequest.

This particular seascape was completed just four years before the Wright Brothers took to the sky. Examine the painting. Much of the work is given over to an endless expanse of blue-green water, its surface flecked with whitecaps. The centerpiece, of course, is a small boat. Did you notice that the craft's mast is missing? It and its lone occupant are in trouble as the boat bobs helplessly on the water. The danger is made greater by a school of sharks circling the boat. Did you notice the creatures' black fins jutting above the water? Look even more carefully, and you will also notice a ship on the horizon. Its sails are barely visible as gray shapes against the white of the clouds. The artist, it seems, has provided a faint ray of hope—or has he? It is up to you, the viewer, to decide how this drama unfolds. Will the ship rescue the man before it is too late? Are those on board even aware of his presence?

Check Your Understanding

1. What is a panorama? Describe the panoramas in the two paintings on these pages.
2. Describe all the dangers facing the figure in the seascape on this page.

STUDIO ACTIVITY

Creating a Panorama

Working with a group of classmates, create a panoramic view of a colorful, highly textured landscape. A winding road should pass through the work, as in Figure 9–15. Begin by arranging sheets of 12 x 18-inch (30 x 46-cm) white drawing paper so that the tops align. There should be one sheet for each group member. One student is to draw a twisting, curving road across the entire surface of the pages combined. Each member is then to work on a single page. Divide your page into eight or more sections. With oil pastels, add and color in houses, fields, forests, and meadows. Use different hues and textures in each section. When finished, your part of the landscape will be joined with those of other group members.

PORTFOLIO

Take a photograph of the panorama you worked on. Add it to your portfolio with a written evaluation of the success of your portion and the way the parts combined to make a panorama.

Figure 9–16 **What do you feel poses the greatest threat to the man on the boat? What type of emotion do you "read" on the man's face?**

Winslow Homer. *The Gulf Stream*. 1899. Oil on canvas. 71.4 × 124.8 cm (28⅛ × 49⅛"). The Metropolitan Museum of Art, New York, New York. Catherine Lorillard Wolfe Collection, Wolfe Fund, 1906.

Creating a Seasonal Panorama

You have examined panoramic views of land and of water. The painting in Figure 9–17 gives you two vistas in one. In the near distance, just below the hill on which the viewer is standing, is a city—Genoa, Italy. Beyond is a stretch of sea rippling and shimmering in the sunlight. Notice how the strong Mediterranean sun glints off the stark white houses. What do you think it would be like to visit this combined city-seascape in person? Do you think cooling breezes from the sea might counter the noonday heat?

In making this painting, the artist faced a challenge. That challenge was capturing the dazzling effects of bright sunlight and its reflected light on a clear summer day. In this lesson, you will face a similar challenge.

WHAT YOU WILL LEARN

You will paint a landscape that shows a particular season. You will begin by selecting hues, values, and intensities that suggest heat or cold, sunlight or shade. You will choose warm or cool hues and vary value and intensity depending on your purpose. For more on hue, value, and intensity, see pages **9–10** in Chapter 1.

WHAT YOU WILL NEED

- Pencils and sketch paper
- White drawing paper, 9 x 12 inches (23 x 30 cm) or larger
- Tempera paints
- Brushes
- Mixing tray
- Paint cloth

Figure 9–17   **Which part of the painting is your eye drawn to first? Why do you think this is?**

Jean Baptiste Camille Corot. *View of Genoa*. 1834. Oil on paper mounted on canvas. 29.5 x 41.7 cm (11⅗ x 16⅖″). Art Institute of Chicago, Chicago, Illinois. Mr. and Mrs. Martin A. Ryerson Collection, 1973.1017

WHAT YOU WILL DO

1. Brainstorm with classmates to create a list of objects associated with landscapes, cityscapes, and seascapes. Name as many features as you can. Record the list in your sketchbook.
2. Choose one of the four seasons. Do not reveal to classmates the season you have chosen. Make several sketches of a panoramic outdoor scene that shows this season. Your panorama may be a landscape, seascape, or cityscape. Include at least four objects from the list you made. Tailor your choices to the season you have selected.
3. Transfer your best sketch to the white drawing paper. Paint your scene with colors that will help convey the season. Choose light values of high-intensity warm colors for warmer seasons. Choose

EXAMINING YOUR WORK

- **Describe**   Did you use at least four objects selected from the list you brainstormed? Can these objects be easily identified?
- **Analyze**   How did you use warm or cool colors to suggest heat or cold? How did you use light and dark values and bright and dull intensities to show sunlight and shadow?
- **Interpret**   How did your color choices contribute to the mood in your painting?
- **Judge**   Are you pleased with your picture? What is its best feature?

dark values of low-intensity cool colors for colder seasons.
4. Display your finished painting alongside those of classmates.

Figure 9–18   Student work. A seasonal panorama.

COMPUTER OPTION

Try This!

■ Select your program's Geometric shape tool. Create landscape objects—trees, hills, a shoreline—as angular abstract shapes. After deciding on a season for your painting, fill each shape with a single color.

Choose light values of high-intensity warm colors for warmer seasons. Choose dark values of low-intensity cool colors for colder seasons. Be sure to save your picture.

Diego Rivera. *Civilizacion Totomac (The Totomac Civilization)*. 1947.

The Development of Communities

In what type of community do you live? Perhaps you live in an apartment building in a large city. Maybe your home is a farm in a rural community.

Communities have existed for thousands of years. In ancient times, before civilizations developed, people moved often. They traveled from place to place in search of food. Then, in about 6500 B.C., farming was developed. With farming, people could count on a regular supply of food. This is when people began settling in permanent communities. They settled in areas near a water source, such as a river.

The first ancient civilizations developed in the Middle East, China, the Indus Valley in India, the island of Crete, and Central America. Although these civilizations were isolated from one another, they had many similarities. The people built cities and raised animals. They also developed systems of writing and created techniques for using metals and making pottery.

In the artwork on this page, Diego Rivera depicts the Totomac civilization. The Totomac are Native South Americans who lived in Mexico.

MAKING THE CONNECTION

- Look carefully at the artwork. Identify some of the tasks being performed by the Totomac.
- How did the discovery of farming lead to the development of communities?
- Draw a picture of the community in which you live. How is it different from the community shown in *Civilizacion Totomac?*

INTERNET ACTIVITY

Visit Glencoe's Fine Arts Web Site for students at:

http://www.glencoe.com/sec/art/students

REVIEW

◆ BUILDING VOCABULARY

Number a sheet of paper from 1 to 10. After each number, write the term from the box that best matches each description below.

architects	façade
cityscape	panorama
columns	Rococo
The Eight	seascape
elevation	staged photograph

1. Vertical posts that rise to support another structure.
2. An art style of the 1700s that emphasized graceful movement, curving lines, and delicate colors.
3. The front of a building.
4. A complete view of an area in all directions.
5. A drawing or painting focusing on large buildings and other objects found in cities.
6. A drawing or painting of the ocean and objects found on or around it.
7. A group of American Realists who worked at the beginning of the twentieth century.
8. Artists who plan and create buildings.
9. A photographic composition that makes use of artificial images or processes.
10. A drawing of an outside view of a building.

◆ REVIEWING ART FACTS

Number a sheet of paper from 11 to 15. Answer each question in a complete sentence.

11. Why did van Gogh choose to paint a picture of his room?
12. What is the meaning of the title of Figure 9–4 on page **166**?
13. What is the name of the palace Louis XIV had built for him? What side of the king's personality does this palace reflect?
14. What change took place in the painting of cityscapes at the turn of the twentieth century?
15. What was the contribution of Louis H. Sullivan to the look of cities today?

❓ THINKING ABOUT ART

On a sheet of paper, answer each question in a sentence or two.

1. **Compare and contrast.** In what way might a room and a city be similar in the eyes of an artist? How are they different?
2. **Explain.** What style did The Eight use to show life in big cities?
3. **Interpret.** What properties or qualities of the sea are reflected in the painting in Figure 9–16?

─ MAKING ART CONNECTIONS

1. **Language Arts.** Imagine that you are a real estate agent. Your job is to describe homes that are for sale. Choose one of the dwellings in Figure 9–6, 9–7, or 9–8. Write a paragraph describing the structure. Identify the type of individual who might feel at home in the dwelling you have chosen. Explain how you came to this conclusion.

2. **Geography.** Genoa, Italy—the city shown in Figure 9–17—has a celebrated past. Among other distinctions, the city was the birthplace of Christopher Columbus. A statue of the explorer even graces the town center. Using an encyclopedia or other resource, find out more about Genoa's past and present. What is the city most noted for today? Share your findings with the class in an illustrated oral report.

Figure 10–1   In what ways is this mask similar to others you have seen? What kind of balance does it have?

New Ireland. *Mask*. c. 1800. Wood and paint. 74.4 × 45.5 cm (29³⁄₁₀ × 17⁹⁄₁₀″). Galerie Ch. Ratton & G. Ladriere, Paris, France.

Examining Objects

Do you have a most prized possession? Maybe you know someone else who does. Some prized possessions are valuable items—a rare coin or stamp, for example. Others have a value that is clear only to their owner—a torn ticket stub, an old toy, a tarnished locket.

It is this second, hidden meaning of objects that makes them candidates for art subjects. In this chapter you will learn about ways in which artists have captured the inner beauty of everyday objects. You will also learn about works of art that are themselves considered *objects*. One of these is pictured at the left. Can you identify the "object" shown? What objects can you identify within the work?

OBJECTIVES

After completing this chapter, you will be able to:

- Explain how artists perceive objects.
- Define the term *applied art*.
- Compare art objects from different cultures and times.
- Use a variety of media to create original art objects.

WORDS YOU WILL LEARN

applied art
jewelry
kiln
pendant
perceive
pottery
slip
vessel
watercolorist

PORTFOLIO IDEAS

From time to time, review your portfolio contents. If you have been using it to hold all of your notes, sketches, and finished artworks, you might want to review your selections and replace some of your entries. Remember, your goal is to present a portfolio of works that communicates your growth as an artist.

Objects in Nature

Artists have a special way of looking at things. They look at the ordinary and see the *extraordinary*. They look at a rain-slicked fence in the countryside and see a study in color and form and texture. They look at a battered old shoe and see a wholeness—a unity—that goes beyond the scuffed leather and tattered laces.

Some artists are born with this ability to "see." Others are trained to **perceive**—to *become aware through the senses of the special nature of objects*. In this chapter, you will share several artists' one-of-a-kind visions of objects in the world around them. You will also sharpen your own ability to perceive.

NATURE STUDIES

"Stop and smell the roses." Are you familiar with this saying? It underscores the idea that there is much that is beautiful and exciting in nature, if only we take the time to notice it.

Artists have been seeking out and perceiving the beauty in nature throughout the ages. The works on these pages are the result of two stops to "smell the roses." The paintings were made at different times and in different places. Yet, a common link exists between them. Both record objects found in nature.

Figure 10–2 The artist explained that her goal was to startle viewers. Do you feel she succeeded? Why or why not?

Georgia O'Keeffe. *Red Cannas*. 1927. Oil on canvas. 91.8 × 76.5 cm (36⅛ × 30⅛"). Amon Carter Museum, Fort Worth, Texas. © 1997 The Georgia O'Keeffe Foundation/Artists Rights Society (ARS), New York, NY

An Object Up Close

The subject of the painting in Figure 10–2 is an object of a type you have seen. Did you immediately recognize it as a brightly colored tropical flower? If you did not, the reason may have to do with the way in which the artist represented it. Notice the size of the painting. Why would any artist choose to magnify an image of a flower many hundreds of times?

The answer rests with events of the period in which the artist, Georgia O'Keeffe, lived. O'Keeffe was active in the early 1900s. The world was changing fast. Tall buildings were going up in big cities such as New York, where O'Keeffe lived. Convinced that people had begun to overlook nature's wonders, O'Keeffe painted her subjects larger than life, just like the buildings.

An Object from Long Ago

The painting in Figure 10–3 focuses on a plant native to its artist's homeland. In this case, the plant is bamboo. The artist was from China. Look closely at this work. See the care given to each small leaf. The elegant lines call to mind *calligraphy* (kuh-**lig**-ruh-fee)—the art of beautiful writing. In fact, the artist was a noted calligrapher in his day. What quality of this work do you think prompted some viewers to call it a portrait of an actual plant?

STUDIO ACTIVITY

Viewing Objects Up Close

With a magnifying glass, study a common object. Choose something so ordinary and familiar that you never take the time to look at it closely. Possibilities include a shell, a leaf, or your thumbprint. Draw the object large enough to fill a sheet of 9 x 12-inch (23 x 30-cm) white drawing paper. Include every detail, every change of value, every line, and every texture.

PORTFOLIO

Write a paragraph describing the experience of perceiving an everyday object. Explore your feelings as you discovered the special nature of the object. Put the paragraph in your portfolio with your artwork.

✔ Check Your Understanding

1. Define the term *perceive*.
2. Why did Georgia O'Keeffe paint flowers on such a large scale?

Figure 10–3 **This ink painting of an actual bamboo plant shows many of its characteristics. How has the artist made some leaves look near and others look farther away?**

Lik'an. *Ink-Bamboo.* (Detail.) 1308. Handscroll, ink on paper. 37.5 × 237.5 cm (14¾" × 7' 9"). The Nelson-Atkins Museum of Art, Kansas City, Missouri. Purchase: Nelson Trust.

Drawing a Magical Forest

Nearly everyone has read a story or seen a cartoon in which non-human objects—houses, trees, or animals—were given a magical feeling. The objects may have looked something like the plants in Figure 10–4. Examine this fanciful work. Notice the color scheme. Are reds, greens, and blues the colors that come to mind when you think of tropical plants? Use your imagination and ask yourself where these plants might be growing.

WHAT YOU WILL LEARN

In this lesson you will learn how, with imagination, ordinary objects can be presented in exciting new ways.

You will use colored markers to create a magical forest of colorful trees and shrubs. Your forest will contain no less than five trees. These will overlap to create a sense of space. The trunks and leaves of the trees will be filled with rich patterns of shapes and lines. These will be drawn with warm colors, as in Figure 10–4. Larger shapes in cool colors will be used for the background.

WHAT YOU WILL NEED

- Pencils and sketch paper
- White drawing paper, 9 x 12 inches (23 x 30 cm) or larger
- Colored markers

WHAT YOU WILL DO

1. Bring to class a small branch. This is to serve as a model for your tree drawing. Make sketches of the branch in several different positions. Each sketch is to represent a different tree in your forest. Include at least five different trees. One of these must lean to the side. Another

Figure 10–4 Notice how the artist has used contrasting shapes for variety. What other element of art is evident?

Paul Sierra. *The Color of Summer.* 1996. 127 × 152.4 cm (50 × 60"). Oscar Friedl Gallery, Chicago, Illinois.

must extend off the top edge of the paper. Overlap the trees and place them to suggest depth.

2. When you are satisfied with your forest, transfer your sketch to the drawing paper in light pencil. Then go over each of the pencil lines with a black marker.
3. Use the colored markers to fill in the trunks and leaves of the trees with a pattern of shapes and lines. These are to be drawn in bright, warm hues.
4. Divide the background space into large shapes. Color in these areas with dark, cool colors, as in Figure 10–4.

Figure 10–5   **Student work. A magical forest.**

Try This! COMPUTER OPTION

■ Arrange objects to show depth. Include changes in size, detail, color, placement on the picture plane, and overlapping. Create an imaginary scene for a story, play, or movie you have imagined, written, or heard about. Think of the kind of setting and objects you will need. Choose from a variety of tools and draw the basic features. Choose the Lasso tool to select, move, and arrange the shapes. Select some of the objects and change their size to larger or smaller if this option is available. Overlap shapes. Move smaller shapes higher on the picture plane. Think of the mood. Select from the Paint tools and add colors and special effects so colors fade in the distance. Title, save, and print.

Grouping Objects

Have you ever been warned that "you can't mix apples and oranges"? Artists have been ignoring this piece of advice for well over 2,000 years. Their works have mixed apples, oranges, and countless other fruits and objects. In this lesson, you will look at two such mixtures. After careful examination, you may decide that the whole *can* be greater than the sum of its parts.

OBJECTS IN STILL LIFES

An important scholar once noted that there are no new ideas, just new combinations of old ones. This statement certainly applies to the works of art called *still lifes*. These are paintings or drawings of *inanimate*, or unmoving, objects.

The objects depicted in still lifes are familiar. What is unfamiliar is their combination—their arrangement. Each still life presents its subject matter in a new, startling way.

A Western Still Life

As a Western art form, the still life is one of the oldest. Descriptions of realistic paintings of grouped objects appear in Greek writings dating back to about 2400 B.C.

A painting fitting this description is shown in Figure 10–6. This still life, however,

Figure 10–6   Compare this still life with the one in Figure 1–2 on page 4. What similarities do you detect? What differences?

Charles Sheeler. *Suspended Forms.* 1922. Charcoal, black and brown chalk, watercolor. 48.2 × 38.7 cm (19 × 15¼"). The Saint Louis Art Museum, St. Louis, Missouri. Bequest of Marie Setz Hertslet, 123:1972

Figure 10–7 Notice the arrangement of the objects in this still life.

Suzuki Kiitsu. *Seashells and Plums.* Japanese. Edo Period. Nineteenth century. Color on silk. 34.6 × 29.2 cm (13⅝ × 11½"). Los Angeles County Museum of Art, Los Angeles, California. Etsuko and Joe Price Collection.

was completed in the twentieth century. Its artist, moreover, was American. Examine the work. It is a detailed, lifelike painting of several ordinary objects. Notice their placement. Would you say they have been arranged haphazardly or with care? Find the single horizontal line in the picture. What does this line represent? In what way does it add a welcome contrast to the design?

An Eastern Still Life

Like the artworks you learned about in Lesson 1, the two on these pages are separated by time and place. The still life in Figure 10–7 was completed more than a century before the one in Figure 10–6. The artist who made this second painting was from Japan. The work, in fact, gives us a sense of traditional Japanese design. It also provides an insight into Japanese culture.

Examine the contents of the painting. These are summed up neatly in the title. What do the first of these items, the shells, reveal about Japan's geography? Look next at the still life's composition. How would you describe the arrangement of the objects? How similar is this arrangement to the one in Figure 10–6? As you study this work, it becomes clear that the artist's goal was to create an elegant, balanced design. Do you think he has succeeded?

✔ Check Your Understanding

1. What is a still life?
2. In what ways are the still lifes on these pages similar? How are they different?

Painting a Watercolor Still Life

To the average person, an eggplant and a green bell pepper are ingredients of a meal. To artist Charles Demuth, these simple vegetables were ingredients of a still life (Figure 10–8). Study this work. It helped secure Demuth's reputation as a great watercolorist. A **watercolorist** is *a painter who works in watercolor.*

In this lesson, you will create your own still life using watercolor and ink. Like the painting in Figure 10–8, yours will feature ordinary vegetables. See if you can paint them in a way that pleases even viewers who usually don't like vegetables!

WHAT YOU WILL LEARN

You will complete a watercolor-and-ink painting of two vegetables and a jar or bottle. Create highlights within your painting by leaving some areas of the paper unpainted. Use broken ink lines to strengthen contour lines and to create details and textures.

WHAT YOU WILL NEED

- Two different vegetables and a jar or bottle as props
- A length of colorful cloth (optional)
- Pencil
- White drawing paper, 12 x 18 inches (30 x 46 cm)
- Watercolor paint
- Large flat brush
- Mixing tray
- Paint cloth
- A wooden skewer
- Black india ink

WHAT YOU WILL DO

1. Begin by studying the watercolor in Figure 10–8. Notice that the artist has left some parts of the paper unpainted. Observe how this helps to suggest highlights, while adding a refreshing sparkle to the entire picture.

Figure 10–8 **What steps has the artist taken to "spice up" his ordinary subject matter?**

Charles Demuth. *Eggplant and Green Pepper.* 1925. Watercolor with graphite. 45.7 × 30.2 cm (18 × 11″). The Saint Louis Art Museum, St. Louis, Missouri. Eliza McMillan Fund, 2:1948

2. With several classmates, select and bring to class two ordinary vegetables and a jar or bottle. These are to be used as subjects for your still life. You may also wish to bring a colorful piece of cloth to serve as a backdrop. Place these objects on a table-top. Strive for an interesting arrangement.

3. Using light pencil lines, complete a drawing of the still life. Make sure to fill the entire sheet of drawing paper.

Figure 10–9 Student work. Watercolor still life.

EXAMINING YOUR WORK

- **Describe**   Identify all the objects in your painting.
- **Analyze**   Did you leave areas of your picture unpainted to suggest highlights and give your work a fresh look? Did you use broken ink lines to sharpen contours and add details and textures?
- **Interpret**   Would you describe your work as light and fresh-looking, or dark and somber?
- **Judge**   Do you think you succeeded in making a visually appealing painting using ordinary vegetables? Why or why not?

4. With a large flat brush, paint your still life. Work with lighter hues first and add darker hues little by little. Use a dry brush technique to apply the paint with single brush strokes. Avoid scrubbing over painted areas. As you move your dry brush over the surface of the paper, some portions will remain unpainted. Leave them this way.

5. Dip the wooden skewer into black india ink. Use this to create broken lines to emphasize contours or edges and to add details and textures.

Try This!

COMPUTER OPTION

■ Select a small Brush tool or the Pencil tool. Draw the shapes of several fruits or vegetables. Use the Selection tool to arrange the shapes to make a still life. Add a setting such as a table or cloth, and include a background. Keep in mind the mood you want to create and the surfaces you will need to communicate that mood.

Choose some hues and the Line tool to add colors and textures. Select Gradients or the Airbrush tool to add shading and emphasize the fruits and vegetables. If available, consider changing the opacity of the colors to transparent hues in order to layer colors and add shading. Title, save and print your work.

LESSON 5

Art Objects

Each of the artworks you have examined thus far in this chapter was created with a common purpose in mind. That purpose was to delight—to appeal to the viewer in terms of its subject, content, or composition. Most fine art shares this purpose. However, some art goes further, serving an everyday use as well. Such *works of art that are made to be useful as well as visually pleasing* are known as **applied art.**

In this lesson, you will examine two examples of applied art from the distant past. In the remaining lessons of the chapter, you will look at other examples of applied art.

VESSEL FROM LONG AGO

The next time you are thirsty, imagine filling the item in Figure 10–10 with water or juice. This art object is a **vessel,** *a hollow utensil made to hold something.* Vessels come in all shapes and sizes. They also serve a wide variety of purposes. The vessel pictured here was used for drinking. Pitchers and vases are other examples of vessels. What objects have you seen in other chapters that might qualify as vessels?

Look closely at Figure 10–10. This drinking vessel is called a *rhyton.* It was created about 2,500 years ago in the ancient kingdom of Persia. The object is made mostly from a single piece of gold. A gold liner at the base of the cup prevented liquid from flowing into the body of the animal. Notice the *flutings,* or bands of rings, etched into the surface of the cup. What other patterns have been used to

Figure 10–10 What animal is depicted on this object? What does that subject and the medium suggest about the person for whom the object was created?

Hamadan (Iran). *Rhyton Vessel in the Form of a Lion.* Fifth century B.C. Gold. 17 × 23 cm (6⅔ × 9"). The Metropolitan Museum of Art, New York, New York. Fletcher Fund, 1954.

decorate this object? What do you think was the social standing of the person for whom it was crafted?

PENDANT FROM LONG AGO

An altogether different function was served by the object in Figure 10–11. That function is clear from the title of the artwork. Like the rhyton, this pendant was fashioned entirely from gold. A **pendant** is *a jewelry item worn suspended from the neck on a string or chain.* Notice its size. For a piece of jewelry that is only 2⅜″ (6.7 cm), the artist has managed to include an amazing amount of detail. Study this object. It portrays a man who projects outward in high relief. Notice the expression on the man's face and the direction of his gaze. What feeling does this portrait communicate?

✔ Check Your Understanding

1. What is a vessel? What are some examples of vessels?
2. Could the work in Figure 10–11 be regarded as both fine art and applied art? Why or why not?

STUDIO ACTIVITY

Creating an Object Design

Look at the object in Figure 10–10. Imagine that you were a goldsmith in Persia, and you were asked to fashion a drinking vessel. Imagine, moreover, that the request was for an original design— something like no other drinking vessel seen before.

Complete a detailed pencil drawing of a cup with a handle. Make your drawing large enough to fill a 9 x 12-inch (23 x 30 cm) sheet of white drawing paper. Use shading to accent the details of your design and to emphasize its three-dimensional form.

PORTFOLIO

Write a paragraph telling how you fulfilled the challenge to create a vessel like no other drinking vessel seen before. Put it in your portfolio with your drawing.

Figure 10–11 Compare the patterns on this object with those adorning the rhyton. How many objects can you identify in this tiny piece of art?

Roman. *Chain with a Portrait Medallion.* A.D. 238–243. Gold. 6.7 cm (2⅜″) in diameter. (Detail.) The Nelson-Atkins Museum of Art, Kansas City, Missouri. Purchase, Nelson Trust.

Building a Clay Musical Instrument

Applied art objects, as you have learned, are meant to serve an everyday function. The object in Figure 10–12 goes a step further. It was designed to have *two* functions. The first, as the credit line reveals, was as a vessel. The item was, in fact, a vase. Can you guess its second function? Would it help you to know that its spout is adorned with finger holes, much like those found on a flute?

WHAT YOU WILL LEARN

In this lesson you will make your own musical wind instrument. Like the object in Figure 10–12, yours will be an example of **pottery.** This is *art, and the craft of making art, from clay.* Your instrument will not only create sound. It will also have the appearance of a real or imaginary bird, animal, fish, or person. You will use a variety of different textures to add interest to your instrument.

WHAT YOU WILL NEED

- Sketch paper and pencil
- Water-based clay
- Clay modeling tools
- A fingernail file, coffee stirrer, or other flat instrument
- A round plastic drinking straw

WHAT YOU WILL DO

1. Make several sketches of animals that might serve as the shape of your pottery object. Choose your best sketch. Set it aside.
2. Make two clay pinch pots in the shape of bowls. The pots should be the same size. (For instructions on joining clay, see Technique Tip **17** on page **285.**) With a modeling tool, *score*—make shallow lines in—the lip of each pot. Add **slip,** *clay with enough added water to give it a runny, liquid consistency.* The slip will function as a kind of glue. Join the edges together firmly.
3. Lightly tap the resulting hollow clay sphere on your work surface. Shape the ball into the form that most resembles the body of the animal you have chosen.

Figure 10–12 **What words would you use to describe this object? What feeling does this object summon up?**

Peru. *Spouted Vessel with Tubular Handle: Man on Fish.* 300–100 B.C. Ceramics. 18.7 × 11.4 × 22 cm (7⁵⁄₁₆ × 4½ × 8⅝″). Dallas Museum of Art, Dallas, Texas. Gift of Mrs. Nora Wise.

Notice, for example, that the fish in Figure 10–12 has a long, tapering, cylindrical body. Refer back to your sketch. Use additional clay to fashion the details for your creature.

4. Choose a body feature to serve as the *windway.* This is the tube or channel of a musical instrument through which air is blown to produce sound. A tail, leg, or mouth will make a good windway.

5. With a fingernail file or coffee stirrer, push a flat hole through the windway. The hole should extend all the way into the body cavity, or *sound chamber.*

6. Push a plastic drinking straw into the opening to create a vertical shaft. This should run perpendicular, or at a right angle, to the windway. Returning to the flat instrument, angle the vertical clay wall opposite the windway.

7. Test the instrument at this stage by blowing into the opening. You should hear a whistle-like sound. If no sound comes out, adjust the clay tip opposite the windway until you can make a sound.

8. Pierce the sound chamber with the straw several times. This will create finger holes. These may be used to raise the

EXAMINING YOUR WORK

- **Describe** Is the subject of your clay musical instrument recognizable? Does your pottery object function as a musical instrument?
- **Analyze** Did you use a variety of textures to add visual interest to your instrument?
- **Interpret** Is your creature pleasing to look at? Does the object produce sounds, and are these pleasing to the ear?
- **Judge** Is your work successful as an example of applied art?

pitch or tone. The location of these holes is not important. You will want to place them, however, where you can reach them easily with your fingers. Use the clay modeling tools to add small details and textures to the surface.

9. Allow your musical instrument to dry completely. Then, with your teacher's help, bake, or *fire,* the instrument in a **kiln.** This is *a special hot oven in which pottery objects are fired.* After firing, apply a glaze carefully. Make sure you do not cover the finger holes. Fire your object a second time.

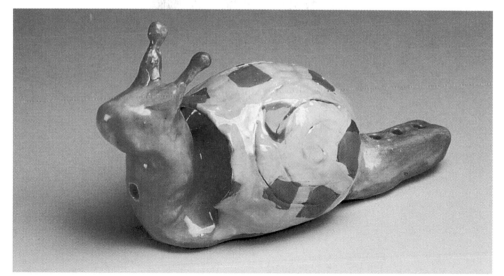

Figure 10–13 **Student work. A musical instrument.**

STUDIO OPTION

■ Use the same procedure—and your imagination—to create a second musical instrument. This instrument should be "from another planet."

Lesson 6 *Building a Clay Musical Instrument* **195**

Decorative Arts

The success of applied art objects is measured not only in terms of their beauty. A second yardstick is how well they do the job for which they were intended.

In this lesson you will learn about objects whose job is to *adorn*, or decorate.

JEWELRY

Some art is made to be worn. Several examples of such objects appear on these pages. Other examples may adorn your own ears, fingers, neck, or waist at this very moment. Such objects are grouped together under the label *jewelry*. **Jewelry** is *art, and the craft of making art, to be worn*. The pendant that you studied in Figure 10–11 on page **193** is an example of jewelry.

The earliest jewelry can be traced to the time of cave dwellers. These objects consisted mostly of shells or feathers strung together on woven leaves or vines. Since that time, the category of jewelry items has been expanded to include rings, earrings, necklaces, pins, and belts. Some, though not all, jewelry contains precious stones or metals.

Jewelry from the 1500s

Imagine that you are living in England during the late 1500s. You have been invited to a *masque ball*. This was a social event of the day that included dancing and a performance by actors in masks.

At such gala events, you were likely to see numerous figures dressed up like the woman in Figure 10–14. Inspect this period portrait.

Figure 10–14 Notice the carefully crafted gems set in gold on this gown. More than ninety appear on the woman's dress.

Unknown British painter. *Portrait of a Noblewoman*. Late sixteenth century. Oil on wood. 113 × 88.3 cm (44½ × 34¾"). The Metropolitan Museum of Art, New York, New York. Gift of J. Pierpont Morgan, 1911.

How many jewels and baubles can you find glinting and sparkling on this grand lady's person? Notice that these adornments are not limited to her splendid silk dress. Jeweled trinkets and pearls sparkle in her hair and on her ears, hands, and neck as well. How would you describe the look of this woman in all her splendor?

Jewelry from the 1700s

In Lesson 6, you learned that applied art objects serve a dual function. At least one item of jewelry shares this distinction. That item is a timepiece, or watch.

STUDIO ACTIVITY

Creating a Jewelry Design

Make several sketches for a jewelry item. Begin with a simple geometric or free-form shape. Choose three shapes and colors of gemstones to appear in your object. Arrange these, as in Figure 10–15, using a variety of shapes and sizes to create a pattern. With pencil, transfer your design to a sheet of black construction paper. Complete the object using light, bright hues of oil pastels or metallic crayons.

PORTFOLIO

Write an advertisement for your jewelry. Describe the item and the jewels and metal from which it is made. List a price for which it would sell. Put this ad in your portfolio with your artwork.

Such an object appears in Figure 10–15. It was made in Germany some two hundred years after the jewelry items shown in Figure 10–14. The timepiece is the circular item at the very bottom of the photograph. The rest of the image is given over to a popular jewelry object of the day called a *châtelaine* (shaht-eh-**len**). This châtelaine contains a key, the watch, and a seal. Notice the repeating gemstone motif. Do you think this repetition adds harmony to the art objects? How has the artist introduced variety?

✔ Check Your Understanding

1. What does the portrait in Figure 10–14 reveal about life in the 1500s?
2. What two functions are served by wristwatches?

Figure 10–15 This object was worn attached to a belt. What objects are suggested in these arrangements?

German. *Watch and Chatelaine*. Eighteenth century, third quarter. Agate, gold, gemstone. 15.3 cm (6"). The Metropolitan Museum of Art, New York, New York. Collection of Giovanni P. Morosini, presented by his daughter, Giulia, 1932.

LESSON 8

Creating a Pendant

Jewelry, like other art, varies from culture to culture. This is true not only of the specific kinds of items crafted but of their design. The three objects in Figure 10–16 are *bolo slides*. You may have seen objects like these. They are decorative jewelry made to wear with string neckties.

Study these objects. Notice the geometric shapes. These are typical of rugs, baskets, pottery, and other art objects of native cultures of the Southwest. Can you identify the simplified figures in these pieces?

WHAT YOU WILL LEARN

You will create a design for a pendant. You learned in Lesson 5 that a pendant is a jewelry item worn suspended from the neck on a string or chain. Like the bolo slides in Figure 10–16, your pendant will use geometric shapes. These will be cut from tagboard. Begin with a single simple shape. Then layer other smaller shapes on top to build a relief design. You will organize your work to create a center of interest by using contrasting geometric shapes.

Figure 10–16 These bolo slides were crafted by Native American artisans. What figures or objects do you recognize?

Bolo Slides. Left: *Trail of Tears* (Colorado). Middle: *The Eagle* (Alaska). Right: *Yee, Sun Spirit* (Arizona). Contemporary. Silver, turquoise, coral, wood. Approx. 2.5–3.8 cm (1–1½"). Private collection.

WHAT YOU WILL NEED

- Sketch paper and pencil
- Tagboard scraps in a variety of sizes, ranging from approximately 2 inches (5 cm) to ⅜ inch (1 cm) on a side.
- Scissors
- White glue
- Paper towels
- Small stiff-bristle brush
- Foil paper or aluminum foil
- Cord or yarn

WHAT YOU WILL DO

1. Create several sketches of pendant designs. Your design should consist of layered geometric shapes. (See the student work in Figure 10–17.)
2. Choose one of the largest tagboard scraps for the base. Following your design, cut the tagboard into a circle, oval, square, rectangle, or other geometric shape.
3. Layer smaller geometric shapes on top of the base. Attach the shapes with white glue. Carefully blot away any excess glue with a lightly dampened paper towel. Work little by little from larger shapes to smaller ones. Make small round shapes with a hole punch. Repeat similar shapes. Create a center of interest by using contrasting shapes or by introducing a pattern.
4. Use a stiff brush to cover the completed design with a layer of thin white glue. Carefully apply a sheet of silver or gold foil paper or aluminum foil. Using your finger, gently push the foil into the corners and creases of the design. Work quickly before the glue dries.

- **Describe**   Describe the shapes and textures in your design. Identify the purpose of the jewelry.
- **Analyze**   Explain how you organized the design to create a center of interest. What shape or patterns add contrast?
- **Interpret**   Could your pendant be worn every day, or does it appear to be better suited for special events? Why?
- **Judge**   Is your work a success? Explain why or why not.

5. Fold back any foil paper edges that extend beyond the borders of the tagboard. Glue these to the back of your ornament. Attach cord or yarn to your pendant.

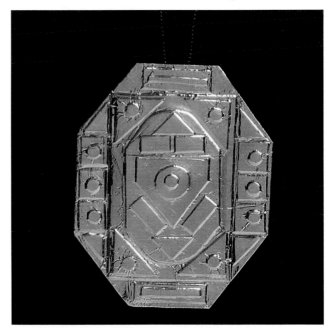

Figure 10–17   Student work. Pendant.

COMPUTER OPTION 🖥

Try This!

■ Choose from the Shape and Line tools. Use a variety of thicknesses. Draw a large geometric shape with a thick line. Add smaller geometric shapes on top to layer the design. Create a center of interest by using a contrasting shape. Use the Selection tool to arrange and duplicate shapes. Think of shiny metal surfaces. Select the Color tool and a hue to match bronze, gold, or silver metal. Choose Gradients, if available, to achieve a reflective look. Fill all the spaces with the same color. (If your program does not have a Multigon tool, use the Line tool to draw triangles and other multi-sided shapes.)

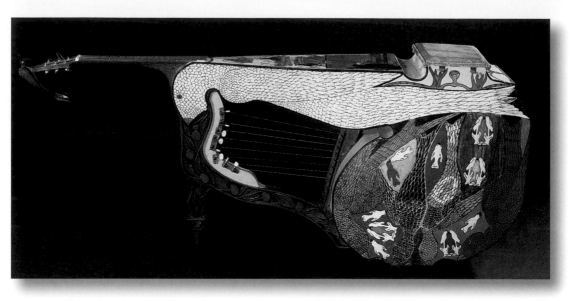

Everald Brown. *Instrument for Four People*. 1986. Wood and paint. 73.5 × 183 cm (29 × 72"). National Gallery of Jamaica, Kingston, Jamaica.

The Language of Music

Try to imagine a world without music. You would not be able to listen to a new CD. Commercials would have no melodies. Your favorite television show would not have a theme song. The school orchestra would not be able to play any instruments, and birds could not sing. Music may play softly in the background, or it may be the main source of entertainment. Regardless of how it is used, music is an important part of our society.

Music is as varied as the people who create and perform it and the instruments they use. All music, however, has four basic elements: melody, harmony, rhythm, and form. Melody is a logical succession of musical tones. Harmony involves tones played together, or chords, and the building of these chords. Rhythm is the combination of long and short sounds that convey a sense of movement. Form is musical design, incorporating repetition and contrast, unity and variety. Musical form should be unified yet varied enough to be interesting.

Take a look at Everald Brown's *Instrument for Four People*. Have you ever seen an instrument like this one? The artist created this unique musical instrument from his imagination.

MAKING THE CONNECTION

✔ What are the four basic elements of music?
✔ Why do you think Everald Brown chose to include birds in *Instrument for Four People*?
✔ Create your own musical instrument. Draw a sketch of the instrument and write a description of how it works.

INTERNET ACTIVITY

Visit Glencoe's Fine Arts Web Site for students at:

http://www.glencoe.com/sec/art/students

REVIEW

BUILDING VOCABULARY

Number a sheet of paper from 1 to 9. After each number, write the term from the box that best matches each description below.

applied art	pottery
jewelry	slip
kiln	vessel
pendant	watercolorist
perceive	

1. Clay with enough added water to give it a runny, liquid consistency.
2. Art, and the craft of making art, to be worn.
3. A jewelry item worn suspended from the neck on a string or chain.
4. A painter who works in watercolor.
5. A hollow utensil made to hold something.
6. A special hot oven in which pottery objects are fired.
7. Works of art that are made to be useful as well as visually pleasing.
8. Art, and the craft of making art, from clay.
9. To become aware through the senses of the special nature of objects.

REVIEWING ART FACTS

Number a sheet of paper from 10 to 13. Answer each question in a complete sentence.

10. What events during her life prompted Georgia O'Keeffe to paint objects "larger than life"?
11. When were the first still lifes in the West produced? By whom were they produced?
12. Based on the objects shown in the still life in Figure 10–7, what can we suppose to be true about the geography and culture of Japan?
13. Name two ways of judging applied art.

THINKING ABOUT ART

On a sheet of paper, answer each question in a sentence or two.

1. **Compare and contrast.** An obvious, if minor, difference between the still lifes in Figures 10–7 and 10–8 is the set of objects in each. What are some other differences?
2. **Analyze.** Early watches, like the one in Figure 10–15, kept time poorly. They were popular nevertheless. What does this reveal about the regard of viewers and users for the two functions of applied art objects?

MAKING ART CONNECTIONS

1. **Language Arts.** Imagine that you are a poet in China during the 1700s. Your friend, Lik'an, has just completed a scroll painting of bamboo, Figure 10–3 on page **185**. Write a two-line poem that sums up the feeling expressed by the painting.

2. **Family and Consumer Sciences.** You have written a cookbook, and your publisher thinks one of the still-life paintings in this chapter would make a good cover illustration. Think about which painting you would choose. Give reasons to explain your choice.

Figure 11–1 Notice the use of bright, lively colors to help capture the mood of this event. What art principles has the artist used to organize the festive scene?

Dorothy Brett. *San Geronimo Day, Taos*. 1924–1965. Oil on canvas. 122 × 137 cm (48 × 54″). In the collection of Glenna Goodacre, Santa Fe, New Mexico.

Recording Events

Life is filled with events that impact us for better or worse. Some events—wars, floods, medical breakthroughs—affect people on a national or even global scale. Others—team championships, birthdays, moving to a new community—affect individuals or smaller groups.

In this chapter, you will learn about different ways in which artists have recorded events, both large and small. You will also come to recognize that a picture often *can* be worth a thousand words.

PORTFOLIO IDEAS

You may be asked to assess the artwork you include in your portfolio. To evaluate a project on your own, begin by asking questions such as:

- Does this artwork meet the assignment requirements?
- Does this artwork demonstrate how I have grown as an artist?
- What improvements could I make?

OBJECTIVES

After completing this chapter, you will be able to:

- Describe various art media and techniques that have been used to capture events.
- Recognize how artists of different times and cultures have recorded events.
- Define *photography* and trace the development of this art form.
- Create several works of art that record events.

WORDS YOU WILL LEARN

camcorder
caricature
frieze
gouache
mosaic
pan
photography
story board
video documentary
videographer

The Media of Visual Reporting

In a way, artists who record events are like newspaper reporters. Like reporters, their goal is to get the whole story and to report the facts accurately and thoroughly. Like reporters, artists always seek out an interesting angle.

Unlike reporters, however, artists are not limited to words when capturing events. Rather, they have at their disposal a wide range of tools. In this chapter, you will learn about some of those tools. You will explore the media of visual reporting.

PHOTOGRAPHY

Open any newspaper or magazine today, and you are apt to see photographs. This wasn't always so. As an art form, **photography**—*the art of making images by exposing a chemically treated surface to light*—is in its infancy. The first photographs were produced just over 150 years ago.

Photograph of an Event

Throughout its brief life, photography has been a key tool of the visual reporter.

Figure 11–2 **After Gutzon Borglum died, his son, Lincoln, took over the project. The last sculpture, of Theodore Roosevelt, remains unfinished to this day.**

Workers on Mt. Rushmore. Photograph. Undated. Mt. Rushmore, South Dakota.

Examine the compelling photograph in Figure 11–2. Like any good reporter, the photographer has answered the "four W's" of journalism—*who, what, when,* and *where.* Look carefully at the photo. The *who* is a crew of workers under the guidance of sculptor Gutzon Borglum. The *when* is 1937, the *where,* a mountaintop in the Black Hills of South Dakota. The *what* is a giant bust of a United States President carved out of the mountain's natural granite face.

Notice that the photographer has raised a fifth question—*how* to get the most interesting "angle." His answer was to take a personal risk and position himself on a rocky ledge a mile high in the sky.

PAINTING

An event no less dramatic is recorded in the painting in Figure 11–3. The *what, when,* and *where* are noted in the credit line below

STUDIO ACTIVITY

Composing a Photograph

Like other works of art, photographs can be judged in terms of composition—the way the parts are arranged. Practice composing and shooting still lifes. Gather three or four objects with different forms, shapes, and textures. Experiment arranging these in various ways on a table or other flat surface. Study each arrangement through your camera's *viewfinder.* This is the hole you peer through to see your subject. When you feel the objects are arranged to your satisfaction, click the shutter.

P O R T F O L I O

Put your photographs in your portfolio along with a self-assessment.

Figure 11–3 The artist has used *abstraction* to record this event. Notice how he has simplified the shapes.

Jacob Lawrence. *Study for the Munich Olympic Games Poster.* 1971. Gouache. 90 × 86.6 cm (35½ × 27"). Seattle Art Museum, Seattle, Washington. Purchased with funds from P.O.N.C.H.O.

the artwork. The *who* is clear from the uniforms and batons. Study the expression on the faces of the front runners. Observe their body language. This is no ordinary relay race. It is a run for the Olympic gold medal. Each sprinter seems to be digging deep into his very being. Each is searching for that burst of energy that will propel him forward across the finish line first.

Look again at the credit line below the picture, this time at the medium. That medium, **gouache** (gwash), is *a form of watercolor that uses non-clear pigments.* Gouache creates flatter, more intense colors than normal watercolor paints. How do the flat areas of color in this painting help convey the intensity of the moment?

Check Your Understanding

1. In what way are artists who record events like newspaper reporters?
2. Each of the artworks on these pages captures a dramatic moment. Tell how each succeeds.

Drawing a Sporting Event in Action

Look back at the painting in Figure 11–3 on page **203.** Much of the drama can be traced to the subject matter—a foot race. Figure 11–4 records another sporting event. It, too, is filled with tense action. Study this painting. Can you identify the event without looking at the title? Notice the feeling of movement suggested by the repeated shapes of the fans dotting the grandstand. Observe the abundant use of diagonals. Even if you've never attended a baseball game, you can sense the excitement as pitcher and batter prepare to compete.

WHAT YOU WILL LEARN

In this lesson, you will create your own artwork based on a sporting event. Begin by gathering magazine or newspaper photographs of baseball, basketball, or football games. Then select a sport. You will do a gesture drawing of a model in an action pose similar to one in a photo. Add background details based on the setting in the picture. Use bright colors in the foreground, dull colors in the background. Include diagonal lines and repetition to give a sense of movement to your drawing.

Figure 11–4   How many diagonals can you count in this painting? What objects have been repeated?

Marjorie Phillips. *Night Baseball.* 1951. Oil on canvas. 61.5 × 91.4 cm (24¼ × 36"). The Phillips Collection, Washington, D.C. Acquired c. 1951.

WHAT YOU WILL NEED

- Photographs of sporting events
- Pencils and sketch paper
- White drawing paper, 12 x 18 inches (30 x 46 cm)
- Fine-tipped black felt marker
- Colored markers, charcoal, or colored drawing pencils

WHAT YOU WILL DO

1. Study the photographs you have gathered. Look for examples that show exciting action. Study the gestures and other body language of the athletes. Note the appearance and fixtures of the stadium or arena pictured.
2. Take turns posing with a fellow student. Ask your model to assume a pose similar to one in the picture. In a basketball drawing, for example, your model might appear with arms raised high and legs outstretched, as though shooting a basket. On sketch paper, do several rapid gesture drawings of your model.
3. Transfer your best sketch to white drawing paper. Still using pencil, add foreground and background details. Foreground details should include a uniform for your athlete and equipment—a ball, bat, basket, and so on. Background details should include crowds of fans and features of the setting—chalk lines or foul lines and a scoreboard, for example. Include as many diagonals as you can.
4. With a fine-tipped black marker, retrace important contour lines. Use color to complete your drawing. Choose markers, colored pencils, charcoal, or drawing pencils. Consider bright colors that capture the mood of the game.

EXAMINING YOUR WORK

- **Describe**   What sporting event does your work show? What moment in the event have you captured? What details of the setting have you included?
- **Analyze**   Have you included diagonal lines? Have you used bright colors?
- **Interpret**   Does you work communicate a sense of vivid action and movement?
- **Judge**   Is your work successful? What would you do next time to increase the excitement of the sporting event?

Figure 11–5   **Student work. A sporting event.**

COMPUTER OPTION

■ Use the Line tool to create a slender, downward-pointing triangle with sharply slanting sides. Make and rotate slightly a copy of this shape. Fill each with a different flat, bright color. Move the two shapes together to form the legs of an abstract action figure. Create arms and a trunk in similar fashion. Switch to the Oval tool. Draw one oval for the figure's head, and a circle to represent the ball. Place this within reach of your athlete.

Lesson 2   *Drawing a Sporting Event in Action*   **207**

The Artist as Historian

"Today's news," someone once noted, "is tomorrow's history." Artists have long been mindful of this bit of wisdom. For centuries, they have used their talents and various tools to record events of the past and history in the making. In this lesson, you will examine some of the events they have captured in their art.

PAST EVENTS

Before the age of photography, portraits were used to provide "visual information" about leaders and celebrities. The painting in Figure 11–6 provides another kind of historical record. Do you recognize the individual at the far left? He was a great military strategist who later went on to become our nation's first president. His name, of course, is George Washington.

In this page from history, General Washington is leading his troops across the Delaware River. The time of year is indicated by large chunks of ice around which the oar operators carefully maneuver. You might wonder why the party is venturing out under such frigid conditions. The answer is that they are planning a surprise attack on the British troops on the opposite shore. Notice that Washington stands taller than any other figure in the painting. The only object rising higher is the American flag. Observe that the diagonal lines of the oars and the flag lend movement to the scene. What do you think might have been the artist's reasons for recording the scene this way? How would you describe the future president's posture as he leads a nation-to-be to its destiny?

Figure 11–6 Notice how the artist has conveyed a sense of forward motion. How has he conveyed a sense of suspense?

Emanuel Leutze. *Washington Crossing the Delaware*. 1851. Oil on canvas. 387.5 × 644 cm (149 × 255"). The Metropolitan Museum of Art, New York, New York. Gift of John Stewart Kennedy, 1897.

RECENT EVENTS

In a sense, the event pictured in the painting in Figure 11–6 paved the way for the one in Figure 11–7. The time is two hundred years later. Do you recognize the individual projected in black and white on the giant TV monitor in the painting? He is Jimmy Carter, our thirty-ninth president. The setting is the 1980 Democratic National Convention. Despite Carter's broad smile and reassuring wave, he lost his bid for re-election to Ronald Reagan.

Inspect this busy painting. Much of it is given over to a sea of politicians. They are represented as dots of color. What other artwork have you looked at in this chapter that depicts crowds in this fashion? Balloons in the colors of the American flag float gaily from the ceiling of the vast room. How has the artist conveyed the mood of this historical event? What art principle organizes the lively work?

✔ Check Your Understanding

1. Which figure stands tallest in Figure 11–6? Why do you think the artist painted the scene this way?
2. What details and properties do Figures 11–6 and 11–7 have in common?

STUDIO ACTIVITY

Recording a Historical Event

With a group of students, brainstorm other events in national or local history. Possibilities include the landing of the pilgrims at Plymouth and the founding of your own town or city. Look in an encyclopedia or similar resource to learn the *who, what, where,* and *when* of the event. Sketch the event you have selected. Complete your drawing using colored pencils, colored markers, or oil pastels.

P O R T F O L I O

In several paragraphs, compose a description of your event. Include the who, what, where, and when of the event, and put the description in your portfolio with your artwork.

Figure 11–7 What three colors has the artist emphasized? Why has he emphasized these colors?

Franklin McMahon. *1980 Democratic Convention.* 1980. Acrylic watercolors and pencil on paper. 22 × 30 cm (8⁷⁄₁₀ × 11⅘"). Courtesy of the artist.

Lesson 3   *The Artist as Historian*   **209**

LESSON 4

Drawing a Cartoon

During a political campaign, newspapers are filled with *editorials*—words that try to persuade you to take a particular position. Television gives or sells time to candidates to speak about their positions. Cartoonists also use their art form to try to persuade their viewers. They use **caricature** (**kar**-ih-kuh-chur), *a humorous drawing that exaggerates features of a person to make fun of or criticize him or her.*

The cartoon in Figure 11–8 uses the elephant and the donkey to symbolize the Republican and Democratic parties respectively. The cartoonist drew them as images on an ancient Greek vase because democracy began in ancient Greece. His title, *Pandora's Ballot Box*, adds another symbol. Do you know the ancient Greek myth of Pandora's Box? She was a very curious girl who opened a forbidden box. By doing so she released troubles into our world. What does this say about the election?

WHAT YOU WILL LEARN

In this lesson, you will create your own cartoon. Think of a neighborhood problem, such as littering, noise, or pollution. You might select a school problem, such as a playground bully. You will draw your characters using exaggeration of facial features, size, and expression to give meaning to your cartoon. You will add background details that help to set the scene and emphasize the problem.

Figure 11–8 How many symbols can you identify in this cartoon?

Kevin Kallaugher. *Pandora's Ballot Box.* 1996. Ink on paper. 15.2 × 16.5 cm (6 × 6½"). Cartoonists and Writers Syndicate.

WHAT YOU WILL NEED

- Examples of cartoons from newspapers
- Pencils and sketch paper
- White drawing paper, 9 x 12 inches (23 x 30 cm)
- Fine-tipped black marker

WHAT YOU WILL DO

1. Study the cartoons to look for ways to use exaggeration.
2. Decide what you want your cartoon to say about the problem you want to solve. Think about ways to *symbolize* your idea. A book can symbolize study, for example.
3. Do several quick sketches, changing size and emphasizing the objects or persons to make your point. Decide whether you need any words in "balloons" or at the bottom of your cartoon.
4. Transfer your best sketch to white drawing paper. Still using pencil, draw

your cartoon lightly, adding foreground and background details.
5. Use your fine-tipped black marker to go over all of your lines. Think about making some lines thicker for emphasis.

Figure 11–9 **Student work. A cartoon.**

EXAMINING YOUR WORK

- **Describe**   What are you saying in your cartoon? What persons or things have you used to make your point?
- **Analyze**   How have you used caricature to exaggerate or symbol to express an idea?
- **Interpret**   How well does your cartoon get its message across?
- **Judge**   Ask your fellow students to decide if you have convinced them about your point.

Try This! STUDIO OPTION

■ Redraw your cartoon. This time add color with watercolors or tempera paints. Use bright colors for emphasis, duller hues for less important details. Go over the outlines with a black marker, making some lines thicker than others. Decide if the color version of your cartoon conveys a stronger message than the black-and-white version.

Recording Exploration

For as long as there have been people, there have been explorers. There have also been countless stories of the brave men and women who ventured into the unknown and forged new paths. In this lesson you will view visual records of two explorations. You will also learn about the media used to create such records.

PAST EXPLORATION

The first explorers were probably cave dwellers curious to know what lay beyond the next hill. It was not until around 1500 that exploration got under way in earnest. During this century, pioneers began embarking on journeys that would, in the end, make the world seem smaller.

Mosaic Frieze

One of these pioneering expeditions is the subject of the colorful work in Figure 11–10. This work is a **frieze (freez)**, *a decorative band running across the upper part of a wall*. This frieze recounts the adventures of French-Canadian explorers Jacques Marquette and Louis Joliet. The two set out in the late 1600s on a quest to locate the source of the Mississippi River. Look closely at the work. All the figures and objects are made up of *small bits of colorful glass and jewels set in cement*. This art medium and the art form that results are known as **mosaic** (moh-**zay**-ik). Notice the care with which the artist mixed and matched pieces to create subtle shadings and depth. Can you find the lifelike images of the two explorers?

RECENT EXPLORATION

Since the time of Marquette and Joliet, our planet's deepest secrets have been laid open. Explorers of the second half of the twentieth century were left with only one direction in which to go. That was up. Many turned their attention to the "final frontier"—space.

Figure 11–10 Look at the detail in this mosaic. What do you think are some of the challenges facing artists working in this medium?

J.A. Holzer. *Departure of Marquette and Joliet from St. Ignace on Their First Voyage to Illinois.* 1895. 1.2 × 2.7 m (4' × 9'). Harr, © Hedrich-Blessing.

Figure 11–11 shows an outpost in this realm of exploration. It is a photo of one of the nine worlds in our solar system. It was taken during a spacecraft "fly-by." Do you recognize this planet? Notice the vivid colors in the photo. What do they reveal about the effects of recent technology on the art of photography?

Check Your Understanding

1. What medium was used for the frieze in Figure 11–10? Describe this medium.
2. What does the photo in Figure 11–11 reveal about the changing face of exploration?

Figure 11–11 This photograph was taken by a camera on a spacecraft. How do you suppose this view differs from ones available to scientists of past centuries?

Jupiter. Photo by NASA.

STUDIO ACTIVITY

Planning a Mosaic

Working in mosaic takes great skill and patience. You can see this for yourself by trying the following activity.

Using pencil, lightly sketch a familiar form, such as an insect, on black paper. Retrace the lines, this time applying a little more pressure. Make ½-inch (1.3-cm) strips of colored construction paper or colored magazine photos. Cut small, square "tiles" from these strips to fill the shapes you drew. Glue the squares down, leaving space between them. Suggest depth and shading by using darker values of a single hue.

PORTFOLIO

Write an evaluation of the technique you employed to complete this work. Add any ideas you might have for improving the method you used.

Creating a Room in Outer Space

During the Age of Exploration, nations established colonies in places where their explorers landed. Someday the citizens of Earth will do the same with planet Mars. To help with this future mission, plans are already under way for an orbiting laboratory where people will work.

What will this space station look like? One artist's answer appears in Figure 11–12. Study this tongue-in-cheek painting. What reality of life far from home has the artist tapped into in his humorous solution? In what way is this space station "homesick-proof"?

WHAT YOU WILL LEARN

In this activity, you will imagine what life is like in a space station. You will construct a three-dimensional room in your family's imaginary space home, including furniture and other objects for work and play. Use a soothing color scheme for your room design and add patterns for variety. The success of your design will be measured in terms of both its usefulness and how well it pleases the eye.

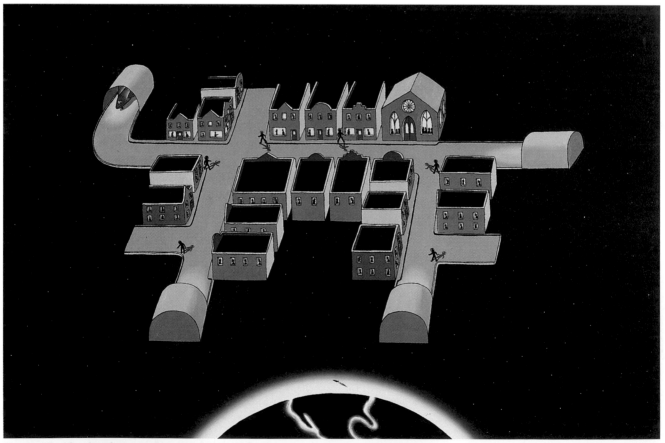

Figure 11–12 In what way has the artist made this space station look like an artist's rendering? How can you tell he is not making a serious design proposal?

Roger Brown. *Homesick-Proof Space Station.* 1987. Oil on canvas. 122 × 183 cm (48 × 72"). Phyllis Kind Galleries, Chicago, Illinois.

WHAT YOU WILL NEED

- Pencil and sketch paper
- Ruler
- Shoe box or other larger box
- Sheets of colored construction paper, 12 x 18 inches (30 x 46 cm)
- Scissors
- White glue
- Scraps of thick cardboard
- Colored markers
- Fabric scraps

WHAT YOU WILL DO

1. Sketch ideas for your space room. Try to picture a room in one of the box-like houses in Figure 11–12. What kind of furniture would you include? Remember that there is no gravity in space. Every surface has the potential to be a floor or wall.
2. With the ruler, measure the height, length, and depth of your shoe box. Note these measurements on scrap paper. With the ruler, measure and draw rectangles of corresponding size on construction paper. These are to be the walls and floor of your room. Choose a soothing color. Cut out the rectangles. Attach these to the sides and bottom of the shoe box with white glue.
3. Design chairs, tables, and other furniture. Cut these out as two-dimensional shapes from cardboard scraps. Arrange these over the inside space of the room. For variety, you might place some furniture on the "walls." Add color and detail to the objects using markers. Paste the furniture in place.

Figure 11–13   Student work. A room in outer space.

EXAMINING YOUR WORK

- **Describe** What furniture and other objects have you included in your space room?
- **Analyze** What colors did you use for the walls and floor? What patterns did you add?
- **Interpret** Is the color scheme of your space room soothing? Do the patterns you chose lend variety to the setting?
- **Judge** Is your work successful? In what way is it useful as well as pleasing to the eye?

4. Choose fabric scraps with interesting patterns or designs. The colors should blend with those of your walls and floor. Glue these down to the walls and floor as "throw rugs."
5. Place your room alongside those of classmates to make a space neighborhood.

Try This!

COMPUTER OPTION

■ Choose the rectangle Shape and Line tools. Draw the outside view of one side of a building using a combination of geometric shapes such as squares, rectangles, and triangles. Pick the Lasso selection tool to select, copy, and paste a duplicate of this side view in front of, but slightly off to one side of, the first building shape. Use the Line tool to connect the corners and make the second side. Erase unnecessary lines. Then choose from a combination of Shape tools to add doors, windows, columns, chimneys, porches, and other details. Use the Bucket tool to fill the spaces with hues and textures. If available, use a Gradient fill to add shading with a consistent light source. Title, save, and print.

Advances in Visual Reporting

Technology and art have always been partners. The invention of paint in tubes in the mid-1800s freed artists for the first time to go outdoors and paint. Advances of the past hundred years have had equal importance and impact. In this lesson you will look at some of these advances and their effect on the field of visual reporting.

MOTION PICTURES

The visual records of generations past, as you have seen, were created using a variety of media. Yet, all shared a common limitation. All, even the camera, provided "frozen" views of an action event. If a still image is worth a thousand words, how many words could be expressed by a *moving* visual record?

An answer to this question came shortly before the beginning of the twentieth century. It was delivered in the form of the technological breakthrough pictured in Figure 11–14. This item, the *kinetoscope* (kuh-**net**-uh-skohp), was a forerunner of the modern movie projector. It was invented by the same person who gave us the electric lightbulb. His name was Thomas Edison. Examine this device. Do any of the parts look familiar? Can you guess what any of them do?

THE VIDEO REVOLUTION

The kinetoscope produced moving images by rapidly stringing together still ones. This same principle is at work in today's movie and video cameras. One advance of the last several decades is the **camcorder,** *a small hand-held video camera.* Camcorders have revolutionized the recording of video events. They have managed this by reducing the cost of the technology while, at the same time, increasing the ease of use.

Figure 11–14 How has the making of motion pictures changed since the days of this device?

A moving picture machine invented by Thomas Edison. 1915. UPI/Corbis-Bettman.

The Video Documentary

The video camera and camcorder have introduced an exciting new type of visual record. This is the video documentary. A **video documentary** is *an in-depth study of a person, place, thing, or event.* Today there are many sources of excellent documentary programming. Nature videos are at the top of the list for artistry. These works have brought the viewer up close to the wonders and mysteries of nature. They have recorded the habits of the tiniest insect to the endless marvels of the vast oceans. See Figure 11–15 for an example of a video documentary crew in action.

 Check Your Understanding

1. What advances in the visual reporting of events have occurred in the last hundred years?
2. What is a video documentary?

Figure 11–15 **This camera crew is about to film a video documentary. What do you suppose is around the bend in the path?**

Photo by Kurtis Productions, Chicago, Illinois.

Planning a Story Board

No video documentary could exist without careful planning. One step in this planning is the creation of a **story board.** This is *a frame-by-frame plan of a video production.*

Think about a video documentary you might like to make. Consider your subject and the points of interest you might emphasize. Think about your audience as well. Then draw lines to divide a 12 x 18-inch (30 x 46-cm) sheet of drawing paper into six sections. In each section, sketch a scene in your documentary. The first frame, for example, might show a person—the narrator—speaking. Include the beginning, middle, and end of your documentary in your story board. Plan the characters, setting, situation, or problem, and solution. Write a script to accompany your images.

P O R T F O L I O

Put your story board in your portfolio with your script.

Making a Video Documentary

When you watch a documentary on TV, do you imagine yourself as the **videographer**—the *person who operates a video camera?* Do you picture yourself trekking deep into the heart of Africa on a safari? Maybe you see yourself scaling a snow-capped mountain peak. In this lesson, you will have the chance to be a videographer. You will probably have to limit your travel to within your own town or city, however. Figure 11–16 shows a student your age "on location" at Chicago's Lincoln Park Zoo. Can you identify her subject?

WHAT YOU WILL LEARN

You will design and videotape your own documentary video. You will begin by choosing a subject. You will then plan and draw a story board. In it, you will identify images that will help give viewers a broad picture of the place or event. Based on your story board, you will shoot your video. You will use a variety of video techniques, including close-ups, long shots, and pans. A **pan** is *a slow, steady, sideways movement of the video camera to capture details in a panorama.*

Figure 11–16 **Sixth-grader Emma Walsh on location during the taping of her video documentary.**

Student using video camera at the Lincoln Park Zoo, Chicago, Illinois.

WHAT YOU WILL NEED

- Writing pad and pencil
- Yardstick or other long straight edge
- Sheet of white drawing paper, 18 x 24 inches (46 x 61 cm)
- Markers
- Camcorder
- VHS videotape cassette
- Tripod (optional)

WHAT YOU WILL DO

1. With a group of students, brainstorm possible events that would make good topics for a video documentary. Choose subjects and locations that are realistic. Possibilities include a race, game, or parade. Locations might include the school grounds, a park, or a zoo.
2. After choosing an event, make a list of ten or more images that are important to your subject. Note these on the writing pad. Organize your images into an outline.
3. Create a story board. With the pencil and yardstick or other straight edge, draw lines to divide a large sheet of drawing paper into sixteen sections. In each section, sketch a scene from your outline. Use markers to add color to your story board.
4. Write an introduction to your documentary. Make sure the camcorder has been loaded with a videotape cassette and that the battery is charged. Set up the camcorder on a tripod if you wish, and tape yourself reading the introduction. Alternatively, you might ask a friend to serve as your narrator.
5. Following your story board, shoot your video scene by scene. Tell what you see

EXAMINING YOUR WORK

- **Describe** Did you plan your documentary? Did you create a story board to help organize the action?
- **Analyze** Did you add variety to your video by including close-ups, long shots, and pans?
- **Interpret** Did you cover the event you set out to cover? How did you capture the mood or emotion of the event?
- **Judge** Hold an "Academy Awards" ceremony for your class. Vote awards for winners in the following categories: Most Interesting Topic; Most Original Coverage; Most Skillful Use of Equipment.

as you tape to provide a running commentary. Include close-up shots, long views, and pans.

6. Plan your closing. Include a wrap-up commentary. Play your finished work for members of your class.

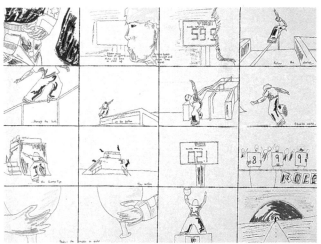

Figure 11–17 **Student work. A story board.**

STUDIO OPTION

■ Do a video interview with a member of your class or community. Prepare by making a list of questions to ask.

Focus on questions that will bring out the interests and talents of your subject. Videotape your interview.

The Book of the Dead by Scribe Nebqued. c. 1400 B.C. Egyptian papyrus with hieroglyphs. Height: 30 cm (11¾"). Louvre, Paris, France. Giraudon/Art Resource, NY

How Do Societies Record Events?

Can you remember what happened on your last birthday? Do you recall how you spent the day? What presents did you receive? If you don't remember, how could you find out? Perhaps you described the day in a diary. Maybe someone took photographs or made a videotape. By keeping a record of the event, you will always be able to remember it vividly.

Throughout time, people have recorded the important events in their history. During the U.S. Civil War, for example, soldiers kept journals of their experiences. Photographers took pictures of soldiers and battlefields. Artists depicted scenes of the war in paintings.

Today, modern technology has provided us with additional ways to record events. The explosion of the space shuttle *Challenger,* for example, was recorded on live television. Through computers via the World Wide Web, we can access sound and video clips of current events, such as the most recent presidential inauguration.

Before modern technology, however, how did societies record events? In the earliest times, people drew pictures on cave walls. In *The Book of the Dead of Nebqued,* the ancient Egyptians told stories by painting them on papyrus, an early form of paper. This work is generally considered the world's first book.

MAKING THE CONNECTION

✔ Identify four ways in which societies record events.
✔ Create a time line of the important events in your life. Start with the day you were born and end with an event that occurred within the past year.
✔ Learn more about *The Book of the Dead of Nebqued.* What was the purpose of the book?

INTERNET ACTIVITY

Visit Glencoe's Fine Arts Web Site for students at:

http://www.glencoe.com/sec/art/students

CHAPTER 11
REVIEW

BUILDING VOCABULARY

Number a sheet of paper from 1 to 10. After each number, write the term from the box that matches each description below.

camcorder	pan
caricature	photography
frieze	story board
gouache	video documentary
mosaic	videographer

1. The art of making images by exposing a chemically treated surface to light.
2. A small hand-held video camera.
3. A form of watercolor that uses non-clear pigments.
4. An in-depth study of a person, place, thing, or event.
5. A slow, steady, sideways movement of the video camera to capture details in a panorama.
6. Person who operates a video camera.
7. Small bits of colorful glass and jewels set in cement.
8. A decorative band running across the upper part of a wall.
9. A frame-by-frame plan of a video production.
10. A humorous drawing that exaggerates features of a person to make fun of or criticize him or her.

REVIEWING ART FACTS

Number a sheet of paper from 11 to 15. Answer each question in a complete sentence.

11. What are the four W's of visual reporting?
12. What personal risk was taken by the photographer of Figure 11–2 to record the event from the best angle?
13. What reasons might the painter of Figure 11–6 have had for making George Washington the tallest figure in the painting?
14. What event was recorded in the frieze in Figure 11–10?
15. When was the kinetoscope invented and by whom?

THINKING ABOUT ART

On a sheet of paper, answer each question in a sentence or two.

1. **Extend.** Look back at Figure 11–6. The painting shows an event at which the artist could not have been present. What details in the painting do you think were accurate? Which might the artist have added for dramatic effect?
2. **Synthesize.** If technology continues on its present course, what developments in the video recording industry do you expect to occur in the future?

MAKING ART CONNECTIONS

1. **Language Arts.** The descriptive recording of events is not limited to the visual arts. Poets are also noted for adding color and immediacy to events from history. Find a copy of the ballad "Paul Revere's Ride" by Henry Wadsworth Longfellow. Read this colorful poem aloud to appreciate its rhythm. If you can locate a copy, study Grant Wood's "visual record" of this historical event.

2. **Science.** The image in Figure 11–11 was taken by a NASA space probe. Using on-line or library resources, learn more about NASA. Begin by determining what the letters in the organization's name stand for. In addition, try to learn when NASA was founded, where it is headquartered, and what work it does. Share your findings in a report.

Figure 12–1 Notice the abundant use of geometric shapes. What art principle has been used to organize these shapes?

John Thomas Biggers. *Starry Crown.* 1987. Acrylic, mixed media on canvas. 155 × 124.5 cm (61 × 49″). Dallas Museum of Art, Dallas, Texas. Texas Art Fund.

Telling a Story

The art of storytelling is as old as humanity itself. Long before people could write, they were telling tales of intrigue and adventure. Some of these stories have been handed down through the ages and teach a lesson or moral. Others offer accounts of real people and events.

Examine the "story" on the facing page. Who are the characters? What is the setting? Does this story tell about people from our own culture or from some distant place?

In this chapter, you will learn how to read stories without words. You will examine works by visual storytellers from different times and places.

PORTFOLIO IDEAS

Artwork doesn't always fit into a folder or even a large portfolio. What if you worked with a group to make a three-dimensional sculpture or a mural? Photographs and drawings are one way to document the experience of working together. Another way is to write about it in detail. When describing work performed in groups, outline the goal and list each member's responsibility. Then focus on your own specific tasks for self-reflection and evaluation.

OBJECTIVES

After completing this lesson, you will be able to:
- Recognize the story that runs through some works of art.
- Explain ways in which different cultures tell stories through art.
- Identify outside factors that impact the creation of visual stories.
- Tell stories using different art media and methods.

WORDS YOU WILL LEARN

cartouche
cutaway
embroidery
font
fresco
gold leaf
Kachina
petroglyph
pictogram

Picture Languages

Ask people to define *story*, and most will mention "words." Few, if any, will include "pictures" in their definition. Yet, in a very real sense, all word stories *are* picture stories. If this statement is confusing, read on. On this page and the next, you will learn about and see examples of images that link the subject areas of writing and art.

EARLY PICTURE WRITING

Do you know someone who reads Korean, Chinese, or Japanese? Maybe you are able to yourself. If so, you are probably aware that these languages use not only letters but pictograms. A **pictogram** is *a small picture that stands for a word or an idea*. Early human languages were written entirely in pictograms. All alphabets today descend from collections of symbols such as these.

Egyptian Hieroglyphic

One of the earliest pictographic languages was that used by the ancient Egyptians some 3,000 years ago. As noted in Chapter 5, this language was a type of *hieroglyphic* (hy-ruh-**glif**-ik), or form of picture writing.

Figure 12–2 shows an object that was common in Egyptian hieroglyphic. That object, a **cartouche** (kar-**toosh**), is *an oval or oblong containing an important person's name*. Study the two cartouches in the picture. Can you make out any familiar shapes? If you cannot, don't be discouraged. It took scholars many hundreds of years to crack the code of this complex language.

Native American Petroglyphs

Even older than the cartouche is the image shown in Figure 12–3. This object is a

Figure 12–2 **The picture writing in these ovals represents people's names. What images can you find?**

Egypt. *Cartouche.*

petroglyph (peh-truh-glif), a *symbolic rock carving or painting*. Objects of this kind were created long ago by Native American artists. Such images have been found in 41 of the 50 states and in Canada. Many petroglyphs are thought to date as far back as 8000 B.C., nearly 10,000 years ago.

Examine the petroglyph in this picture. Can you identify the creature shown? The four pairs of legs should provide a clue to its identity. It is a spider. Note that this is no ordinary spider. Rather, it is the Spider Woman. This is a goddess-like figure common to the teachings of the Hopi and Zuni peoples of the American Southwest. The petroglyph symbolizes the story of creation. According to this tale, the Spider Woman formed all living creatures out of clay using her many slender fingers. A second figure, the Sun God Tawa, sent glowing rays to warm the creatures, thus breathing life into them. How does this creation story compare with others you may have heard? What does it reveal about the role of nature in the Hopi and Zuni system of beliefs?

STUDIO ACTIVITY

Designing a Cartouche

Design your own personal cartouche. Begin by cutting a 4 x 9-inch (10 x 23-cm) rectangle from a large brown paper bag or from a sheet of brown butcher paper. Using pencil, draw an oval that fills most of the surface area. Within the oval, sketch images that correspond to letters in your name—a cat for *Catherine*, a car for *Carl*. Alternatively, sketch objects that symbolize your interests or hobbies. Go over all lines in fairly wide-tipped dark brown, red, and black markers. Allow a few minutes to make sure the markers have dried. Crumple the paper, then carefully smooth it out. The remaining creases will give your art an aged look.

PORTFOLIO

In self-reflection, write what you learned about symbolizing your name for a cartouche.

✔ Check Your Understanding

1. What type of language was used by the ancient Egyptians?
2. What is a cartouche?
3. How were petroglyphs made?

Figure 12–3 **What type of balance has been used in this image?**

Native American. Petroglyph. *Spider Woman*. Nina River, Wyoming. Photo by Andrea Bush.

Lesson 1 *Picture Languages* **225**

Making a Visual Autobiography

Who am I? That question might at first seem easy for most of us to answer. Careful thought, however, reveals that each of us is a complex, one-of-a-kind individual. The person you see when you look into the mirror has a story to tell unlike anyone else's. Some writers have, in fact, written entire books about themselves and their lives. These are called *autobiographies*.

The painting in Figure 12–4 is an autobiography of sorts. In this case, the artist has answered the question *Who am I?* without using words. Study the painting. The artist has painted herself three times. What differences can you find among the three self-portraits? Notice the images—an eye, a shoe, a factory, a chicken—which the artist has placed in front of her own image. What meaning do you suppose she wants us to "read" into these?

WHAT YOU WILL LEARN

In this lesson, you will make your own "visual autobiography." Think of qualities and traits that make up the one-of-a-kind individual that is "you." Use a combination of found and original images to tell your story. You will emphasize the importance of events and objects in your picture through size and color contrast.

WHAT YOU WILL NEED

- Sheet of lined notebook paper and pencil
- Used magazines
- Scissors
- Sheet of white or colored drawing paper, 9 x 12 inches (23 x 30 cm)
- White glue
- Markers and oil pastels

Figure 12–4 **The images of hands and other objects are painted metal cutouts. They stand out in relief from the large triple self-portrait.**

Marina Gutierrez. *Biography.* 1988. Acrylic on Masonite with painted metal. 122 × 183 × 15.2 cm (48 × 72 × 6"). Courtesy of the artist.

WHAT YOU WILL DO

1. Divide a sheet of lined paper into two columns. In one column, list your hobbies, interests, likes, talents, and so on. Also include memories that have special meaning to you. In the second column, note images that relate to the items in the first column. If you play an instrument, for example, you might draw several musical notes in the image column.

2. Look through old magazines for photographs of about half of the images you have recorded in your second column. Choose photos in a variety of sizes. Clip these out and arrange them in an interesting fashion on the sheet of drawing paper. When you are happy with the composition, glue the images in place.

3. Fill most of the remaining space on your paper with pencil sketches of other images from your list. Make some of the images larger than others. Leave some negative space between them. Write your name in a creative way between some of the images. Use block letters, squiggly lines, connected circles, and so forth.

4. Complete your illustrations with markers and oil pastels. Use bright hues for some images, contrasting duller hues for others.

EXAMINING YOUR WORK

- **Describe** What images appear in your artwork?
- **Analyze** How have you used size and color contrast to suggest the importance of some images?
- **Interpret** What does your artwork tell about you as a person? What title would you give your work?
- **Judge** Decide whether your autobiography is effective in terms of its design. Decide whether it is effective in telling about your life.

Figure 12–5 **Student work. A visual autobiography.**

Try This! COMPUTER OPTION

■ If you have access to a scanner or digital camera, scan a photograph of yourself into the computer, or have a friend capture a portrait of your face with a digital camera. Open the image in an art application. Title and save. On a new page in your application, draw six or more images and objects that reveal your interests and traits.

Select, Copy, and Paste these images, one at a time, onto the page with your portrait. While selected, resize each image and arrange around your likeness so they overlap your portrait. Consider adding images from your clip-art files. Surround your portrait with images. If available, select and apply special effects that match the mood. Title, save, and print.

Myths and Legends

Do you know the story of how the giraffe got its long neck? Maybe you are familiar the legend of Hercules, the mighty Greek warrior. Myths and legends like these have been passed down through generations. They have also crossed many cultural boundaries.

In this lesson, you will learn about myths and legends from around the world. You will take a quick look at visual retellings of two such legends.

LEGENDS BASED ON HUMAN TRAITS

"They all lived happily ever after." You almost certainly know these words. You probably have heard them countless times at the end of bedtime stories when you were young. These words reflect our fondness for happy endings. They also reveal our desire to overcome evil, whether it is a wicked witch or the misdeeds of real people.

Figure 12–6 Notice how balance is used to organize this object. What role does color play?

Chinese Dragon. Photo by Brian Lee.

Figure 12–7 Did you recognize Ganesha as an elephant? Are you familiar with other tales or legends based on this jungle creature?

The Hindu God Ganesha and His Consorts. Early eleventh century. Cream sandstone. 41.5 cm (16⅓"). John H. and Ernestine A. Payne Fund, Helen S. Coolidge Fund, Asiatic Curator's Fund, John Ware Willard Fund, and Marshall H. Gould Fund. Courtesy of Museum of Fine Arts, Boston, Massachusetts.

Object Based on Myth

The subject of Figure 12–6 is a creature that is often used to represent evil in the legends of our own culture. Can you identify this mythical beast? It is a fire-breathing dragon. Study the menacing frown, flaring nostrils, and glowing red eyes. Don't bother looking for the brave knight you are accustomed to seeing wherever dragons lurk. In the culture of China, where this object was created, dragons are a symbol of good luck. A costume like this is typically worn by the lead figure in a parade to bring in the Chinese New Year. Can you think of other cultures you have learned about in which frightening masks are worn on happy occasions? How has the artist used the element of line to emphasize the dragon's fierceness?

STUDIO ACTIVITY

Sketching a Mythical Beast

Another mythical beast appears in Chapter 7 on page **136.** That creature is a unicorn. Take a moment to return to that page and examine the creature. Notice ways in which it is similar and different from the mythical creatures in this lesson.

Based on your comparisons, do sketches for a mythical beast of your own invention. Decide what trait or quality your beast will represent. Decide whether it will have legs, wings, horns, a tail, scales, or feathers. Set your sketches aside in a safe place for use in the following lesson.

PORTFOLIO

Make a list of other characteristics you might like to consider for your mythical beast. Put them with your sketches and review them before you begin Lesson 4.

Sculpture Based on Myth

The sculpture in Figure 12–7 depicts another creature meant to bring luck. The work is a product of a culture neighboring that of China. That culture is India.

This mythical figure is Ganesha, the ancient Hindu god of good fortune. Works like this once adorned the outsides of Hindu temples. People about to embark on a new undertaking would bring offerings in the form of sweets before the god's likeness. What kind of creature is Ganesha? How did the sculptor go about breathing life and energy into this mythical being?

Check Your Understanding

1. What do the two artworks on these pages share in common?
2. What differences do you detect?

Creating a Mythical Creature

In the previous lesson, you learned about two mythical creatures. Figure 12–8 shows an object based on another. This object is a **Kachina** (kuh-**chee**-nuh), a *hand-crafted statuette that represents spirits in Pueblo rituals.* Kachinas are used to teach Native American children about the traditions of their people. Such figures were long believed to embody Kachina, spirits who once dwelled among the Pueblo. Examine this object closely. What features of the bird in the object's title are represented in this statuette? How would you describe the use of color?

WHAT YOU WILL LEARN

You will use the sketches you made in the previous lesson as a jumping-off point for creating your own Kachina. Everyday found objects will be used to construct your Kachina. Your finished object, like the one in Figure 12–8, will exhibit formal balance and rhythm based on color and pattern.

WHAT YOU WILL NEED

- Three cardboard tubes from paper towels
- Colored construction paper
- Transparent tape
- Wrapping paper
- Scissors
- Work gloves (optional)
- Tempera paints, brushes
- Found objects such as fabric scraps, raffia, and feathers
- Stapler or white glue
- Jewelry boxes or other small boxes

WHAT YOU WILL DO

1. Begin construction by cutting one of the cardboard tubes in half lengthwise. The two narrow half-cylinders that result are to be the creature's legs. Wrap a scrap of brightly colored construction paper around the left leg. Secure it with transparent tape. Use a scrap of wrapping paper in a busy pattern to cover the right leg.

Figure 12–8 How would you describe the figure's stance? What principle of art has been used to organize this object?

L. Joe. *Eagle Kachina*. 1990. Wood, leather, feathers, yarn, and fur. 30 cm (12"). Private collection.

2. Follow a similar procedure with a second tube to form the arms. This time, begin by cutting away about three inches of the tube. Then cut the remaining part in half lengthwise. Again, attach colored paper and wrapping paper, this time to the opposite limbs. Attach arms to body with tape.

3. Cut two slits into the top of each leg. Slide the upper body down into the slits.

4. Create the Kachina's head by painting the top of the body tube. Use a medium brush to apply the base paint for the head. Add facial features—eyes, nose, mouth—with contrasting hues. Use a fine brush for this task. The features and other decorations should be highly geometric, as in Figure 12–8.

5. Look back at the sketches you made for the Studio Activity on page 229. Choose your best sketch. Identify your mythical beast's most interesting parts and features. These might include wings, scales, a tail, or another such part. Use found objects such as fabric scraps, raffia, and feathers to create these features. Add the features to your Kachina with a stapler or white glue.

6. Use jewelry boxes or other small boxes for the Kachina's feet. Notch the bottoms of the legs and glue them to the boxes. Paint the feet.

EXAMINING YOUR WORK

- **Describe** Point out the arms, legs, and body of your figure. Identify wings, scales, or other such features.
- **Analyze** Does your Kachina exhibit formal balance and rhythm based on color and pattern?
- **Interpret** What feeling or mood is communicated by your Kachina?
- **Judge** What are the best features of your figure? What would you do differently if you were to repeat the lesson?

Figure 12–9 Student work. Kachina.

Try This!

STUDIO OPTION

■ Make a soft-sculpture doll to represent a legend you know. Draw your design on paper. Place the paper over a length of fabric and cut out the shape. Repeat this step so that you have two identical shapes. Place the fabric shapes with right sides together. Sew the pieces together, leaving a section unsewn. Clip seams with scissors up to stitching. Turn inside out. Fill with fiberfill, then finish sewing the open section. Use markers and add beads, trims, and buttons to complete your doll.

Art Stories Larger than Life

Some storytellers create *short* stories. These tell about an event or experience so specific that it may be recounted in just a few pages. Other stories are told on a much grander scale. These stories focus on events that are more complex or of great importance. They require hundreds and sometimes thousands of pages.

Visual stories, too, may be told on a large or small scale. In this and the following lesson, you will look at stories that are larger than life.

FRESCOES

When you were little, you may have been scolded for drawing on the wall. Some professional artists make a living doing just that. They create frescoes (**fres**-kohz). A **fresco** is *a painting created when pigment is applied to a section of wall spread with fresh plaster.* The word *fresco* is Italian for "fresh." The technique of fresco painting got its start in Italy during the late Middle Ages.

Frescoes that Tell a Story

The fresco in Figure 12–10 was painted closer to our own time. Observe the work's

Figure 12–10 Notice that the figures in the room at the viewer's lower right are wearing lab coats. What service do you think they provide to city dwellers?

Diego Rivera. *The Making of a Fresco Showing the Building of a City.* 1931. Fresco. 6.9 × 9 m (22' 7" × 29' 9"). Located at the San Francisco Art Institute, San Francisco, California.

Figure 12–11 This building, which was completed the year the artist died, bears his name. The mural shown covers 274 square meters.

David Alfaro Siqueiros. *Poliforum.* 1974. Acrylic enamel on asbestos-cement and steel. 15 m (49′ 2½″). Mexico City, Mexico. Mexican Government Tourism Office, New York.

physical dimensions. The figures and objects in it have been painted life-size. You may have been struck by the painting's unusual shape. The artist has provided a **cutaway** of a house under construction. This is *a view in which an outside wall has been removed to reveal the scene within.* Most of the details in this painting are activities you would expect to find in such a scene. There are workers in coveralls laying foundations. In the center room on the ground floor, men in business suits—the architects, maybe—review plans.

The story seems straightforward enough. Yet, there is more to this painting than meets the eye. Notice the title. The fresco depicts not the building of a house but of a city. People from all classes and walks of life work cooperatively toward a common goal. What is that goal? In what way is a house a fitting symbol of a city?

MURALS

The artist who painted the fresco in Figure 12–10, Diego Rivera, was a notable Mexican artist. So was the individual responsible for the work in Figure 12–11. His name was David Alfaro Siqueiros (ahl-**far**-oh see-**cay**-rohs). This gigantic work is a *mural,* a type of public art done on a wall. The mural shown here graces the outside of an arts center in Mexico City. There are twelve such works, one for each of the sides of this oddly shaped building. Each mural addresses a different theme. Examine this giant artwork. What story does it tell? How would you describe its composition?

✔ Check Your Understanding

1. What is a fresco? What is the origin of the word?
2. In what ways are the works on these pages similar? How are the two different?

Painting a Mural About School Life

As an art form, murals date back to ancient Egyptian times. They have remained popular ever since for telling stories in a larger-than-life way. Consider the mural in Figure 12–12—that is, if you can find it. You may have trouble because the work was painted in a *trompe-l'oeil* style. As noted in Chapter 8, this is a style of painting in which objects are depicted with photographically realistic detail. Furthermore, the subject, building façades, blends in with its surroundings. This is because the mural covers the side of a building! The work pays tribute to the architects who designed the city of Chicago. You may recall learning about one of these pioneers, Louis H. Sullivan, in Chapter 9. Do you remember what Sullivan was famous for?

WHAT YOU WILL LEARN

You will work with a group of five or six classmates. Together you will plan and paint a mural for your school or classroom. Emphasize key images in your mural by making them larger and brighter in color. Introduce harmony by repeating shapes.

WHAT YOU WILL NEED

- Sketch paper and pencils
- Butcher or plain wrapping paper, 36 inches (1 m) wide by 6 feet (2 m) long
- Masking tape
- Sheets of newspaper
- Brushes of various sizes
- Tempera paints, water

WHAT YOU WILL DO

1. Brainstorm with group members for a theme for your mural. Jot down ideas for images associated with particular themes.

Figure 12–12 **What is the size of this painting? What is the style of the buildings shown?**

Richard Haas. *Façade of Chicago Building*. 1984. Keim silicate paint on brick. Chicago, Illinois. © 1988 Richard Haas/Licensed by VAGA, New York, New York.

234 Chapter 12 *Telling a Story*

2. Plan the creation of the mural so that each group member works on a separate section. Begin by working individually on sketches of background objects and details. Stop from time to time to share and compare your work with that of other group members. Strive for a single, consistent style.

3. Concentrate next on any images of people that might be pictured. Again, pause and compare your efforts with those of group members. Emphasize important people and images by making them larger.

4. Lay out all of the sketches on a large work surface. Working as a team, decide which images to include and where to place them.

5. Complete a finished sketch of your portion of the mural. Use the method outlined in Technique Tip 5 on page 281 to impose a grid over your sketch. Still working in pencil, re-create your grid on the butcher or wrapping paper. Transfer the enlarged image to the butcher paper using the grid.

6. Use the masking tape to connect sheets of newspaper. These are to protect the

EXAMINING YOUR WORK

- **Describe** What images did you include in your mural?
- **Analyze** Did you emphasize important images by making them larger and brighter? Did you add harmony by repeating shapes throughout?
- **Interpret** What theme does your mural express? Which objects help convey this theme?
- **Judge** How effectively did you and your fellow group members work together? Did you succeed in your goal as a group?

surface on which you will work during the painting stage.

7. Using a fairly large brush loaded with tempera paint, begin coloring in background objects, such as sky. Switch to a finer brush for small details. Use bright hues for important images, duller hues for less important ones.

8. When the mural has dried completely, hang your mural on a wall by affixing loops of tape along the back.

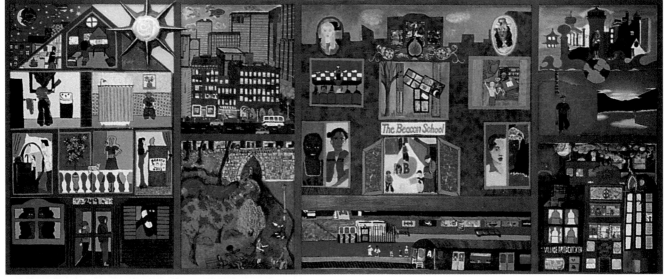

Figure 12–13 **Student work. A mural about school life.**

Try This!

STUDIO OPTION

■ With several classmates, design and create a mural made up of abstract shapes. Transfer your image to a long strip of cloth. Use colored markers to complete the mural. What idea or mood does your mural communicate?

Book Illustration

As has been noted, some stories are told in words, others in pictures. In this lesson, you will look at picture stories that co-exist successfully side by side with the printed word. Pictures of this kind appear scattered throughout the book you are holding at this moment. They are called *book illustrations.*

MANUSCRIPT ILLUMINATION

The practice of illustrating books goes back some eleven hundred years. The earliest such illustrations were tiny paintings known as *illuminations.* They were so called because their job was to illuminate—or shed light on—the words on the page. Illuminations were common in Europe at a time when most people could not read. These illustrations thus served a function that went beyond mere decoration. Do you recall the name for art of this type?

The object in Figure 12–14 is an illuminated page from a book produced around the turn of the fifteenth century. This book was called a *missal* (**mis**-uhl). Its purpose was to teach. The bulk of the instruction was provided by miniature framed images of the sort appearing at the top of the page shown. Notice the richly colored border of fanciful plants and creatures. Each of these objects was individually hand-painted. What kind of lessons do you think missals taught? Do you know the story narrated by the framed picture on this missal page?

BOOK ILLUSTRATION OF TODAY

The invention of the printing press in the 1400s changed for all time the way books were made and illustrated. At first, all illustrations were done as woodcuts. The printing plates for such illustrations

Figure 12–14   In what ways is this book page similar to others you have seen? How is it different?

Artist unknown. Missal. 1389–1404. Tempera colors, gold leaf and gold paint on vellum in a medieval, blind-stamped binding. 33 × 24 cm (13 × 9 7⁄16"). The J. Paul Getty Museum, Los Angeles, California.

Figure 12–15 The artists have used the art element of line to suggest action. What role does proportion play in this book illustration?

Leo and Diane Dillon. *Marie and Redfish*. Illustration by Leo and Diane Dillon from *Her Stories: African American Folktales, Fairy Tales and True Tales* by Virginia Hamilton. Illustrations copyright © 1995 by Leo and Diane Dillon. Reprinted by permission of Scholastic, Inc.

STUDIO ACTIVITY

Designing a Letter

Look back at the book illumination in Figure 12–14. Note, in particular, the care that has gone into crafting simple capital letters. Each is a miniature artwork unto itself. The shimmering gold effect here and elsewhere is the result of **gold leaf.** This is *a very thin layer of gold glued to a surface for decoration.*

Choose a letter of the alphabet and decorate it in the manner of early illuminated manuscripts. Lightly draw the capital letter at least six inches high and one inch wide. Follow the graceful lines of the capitals in the missal, or create your own design. Add flowers or other decorations in and around the letter shape. You may want to set the letter in a rectangle. Use fine-tipped colored markers to capture details. Use gold or silver crayons to create rich effects.

P O R T F O L I O

Write a short paragraph describing how you used the elements and principles of art in your illumination. Keep the paragraph and the drawing together in your portfolio.

could be arranged conveniently alongside the type.

In time, changes brought about through advances in technology simplified this process. Artists today are free to create book illustrations in any medium they choose. One recent illustration appears in Figure 12–15. Examine this artwork. It was created to accompany a story titled "Marie and Redfish." The story tells of a teenager whose path crosses that of a prince. Find the "prince" in the picture. In what ways does this creature remind you of the mythical beasts you learned about in Lesson 3? In what ways does this illustration help the story come alive in the same way as the missal illustrations did?

✔ Check Your Understanding

1. What is an illumination? What is a missal?
2. How have book illustrations changed since the Middle Ages?

Creating a Book Cover

Despite what you may have heard, you *can* tell a book by its cover. For proof, examine the center portion of the quilt in Figure 12–16. It was used for a book cover. The group is having a "picnic" on the tar roof—the "tar beach"—of an apartment building in a big city. Notice how the illustration draws you right into the story. Do you think this art makes a good book cover?

WHAT YOU WILL LEARN

In this lesson, you will design a book cover of your own. Begin by finding a story or making one up. Then plan a cover design that will invite readers to pick up your book and read it. You will create the title and author's name in a type style that suits the story theme or topic. The colors used for the title and the author's name should contrast with the colors of the illustration. Complete a picture to fit your chosen theme or topic.

WHAT YOU WILL NEED

- Sketch paper and pencil
- Sheet of white drawing paper, 9 x 12 inches (23 x 30 cm)
- Sheet of colored construction paper
- Colored markers, crayons, or tempera paints and brushes
- Ruler

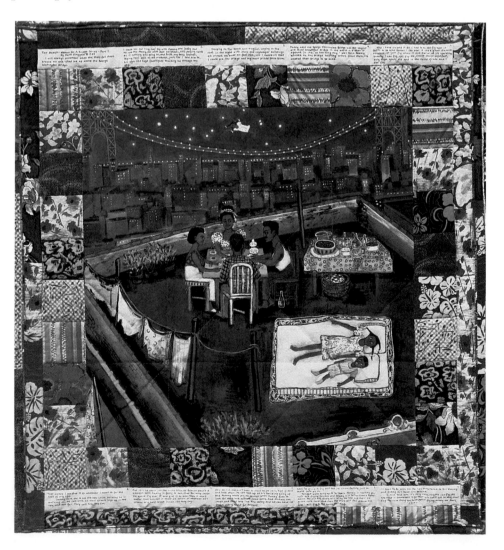

Figure 12–16 How would you describe the style of this artwork? How does the artist draw your attention to the figures?

Faith Ringgold. *Tar Beach.* 1988. Pieced and printed fabric. 188 × 175.3 cm (74 × 69"). Faith Ringgold, Inc. © Solomon Guggenheim Collection.

- Compass
- Scissors
- White glue

WHAT YOU WILL DO

1. In the school library, examine several books. Notice the covers or book jackets. Pay attention to the cover illustration and to the **font**, or *typeface*. In what way does the font add to the impact of the illustration?

2. Choose a book that you like. The book may be a made-up story, like *Tar Beach*, or it may be a book about science or some other subject. If you prefer, you may make up a story and title.

3. Think of a picture that will attract readers to your book. Decide how large your picture will be. Will it fill the cover, as in *Tar Beach*, or will it fit into a smaller space? Make several sketches. Transfer your best sketch to a sheet of white drawing paper. Complete your illustration using markers, crayons, or tempera paints.

4. Think next about lettering styles for the title. Look through books for fonts that fit in with your story. If the story is humorous, you might choose rounded letters. A frightening story might call for tall, pointed letters.

5. Imitating the font you have chosen, carefully letter your title on colored construction paper. Choose a color that will stand out against your illustration. To control the height, measure and cut a strip from the construction paper about one inch wide. Draw the title on this strip. Use a ruler for the straight edges on letters such as *m* or *t*. Make the round parts of *p* and other letters by using a compass. Draw letters for the author's name in a similar fashion. These should be smaller than the title. Cut a half-inch-wide strip of construction paper to help

EXAMINING YOUR WORK

- **Describe**   What part of the story did you choose for the cover picture? What images appear in this illustration? What kind of font did you choose?
- **Analyze**   Does color of the lettering in your title stand out vividly against colors of the illustration? Is the author's name smaller than the title?
- **Interpret**   Does the font you chose fit the theme or message of your story? Is the message clear?
- **Judge**   Tell whether your book cover would draw readers in and why.

guide you. With scissors, cut out the letters when you have finished.

6. Organize the design of your book cover. Experiment placing the words in relation to the illustration. When you are satisfied, glue the words in place.

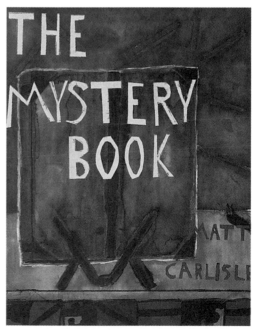

Figure 12–17   **Student work. A book cover.**

Try This! COMPUTER OPTION

■ Select the Text tool in your program. Experiment with creating titles in different fonts and sizes. Choose different fill and outline colors for your wording. If your program has special effect filters, such as an Extrude command, try applying a filter.

Pieter Bruegel. *Fall of Icarus.* c. 1555. Oil on canvas. 73.5 × 112 cm (29 × 44"). Musees Royaux des Beaux Arts de Belgique/The Bridgman Art Library, London.

What Is an Allegory?

When you were a child, your mother or father taught you many essential life lessons. "Look both ways before you cross the street," "Respect your elders," and "Don't talk to strangers." You also learned many other important truths in the stories you read.

In literature, these truths are often presented as allegories. An allegory is a narrative that conveys a symbolic meaning. This meaning is in addition to the literal meaning of the story. On the surface, for example, *Beauty and the Beast* is a love story. The underlying truth, however, could be summarized by the saying "You can't judge a book by its cover."

Allegories are also told in artwork. In *The Fall of Icarus*, Pieter Bruegel presented a classic myth. Look carefully and you will see the legend of Icarus. In this story, Icarus escaped from jail using wings made of wax. Although his father told him not to fly too close to the sun, Icarus ignored the warning. When Icarus flew near the sun, his wings melted and he fell to his death.

MAKING THE CONNECTION

- ✔ Describe how Bruegel conveyed the story of Icarus in this painting.
- ✔ What do you think is the lesson to be learned from the legend of Icarus?
- ✔ Find another example of allegory in literature or art. Describe the literal and symbolic meanings of the story.

INTERNET ACTIVITY

Visit Glencoe's Fine Arts Web Site for students at:

http://www.glencoe.com/sec/art/students

CHAPTER 12
REVIEW

BUILDING VOCABULARY

Number a sheet of paper from 1 to 9. After each number, write the term from the box that matches each description below.

cartouche   gold leaf
cutaway   Kachina
embroidery   petroglyph
font   pictogram
fresco

1. A very thin layer of gold glued to a surface for decoration.
2. A view in which an outside wall has been removed to reveal the scene within.
3. Typeface.
4. A symbolic rock carving or painting.
5. A painting created when pigment is applied to a section of wall spread with fresh plaster.
6. The art of making ornamental designs with needle and thread.
7. A hand-crafted statuette that represents spirits in Pueblo rituals.
8. An oval or oblong containing an important person's name.
9. A small picture that stands for a word or an idea.

REVIEWING ART FACTS

Number a sheet of paper from 10 to 15. Answer each question in one or two complete sentences.

10. What is a hieroglyphic? When did ancient Egyptian hieroglyphic come into being?
11. How old are Native American petroglyphs?
12. How is the dragon viewed in the culture of the Chinese?
13. What are Kachinas believed to represent?
14. From what language does the word *fresco* come? What does it mean in that language?
15. Why were illuminations common in the Middle Ages?

THINKING ABOUT ART

On a sheet of paper, answer each question in a sentence or two.

1. **Compare and contrast.** The cartouche in Figure 12–2 and the petroglyph in Figure 12–3 have many similarities. Yet, in many ways, the objects are different. What are some of these ways?
2. **Synthesize.** How has the art of visual storytelling changed from earliest times through the present?

MAKING ART CONNECTIONS

1. **Language Arts.** With the school librarian's help, find the poem "Ganesha, Ganesh" by Myra Cohn Livingston, "Dragon" by Karla Kuskin, or another such poem. Compare the poem's subject and meaning with what you learned in the chapter about such mythical creatures. Share your findings with the class, along with a reading of the poem you chose.

2. **Technology.** Computers have had an impact not only on book production but on book illustration as well. Speak with a teacher in your school's computer department or, if possible, with a local computer artist. Find out from this expert about advances in book illustration. Share the information with classmates, along with any tips you pick up.

Figure 13–1 Notice the title of this painting. Do you know when and for what a maypole was used?

William Glakens. *May Day, Central Park.* c. 1905. Oil on canvas. 63.8 × 76.8 cm (25⅛ × 30¼"). The Fine Arts Museums of San Francisco, California. Gift of the Charles E. Merrill Trust with matching funds from The de Young Museum Society.

CHAPTER 13

Celebrations

What do you think of when you hear the word *celebration*? If you are like most people, you probably picture festive food, smiling faces, and lively activity. Songs and dances may be part of the image as well.

The painting on the facing page reveals that some of these features were common in celebrations a century ago. Examine this painting. What is being celebrated? Where is the celebration taking place? What is the mood? How are the participants dressed?

In this chapter, you will learn about the ways in which artists have recorded celebrations through the ages. You will glimpse visual celebrations of many cultures.

OBJECTIVES

After completing this chapter, you will be able to:
- Identify media and methods artists have used to capture celebrations.
- Describe how artists of different periods and places have depicted celebrations.
- Create several works of art that focus on celebrations.

WORDS YOU WILL LEARN

adenla
kinetic art
pueblo
seal
shadow puppet
tricolor

PORTFOLIO IDEAS

A portfolio can serve a number of purposes. The work you include will demonstrate what you have done and how you did it. Written self-reflections and evaluations help you define goals and recognize achievements. A teacher may use your portfolio to evaluate your progress too. In any case, a portfolio is evidence of your participation, understanding, and growth as an artist.

Holiday Celebrations

Every culture around the world celebrates holidays. Some holiday celebrations are joyous occasions. They are marked by parades, decorations, and possibly the exchange of gifts. Other holidays are times of solemn remembrance.

One common link among all holiday celebrations is the frequency with which they have turned up through the centuries as art subjects. In this lesson, you will examine two such artworks. Both celebrate a single holiday as it is observed in two different cultures.

HOLIDAY ART

If you look up *celebrate* in a dictionary, you discover that the word has many meanings. One of these is "to give thanks for." The painting that opened this chapter depicts a holiday event that is all but forgotten in our own country. That event is the giving of thanks for the coming of spring. The holiday is May Day.

Art Celebrating American Independence

A "thanksgiving" of a different sort is pictured in Figure 13–2. The subject is obvious from the title. The setting is a small New England town. Even without glancing at the credit line, you can probably guess the year this work was done. The clothing styles and presence of horse-drawn vehicles offer clues.

Take a moment to study this painting. Notice how the artist has used lighter color values to focus the viewer's attention on the parade. A careful inspection reveals that this is no well-disciplined, uniformed marching band. Rather, it is a random gathering of

Figure 13–2 **What colorful associations do you have with the holiday shown in this painting? Would you describe this work as realistic?**

Alfred C. Howland. *The Fourth of July.* 1886. Oil on canvas. 60.8 × 91.6 cm (24 × 36⅟₁₆″). High Museum of Art, Atlanta, Georgia. Gift of Life Insurance Company of Georgia in celebration of the Nation's Bicentennial.

townspeople. They are simply bound together by their patriotic spirit and the steady boom of the bass drums. What mood or feeling does this work bring to mind?

Art Celebrating Mexican Independence

Compare the style and subject matter of Figure 13–2 with those of the picture on this page. This work, too, celebrates Independence Day—in this case, Mexico's. Like the painting at the left, the centerpiece of this one is a parade. Unlike Figure 13–2, the marchers in this work are schoolchildren. All are dressed in white, and each carries a miniature Mexican **tricolor** (**try**-kuhl-uhr). This is *a flag with three broad bands of color*. In stark contrast to the children's costumes is the black suit worn by the man leading the procession. Who do you suppose he is? Note the serious expressions on the people's faces. What do these suggest about the tone or mood of the celebration?

 **Check Your Understanding**

1. How does the artist of Figure 13–2 draw your attention to the parade?
2. What difference in mood do you detect between the paintings in Figures 13–2 and 13–3?

STUDIO ACTIVITY

Making a Tricolor

Design a tricolor to represent your class, school, or community. Choose colors with symbolic value. Use red, for example, for courage, blue for loyalty. Begin with a 9 x 12-inch (23 x 30-cm) sheet of paper. Divide it into three geometric shapes—squares, circles, rectangles, triangles, or a combination. Measure and cut from colored construction paper the three shapes in the colors of your choice. Using white glue, attach these so as to fill the sheet of drawing paper. Complete your flag by creating an official **seal**—a *symbolic image or emblem*—on a sheet of white paper. Color the seal with markers. Cut it out and glue It to the center of your tricolor.

 P O R T F O L I O

Write a short paragraph describing what your tricolor symbolizes and what each color stands for. Put the paragraph in your portfolio along with the tricolor.

Figure 13–3   What art principle is used to organize this painting? What art elements does it control?

Antonio M. Ruiz. *School Children on Parade.* 1936. Oil on canvas. 24 × 33.8 cm (9½ × 13¼"). The Metropolitan Museum of Art. Secretaria de Hacienda y Credito Publico, Mexico City, Mexico.

Lesson 1   *Holiday Celebrations*   **245**

LESSON 2

Creating an "Event" Quilt

The painting you looked at in Figure 13–2 celebrates a milestone in the growth of our nation. The work in Figure 13–4 celebrates *eight* such milestones. On the surface, the painting shows a simple and distinctly American pastime—a quilting bee. Eight women appear seated around the quilt they have sewn. A deeper meaning begins to form when the viewer learns the identities of these individuals. The figure in the blue suit at the center is Harriet Tubman. The person in the polka-dot dress to her left is Rosa Parks. What personal sacrifices did these women make? What did they fight for?

WHAT YOU WILL LEARN

A quilt is a fitting symbol for the contributions of people who are working together in a group effort. With classmates, you will make a quilt that celebrates an important group effort you or others in your community have made. Working alone, each of you will create a quilt square from fabric scraps and paint. This will help introduce variety. All the pieces will then be glued or sewn together. You will complete your quilt by creating a large frame or border that adds harmony and unifies the work, as in Figure 13–4.

Figure 13–4 How has the artist added harmony to this busy painting? How has she introduced variety? Can you appreciate why this scene is an impossible one?

Faith Ringgold. #4 *The Sunflowers Quilting Bee at Arles.* 1991. Acrylic on canvas, pieced fabric border. 188 × 203.2 cm (74 × 80"). Faith Ringgold Inc., © Oprah Winfrey Collection.

WHAT YOU WILL NEED

- Sketch paper and pencil
- Assorted scraps of fabric
- Fabric pieces (to be the basis for the quilt)
- Fabric glue or fusible webbing
- Needle and thread
- Fabric paint

WHAT YOU WILL DO

1. With group members, brainstorm an event to celebrate. Possibilities include a successful school fund-raising drive, a cleanup campaign, or an effort to save a local park.

2. After choosing an event, select colors and materials that reflect the theme and help create the mood. For example, you might choose green and blue for a Save the Earth campaign.

3. Working by yourself, make several pencil sketches for a quilt square. Look through the fabric pieces to see if any of the designs suggest ideas. Decide whether you will cut out figures and objects or use shapes and symbols to tell about the theme.

4. Using your best sketch as a guide, cut out shapes from a variety of fabrics. Arrange and overlap these on a piece of fabric. Attach the shapes using either fabric glue, fusible webbing, or needle and thread.

5. Decide if a title will be part of the entire quilt design. Letters may be cut from felt or fabric. The letters could be accented with hand sewn stitches or fabric paint.

6. Stitch all the quilt squares together. Make an overall border for the entire quilt out of fabric scraps.

EXAMINING YOUR WORK

- **Describe**   Identify the objects and figures in your quilt square. Identify the event the quilt celebrates.
- **Analyze**   Explain how you organized the art elements in your quilt to create harmony, variety, and unity.
- **Interpret**   Explain how your square helps capture the event. Describe the mood and idea your square communicates.
- **Judge**   Were you successful in creating a quilt that celebrates an event?

Figure 13–5   Student work. Quilt: Four seasons in Western New York.

STUDIO OPTION

■ Make a paper quilt that tells a story. Choose a favorite story or historical event. Choose colors and textures to emphasize the idea and mood. Use a variety of paper media, including construction paper, butcher paper, foil, tissue, and wallpaper. Cut out and layer shapes, symbols, or objects that relate to your story. Imitate cross-stitches by drawing parallel diagonal lines or X's with pen or paint.

Lesson 2   *Creating an "Event" Quilt*   **247**

Celebration Dances in Art

Does your school sponsor dances? Maybe a youth or social club in your community does. With few exceptions, such events in our society are leisure-time activities. Yet, in some cultures, dance plays a featured role in important celebrations.

In this lesson, you will explore two such celebrations. You will view artistic interpretations of dances that are part of these events.

A NATURE DANCE

Most of our dances are recreational. A few, however, have some special meaning. The opposite is true for the Hopi people of the American Southwest. In their culture, only a small number of dances are considered social events. The majority occupy an important place in rituals celebrating their people's oneness with nature.

One of these, the Green Corn Dance, is pictured in Figure 13–6. Examine this painting. Did you find your eye drawn to the sweeping curve formed by the ceremonial procession on the right side? The people in this line are the dancers. They are dressed in traditional clothing. Within the semi-circle is a second, smaller group that includes a drummer. Notice the dancers' upright posture. What does their body language suggest or tell about the *tempo,* or speed, of the music? Find the figure in the feathered headdress standing atop the **pueblo** (**pweh**-bloh), or *dried-clay dwelling.* Who do you think this person is?

A VICTORY DANCE

Some dances, like the one in Figure 13–6, are calm and dignified. Others are fast-paced and frenzied. How would you characterize

Figure 13–6 What do you think is the purpose of this dance? What role do the repetition of colors and forms and the use of vertical lines play in creating the painting's mood?

Fred Kaboti. *Pueblo Green Corn Dance, Hopi.* 1947. Oil on canvas. 75 × 64.8 cm (29½ × 25½"). The Thomas Gilcrease Institute of American History and Art, Tulsa, Oklahoma.

the dance pictured in Figure 13–7? Without looking at the title, you can probably sense the joyous mood and high energy level of the dancers. The painting captures a part of a victory celebration in the artist's native island of Jamaica. Can you think of a dance or "ball" with a similar purpose in our own country?

Look closely at this painting. It is divided into three main sections. The top and bottom thirds of the picture plane are given over to musicians in brightly colored costumes. At the center are the dancers, framed against a field of vivid orange. Observe how the angled lines of their arms, legs, and bodies help convey a strong sense of urgent movement. Notice the array of bold colors that make up the buildings and plant life. What art principle has the artist used to control the many colors and shapes in this action-filled painting?

✔ Check Your Understanding

1. What do most Hopi dances celebrate?
2. What event is the focus of the painting in Figure 13–7?

 **STUDIO ACTIVITY**

Dance Gesture Drawing

Work with a group of about six classmates to learn and perform a popular dance step. The group is to repeat the same movements over and over. While they perform, the remainder of the class is to make individual gesture drawings of the event. Sketching rapidly in pencil, the students should try to capture the sense of movement, paying close attention to the angles of arms and legs. After completing their sketches, a second group of volunteers should perform the same step to allow the dancers to do their own gesture drawings.

portfolio

Write an evaluation of your gesture drawings. Did they capture movement? Were they in proportion? Put your critique in your portfolio with your drawings.

Figure 13–7 Would you describe this treatment as realistic? Has the artist used linear perspective or any of the other space-giving techniques described in Chapter 1?

Everald Brown. *Victory Dance.* 1976. Oil on canvas. 83.8 × 124.5 cm (33 × 49″). Organization of American States Museum, Washington, D.C. Collection of the Art Museum of the Americas.

Creating Kinetic "Festival" Art

The Pueblo Green Corn Dance in Figure 13–6 is an ingredient in a Hopi *festival*. Festivals are colorful events that include food, music, dancing, and other forms of entertainment. They are celebrated in every culture. The purpose of some festivals is to usher in a new year. Others are meant to ensure a bountiful harvest.

No festival would be complete without live performances. The "performer" in Figure 13–8 is a **shadow puppet.** This is *an art object in the shape of an animal or human attached to a wand or stick.* Shadow puppets are popular throughout much of Asia, where they are featured in special events known as *shadow dances.* In these events, the puppets are made to sway gracefully to and fro behind a screen on which a bright light has been trained. Each figure appears to be dancing with its shadowy partner. Can you guess the type of festival to which this art object relates?

WHAT YOU WILL LEARN

Shadow puppets are an example of **kinetic** (kuh-**net**-ik) **art.** This is *an art style in which parts of a work are set into motion by a form of energy.* In this lesson, you will design and create your own piece of kinetic art for a festival. You will begin by deciding what form your art object will take. Then you will create the object out of tagboard. You will add visual texture to emphasize a specific part. You will repeat lines or shapes to create rhythm, as in Figure 13–8.

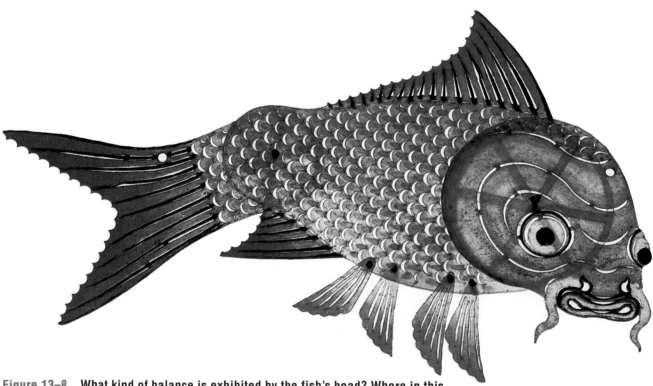

Figure 13–8 **What kind of balance is exhibited by the fish's head? Where in this object has the artist used the principle of repetition?**

China. *Fish Shadow Puppet.* c. 1900. Leather with color. 13.5 × 30.5 cm (5⅜ × 12″). Museum of International Folk Art, a unit of The Museum of New Mexico, Santa Fe, New Mexico. The Girard Foundation Collection.

WHAT YOU WILL NEED

- Sketch paper and pencil
- Sheet of tagboard, 14 x 22 inches (35.6 x 56 cm)
- Pens, watercolors, or markers
- Brushes
- Scissors
- Hole punch, book brads
- String or wooden dowel ¼ inch (6 mm) or less in diameter

WHAT YOU WILL DO

1. With classmates, brainstorm a list of joyous festivals. Exchange information on animal shapes and other images associated with these festivals.
2. Working alone, choose a festival. Make several sketches of an image connected with it. The image should be one that has potential for a kinetic art project. This might be a shadow puppet, a kite, or a lantern. Your object should have at least two parts, such as a body and tail (see Figure 13–8). Arms, legs, and a head are other possibilities.
3. Transfer your best sketch to tagboard. Draw outline shapes for all of the parts of your object. Fill as much of the surface as possible. Add details and color with pens, watercolors, or markers. Cover the entire surface of each part with color. Repeat lines and shapes to create a rhythmic pattern. Emphasize one part by introducing visual texture.
4. With scissors, carefully cut all parts out of the tagboard. Use a hole punch to make holes at the points where the parts will be joined. Use book brads to attach the parts. Make an additional hole in either the top

EXAMINING YOUR WORK

- **Describe** Identify the type of kinetic art you have created. Indicate the energy source—the wind or muscle power, for example.
- **Analyze** Tell whether you repeated lines and shapes to create a rhythmic pattern. Point to a part you emphasized by adding visual texture.
- **Interpret** Explain how the art object will be used. State whether it expresses the joyous mood of the festival.
- **Judge** Explain whether your artwork is successful. Tell whether the parts move freely.

or bottom of your creation. Tie string through this hole if your object is to be hung. Insert a wooden dowel as support if your object is a shadow puppet.

5. Share your work with classmates. Can they identify the festival you have chosen?

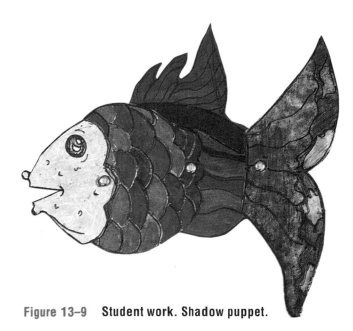

Figure 13–9   Student work. Shadow puppet.

Try This! COMPUTER OPTION

■ Use the Rectangle and Oval tools in your program to create outline shapes for body parts of a fish or other creature. Fill each shape with a bright, festive hue. If your software offers gradient fills, use these to create shading. Place the parts in their proper locations with respect to one another. In a free area of the screen, create a small shape in a contrasting color. Using the Duplicate or Copy and Paste commands, create many copies of the shape. Arrange these in a pattern. Group or select all the shapes and place them over the body of your creature.

Celebrating Rites of Passage

Of all the events you celebrate, probably none is more special to you than the anniversary of the day you were born. On your birthday, *you* are the "celebrity." Friends and loved ones gather around you. Bearing presents and good wishes, they help you celebrate your passage into another year of life.

The special quality of birthdays and other "passages" is not lost on artists. In this lesson, you will look at two art objects celebrating rites, or ceremonies, of passage.

RITE OF PASSAGE ART

What do you plan to be when you grow up? This is a question you probably have been asked many times. You may have asked it of yourself as well. Growing into adulthood is a big step. With it comes more privileges and more responsibilities. Many cultures observe this "coming of age" with a special celebration. Graduating, obtaining a driver's license, and being able to vote are examples of coming of age that bring a feeling of excitement and a desire to celebrate.

Chinese Rite of Passage Object

In some cultures, rites of passage include the wearing of special articles of clothing. One such article appears in Figure 13–10. Did you recognize this colorful creation as a hat? In China, it is a tradition—and an honor—to wear a hat like this on the birthday marking one's passage into adulthood. You may be reminded of the paper hats you wore at birthday parties when you were younger.

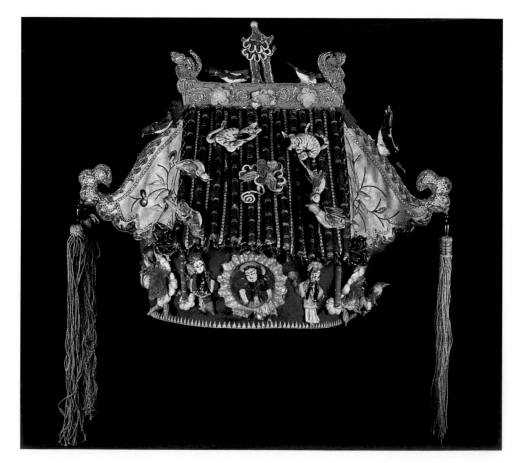

Figure 13–10 Color helps create visual interest in this object. What other art elements contribute?

China. *Coming of Age Hat.* Mixed media, embroidery. 31 × 38 cm (12 × 15"). Private collection.

Figure 13–11 What kinds of shapes appear throughout this object? How would you describe the colors that have been used? What steps has the artist taken to achieve harmony?

Africa. Yoruba. *King's Crown (adenla)*. c. 1930. Bamboo framework, beads, cloth, leather. H: 50.8 cm plus 58.4 cm beaded fringe (20″ plus 23″ fringe). Diameter: 31 cm (12″). The Saint Louis Museum of Art, St. Louis, Missouri. Purchase: Museum Shop Fund.

Examine this festive object. It has been richly embroidered with beads. Notice the attention to detail. Who do you suppose the human figures toward the base of the hat might be?

African Rite of Passage Object

The custom of wearing a birthday hat in China is widespread. The "hat" in Figure 13–11, by contrast, is worn by a chosen few. This object is an adenla (uh-**den**-luh), or

"King's Crown." It was created by an artist of the Yoruba people of West Africa. An **adenla** is *a sculpted ceremonial headdress used in rites of passage.* The privilege of wearing an adenla is reserved for royalty.

As you study this object, take note of the bird-like figure at the top. Many Yoruban adenla are decorated with woodpeckers. These are symbolic of the class structure—the "pecking order"—in this West African society. The long beaded threads extending from the brim form a *veil* of sorts. The purpose is not to protect the new king from curious glances. Rather, it is to force his own gaze inward, to remind him of his obligation to serve his people well.

✔ Check Your Understanding

1. Identify similarities and differences between Figures 13–10 and 13–11.
2. What is an adenla?

Collage of a Family Gathering

Study the painting in Figure 13–12. You don't have to speak Spanish to know that *cumpleaños*, the first word in the title, means "birthday." The frosted, decorated cakes and festively wrapped presents on the table are dead giveaways. Notice the blindfolded child in the pink party dress waving a stick. Do you know what game she and the other children are playing? Can you guess what treasures await inside the blue fish piñata suspended from a tree branch?

Like the birthday parties you may have attended, this one is a family gathering.

Notice the grownups and children who form a circle around the center of attention. Even the family dog is on hand to take part in the celebration.

WHAT YOU WILL LEARN

You will make a collage that celebrates a special family gathering. Your collage will use a variety of objects and materials. These will include items that help recall and identify the gathering, such as photographs and souvenirs. You will use size and color contrast to add variety to your composition.

Figure 13–12 What reason may the artist have had for placing the figures at this celebration in a circle? What symbolic meaning can you attach to this shape?

Carmen Lomas Garza. *Cumpleanos de Lala y Tudi (Lala's and Tudi's Birthday Party).* 1989. Oil on canvas. 91.4 × 122 cm (36 × 48"). Private collection.

WHAT YOU WILL NEED

- Photographs and assorted found objects
- Sheet of sturdy cardboard or tagboard, 18 x 24 inches (46 x 61 cm)
- White glue
- Colored felt-tip markers
- Sheets of white drawing paper
- Sheets of colored construction paper
- Scissors

WHAT YOU WILL DO

1. Choose a memorable family gathering as the subject of your collage. It may be a birthday celebration, as in Figure 13–12, or some other event. If you like, you may focus on an event involving your "family" at school, such as a class party.
2. Collect snapshots and other objects that help to recall the event. These might include a program from a grade-school graduation ceremony or a birthday card.
3. Arrange the materials you have gathered on a sheet of cardboard or tagboard. As a way of adding variety, try placing larger objects next to smaller ones, brighter-hued pieces next to duller ones. Leave some negative space between objects. When you are pleased with your composition, glue the objects in place.

EXAMINING YOUR WORK

- **Describe** Identify the materials you used for your collage. Point to hand-lettered words and phrases that you added.
- **Analyze** Did you place objects of contrasting sizes and colors side by side to add variety?
- **Interpret** What is the theme of your collage? Write a paragraph about the event.
- **Judge** Does your collage successfully convey that the event was a family celebration? What would you change?

4. Think of single words and short phrases that capture the theme of the event. For a graduation or confirmation, the phrase *rite of passage* might come to mind. Using colored markers, hand-letter at least three such words or phrases on white drawing paper. Experiment with different letter styles. If you prefer, you might want to outline your letters on colored construction paper.
5. With scissors, cut out the words and phrases you have created. Glue these to your collage. When the glue has dried, display the finished work.

Figure 13–13 **Student work. Family celebration.**

STUDIO OPTION

■ Make an abstract clay sculpture or relief that captures the idea of a family celebration. Do not include obvious forms such as human figures. Concentrate instead on a symbolic shape or abstract form. Be inventive! With your teacher's help, fire your sculpture. Give the work a title.

Art that Celebrates Life

In this chapter, the focus has been on celebrations that relate to important dates on the calendar. Not all celebrations, however, revolve around "red-letter days." Some causes for celebration are simple, everyday events—skating with friends on a perfect fall afternoon, gazing out the window at a gentle spring rain, or waking up to the first snow. Can you think of similar occasions that made you feel glad just to be alive?

Every now and then life serves up such priceless moments. These celebrations of life know no cultural boundaries. In this lesson, you will look at two artists' views of such celebrations.

INUIT SUBJECTS

The painting in Figure 13–14 captures a rare moment for both the artist and her subjects. Study the work. In it, two Inuit women

Both the Sun and the Moon Belong to Women

RIE MUÑOZ

• Alaska Women's Commission •
CELEBRATING WOMEN IN THE ARTS

Figure 13–14 **Notice how the artist uses the sun, moon, and stars to symbolize the universal nature of artistic expression. How has she symbolized day and night?**

Rie Munoz. *Both the Sun and Moon Belong to Women.* 1990. Watercolor. 48.2 × 55.9 cm (19 × 22"). Rie Munoz Ltd., Juneau, Alaska.

Creating an African Design

In addition to suggestions of masks, Figure 13–15 contains a number of other traditional African designs. Many are organized by means of radial balance. Make an African design of your own. Begin by folding a 12-inch (30-cm) square sheet of white drawing paper in half. Fold the resulting rectangle in half again to form a smaller square. Unfold the page. Then fold it diagonally to make a triangle. Open and fold it diagonally the other way. Unfold. Beginning in the center, draw lines or shapes to make a pattern on the fold lines or spaces in between. Turn the paper as you work to make sure your shapes and lines are repeated evenly. Continue until you have completed the pattern. Add color to your design using oil pastels, crayons, colored pencils, or colored markers.

PORTFOLIO

Write a description of your design listing the elements and principles of art you used. Put this written description in your portfolio with your artwork.

Figure 13–15 Can you find objects in this painting that exhibit radial balance? What other art principles are evident in this work?

James Phillips. *Ancestral Dream.* 1991. Acrylic on paper. 120.6 × 106.7 cm (47½ × 42½"). Private collection.

appear. The similarity of their positions indicate that they are celebrating. Imagine the artist's own delight in creating this scene. She expresses her feelings by recording a celebration in a symbolic way. Notice the stylized use of shape and color.

AFRICAN AMERICAN PAINTING

Some celebrations of life do not come from how we feel. They come instead from a sense of pride in who we are. The abstract artwork in Figure 13–15 is such a "celebration." The work celebrates the artist's African roots.

As you explore this busy painting, your eye never stays in one place for long. It is forever moving, much like the pulsing colors and vibrating geometric shapes that make up the work. Pause for a moment to focus on the yellow-and-black bull's-eyes nested within the

blue circle at the upper left. These objects may remind you of a face. If so, this is no accident. Similar arrangements throughout this painting are efforts to re-create, at least in spirit, the ritual masks of the artist's African ancestors.

✔ Check Your Understanding

1. What event is celebrated in the painting in Figure 13–14?
2. What kinds of traditional images appear in Figure 13–15?

Celebrating a Role Model

Are there grownups whose footsteps you hope to follow in someday? Maybe your role model is a person like the one whose sculpted likeness appears at the center of the work in Figure 13–16. This man is C. J. McLin. He was the first African American to be elected to public office in the artist's home state of Ohio. The work is the artist's personal tribute to McLin. It is more than just that, however. It is also intended as a message to young people—a call to them to find heroes truly worthy of admiration. What qualities of this work reveal the artist's own admiration for a leader and pioneer?

WHAT YOU WILL LEARN

You will create a three-dimensional mixed-media tribute that honors a person whose life or work inspires you. Your design will include a variety of media. The objects you choose will connect in some way with your theme. Your design will include colored yarn or paper strips that create harmony with the rest of the media. The yarn will be woven and arranged in an interesting pattern.

WHAT YOU WILL NEED

- Photographs and old magazines
- Compass
- Sheet of construction paper, 9 x 12 inches (23 x 30 cm)
- Scissors
- White glue
- Tissue paper, gold or aluminum foil
- Assorted yarns, colored paper, or colored markers
- Plastic lid from an ice-cream or coffee container

Figure 13–16 How does the artist emphasize the image of the figure whose achievements this work celebrates?

Bing Davis. *Puberty Ritual Image #10*. 1992. Clay and found objects. 91.3 × 45.7 cm (36 × 18″). Private collection.

WHAT YOU WILL DO

1. Select a person whom you admire. This might be a relative, a leader in your community or state, a teacher, or anyone else who inspires you.
2. Think about images that communicate information about this person's appearance and accomplishments. These might include photographs and pictures clipped from magazines that symbolize the person's importance to you. Gather an assortment of such materials.
3. Trace a circle that will fit the outside measurement of the lid on colored construction paper. Choose a color that is in keeping with your tribute. Make a second circle the same size on a thin sheet of cardboard. Cut out both circles. Glue them together.
4. Arrange the photographs and images you have gathered on the colored construction paper circle. When you are satisfied with the arrangement, glue these in place. Fill the negative spaces between and around the images with strips of tissue paper, gold foil, or colored lines. Be creative! Set this object aside to dry.
5. Gather strands of thin yarn or cut paper strips in several colors. These should blend with those of the construction paper and images, so as to create harmony. Form an interesting pattern with the yarn or paper strips and glue them to the edge of the plastic lid to make a border and add repetition to the work.
6. Glue your circle to the flat surface of the lid.

EXAMINING YOUR WORK

- **Describe** Describe the materials used in your tribute. Identify the individual you are honoring.
- **Analyze** Does your work achieve harmony through the use of color? Have you used interesting patterns in the border as an organizing principle?
- **Interpret** Explain the idea, mood, and message your work expresses about its subject.
- **Judge** How does your work compare with that in Figure 13–16? In what ways is it similar? How is it different?

Figure 13–17 **Student work. A role model.**

COMPUTER OPTION

Try This!

■ On the computer, design a certificate for a special personal achievement. Include a variety of fonts in different sizes and styles. Add graphics, either in the form of clip art or original illustrations. Complete your certificate with a decorative border that uses a repetitive pattern. Print and present copies of your certificate to deserving individuals.

Thomas Hart Benton. *The Sources of Country Music.* 1975. Acrylic on canvas. 1.8 × 3 m (6 × 10'). The Country Music Hall of Fame and Museum, Nashville, Tennessee. ©1998 Thomas. H. Benton & Rita P. Benton Testamentary Trusts/Licensed by VAGA, New York, NY

Celebrating Music and Dance

Have you ever danced to "The Hokey Pokey" or "The Bunny Hop" at a wedding or other event? Perhaps your family does the Irish jig or the Polish polka during family celebrations. Music and dance have been a part of celebrations and rituals since ancient times.

One type of dancing—folk dancing—developed when people lived in simple, rural societies. Back then, people did not have many forms of recreation. They did not have televisions, VCRs, computer and video games, or stereos. Traveling was difficult, and most people did not know how to read.

Dancing, however, was something that almost everyone could do.

Some types of folk dancing are associated with certain cultures and traditions. The Highland Fling, for example, is a Scottish folk dance. The Hora is a Romanian and Israeli folk dance. Dancers lock their arms together or hold hands. They move counterclockwise in a circle. The dance is often performed at Jewish weddings and other celebrations. In *The Sources of Country Music,* Thomas Hart Benton depicts a celebration with music and dancing.

MAKING THE CONNECTION

- ✔ Identify some of the musical instruments shown in *The Sources of Country Music.*
- ✔ How did Benton create a sense of movement in this work?
- ✔ Find other examples of music or dancing depicted in artwork. What are the similarities and differences with Benton's piece?

INTERNET ACTIVITY

Visit Glencoe's Fine Arts Web Site for students at:

http://www.glencoe.com/sec/art/students

BUILDING VOCABULARY

Number a sheet of paper from 1 to 6. After each number, write the term from the box that matches each description below.

adenla   seal
kinetic art   shadow puppet
pueblo   tricolor

1. An art style in which parts of a work are set into motion by a form of energy.
2. An art object in the shape of an animal or human attached to a wand or stick.
3. Dried-clay dwelling.
4. A sculpted ceremonial headdress used in rites of passage.
5. A flag with three broad bands of color.
6. A symbolic image or emblem.

REVIEWING ART FACTS

Number a sheet of paper from 7 to 12. Answer each question in a complete sentence.

7. What is the purpose of May Day?

8. What do the paintings in Figures 13–2 and 13–3 "give thanks" for?
9. In what ways might Figure 13–4 be said to be an example of *impossible art*?
10. What two types of dance are featured in Hopi culture? Which type is most common?
11. Name two purposes of festivals in various cultures of the world.
12. What is a rite of passage?

THINKING ABOUT ART

On a sheet of paper, answer each question in a sentence or two.

1. **Extend.** Which of the artworks in this chapter would you identify as having joyous subjects? Explain your choices.
2. **Analyze.** What principles of art has the artist used in Figure 13–14 on page **256** to create a feeling of celebration?

MAKING ART CONNECTIONS

1. **Social Studies.** One of the historical figures celebrated in Figure 13–4 is Harriet Tubman. With several classmates, research Harriet Tubman's life. Use your findings as the basis for a multimedia presentation. Include readings from poems and stories about the Underground Railroad, such as Jim Haskins's *Railroad Songs.* You may also want to display images from artist Jacob Lawrence's narrative series on Harriet Tubman.

2. **Community Connection.** Different states and locales have their own specific holidays. Residents of Massachusetts, for example, celebrate Patriot's Day. Find out about holidays specific to your town or community, such as Founder's Day. Design and create visual materials—posters and a logo, for example—for the next celebration of this event. Share your creations with community members.

Figure 14–1 Marc Chagall used his imagination to create this artwork. How many examples of fantasy can you find?

Marc Chagall. *Green Violinist*. 1923–24. Oil on canvas. 198.1 × 108.6 cm (78 × 42¾″). Solomon R. Guggenheim Museum, New York, New York. © 1997 Artists Rights Society (ARS), New York/ADAGP, Paris

Creating Fantasy

The imagination is a wonderful thing. When you are small, it transforms a plain box into a house or pirate ship, a stuffed animal into a living, talking friend. When you are older, it unlocks the door to creative ideas and solutions to problems.

The painting at the left is the product of an active imagination. Study the work. What mood or feeling does this unusual work arouse? In this chapter, you will look at a number of artworks that, like this one, are fueled by the power of imagination.

PORTFOLIO IDEAS

When you have completed this class, your portfolio will be the evidence of all you have learned about art. Your art portfolio shows personal achievement. Use it as a motivation to continue communicating your ideas and feelings through new artworks. As long as you continue to work, you will continue to grow as an artist.

OBJECTIVES

After competing this chapter, you will be able to:
- Define fantasy art.
- Determine what the Surrealists were trying to accomplish.
- Identify links between fantasy art of this and other cultures and times.
- Complete several fantasy artworks using different media and techniques.

WORDS YOU WILL LEARN

architectural rendering
belvedere
fantasy art
juxtapose
social protest painting
Surrealists

Dreams and Nightmares

Do you remember what you dreamed last night—or *if* you dreamed? Dreams are our lone connection with a world that is otherwise lost to us. This is the hidden world of sleep. It is a place where we spend eight of every twenty-four hours each day—a full third of our lives. Is it any wonder that this uncharted territory has long held fascination for artists?

In this lesson, you will look at two "dreamscapes." You will explore visual interpretations of the strange kinds of images that visit us during our slumber.

DREAM ART OF THE PAST

Depicting dreams in art is nothing new. As a branch of **fantasy art**—*art that focuses on make-believe or imaginary subjects*—dream art dates at least to the time of the ancient Greeks. During the Middle Ages, demons and other "night visitors" were frequent subjects of paintings and illustrations.

The work in Figure 14–2 is more recent. The artist, who was active during the mid-1800s, worked chiefly as a sculptor. The painting is based on a dream he actually had. In the dream *and* the painting, the figure

Figure 14–2 Look at the title and then at the painting. What principle of art has been used to heighten the suspense in this work?

William Rimmer. *Flight and Pursuit.* 1872. Oil on canvas. 46 × 66.7 cm (18 × 26½"). Museum of Fine Arts, Boston, Massachusetts. Bequest of Miss Edith Nichols.

Figure 14–3 What properties are shared by this painting and the one opposite? How has the artist of this work suggested deep space?

Kay Sage. *No Passing*. 1954. Oil on canvas. 130.2 × 96.5 cm (51¼ × 38″). Collection of Whitney Museum of American Art, New York, New York. Purchase.

running in the foreground is the artist. That he is being chased by someone is clear not only from the title. It is equally evident from the scary shadows on the floor behind him. Who is chasing the artist? Why are they after him? Most baffling of all is the ghostlike image in parallel stride in the background. From whom is *he* running?

RECENT DREAM ART

During the first half of the twentieth century, artists struck out in many bold new directions. Some turned to their conscience for inspiration and subject matter. Others looked to their emotions. Yet others probed the inner workings of the mind. This *group of artists who explored the realm of dreams and the subconscious* called themselves **Surrealists** (suh-**ree**-uh-lists).

STUDIO ACTIVITY

A Drawing in the Surrealist Style

Use your imagination to come up with an image you might expect to find in a nightmare. On a sheet of lined paper, note details of this image. Do not include people among your details. Using pencil, sketch your image lightly on a sheet of drawing paper. Imitate as much as possible the style of the painting on this page and in Figure 14–1. Use colored pencils, markers, or oil pastels to complete your work. Choose hues that help communicate a sense of fear.

P O R T F O L I O

In self-reflection, write what you learned about selecting a nightmarish image and using the Surrealist style to portray the image.

The name comes from a word whose initial part, *sur-*, means "beyond or above."

The painting in Figure 14–3 was created by a Surrealist. Examine this unusual work. Beneath a sullen sky, collections of flat building-high objects (some wrapped in what looks like canvas) stretch endlessly to the horizon. Scraps of these same materials litter the ground, providing a possible clue to the work's title. Typical of Surrealist art, this "landscape" is bathed in an unnatural light that casts shadows on some of the towering structures. What is the source of this light? The answer to that question, like the meaning of the odd shapes themselves, remains a mystery.

✔ Check Your Understanding

1. What is fantasy art? What are its roots?
2. To what did the Surrealists turn for inspiration?

Creating a Fantasy Bird Collage

The world of fantasy art is filled with curious creatures. Some, like the tropical plants in Figure 10–4 on page **186,** are light-hearted. Others, like the bird in this picture, are not. Study this painting. Without glancing at the title, you can still sense the girl's sheer terror. Have you ever seen a bird like this? Perhaps the artist saw it in a dream.

Figure 14–4 **Does the use of abstraction in this painting take away from the feelings the work communicates? Why or why not?**

Rufino Tamayo. *Girl Attacked by a Strange Bird.* 1947. Oil on canvas. 178 × 127.3 cm (70 × 50⅛"). The Museum of Modern Art, New York, New York. Gift of Mr. and Mrs. Charles Zadok.

WHAT YOU WILL LEARN

In this lesson you will have a chance to use your own imagination and create an image of a bird. You will use this image, along with an assortment of art media, to create a collage. Begin by discussing with classmates the various features of birds. A class member will list these features on the board. For each feature the class will brainstorm descriptive words. These will be written next to the feature. Using this list as a starting point, make several pencil sketches of birds. Transfer the best of these to drawing paper. You will use tissue paper and other materials to give your bird color and texture.

WHAT YOU WILL NEED

- Pencil and sketch paper
- White drawing paper, 12 x l8 inches (30 x 46 cm)
- Scissors
- Sheets of colored tissue paper
- White glue, water, brush
- Yarn
- Black markers or pen and black ink

WHAT YOU WILL DO

1. Working with classmates, discuss features common to birds. These might include wings, legs, claws, beak, and feathers. One class member is to write these features on the board. Space for additional words is to be left alongside each feature.
2. Still working as a class, brainstorm words to describe each feature. Let your imagination run free. For *eyes,* for example, you might mention words such as *large, narrow,* and *yellow.* The volunteer at the board should list suggested words in the space after each feature.

3. Working alone, use the lists on the board to form a picture of a bird in your "mind's eye." Your bird might terrify your viewers or it may make them smile and even laugh. Make several sketches of your bird.

4. Using your best sketch as a model, re-draw your bird on a sheet of drawing paper. Make sure that the drawing fills the paper. Use a firm, continuous line.

5. Cut a variety of large and small shapes from sheets of colored tissue paper. When you have enough to cover your drawing, glue these carefully in place. Use white glue thinned with water for this purpose. Then lay the tissue paper on the damp surface. Smooth it out gently with your hand. Then carefully brush a second coat of glue across the surface of the tissue. If your brush picks up any color from the wet tissue, wipe it off on a paper towel.

6. Continue in this fashion, adding layer upon layer of tissue paper. Always glue

EXAMINING YOUR WORK

- **Describe** Is your drawing easily identified as a bird? Can you point to the different features of your bird?
- **Analyze** Is your bird large and colorful? Does it contain a variety of textures?
- **Interpret** What kinds of emotions or feelings do you think your bird collage will arouse in viewers?
- **Judge** Do you think your bird is a success? Do you feel it can be described as fantasy art?

the darkest colors of tissue in place first. Add subtle shadings of color by adding pieces of lighter tissue over pieces of darker ones.

7. When all the tissue is dry, add lines to suggest feathers or other designs. Do this with lengths of colored yarn or with a black marker or pen, or with both.

Figure 14–5 **Student work. Fantasy bird collage.**

Try This! STUDIO OPTION

■ Create another imaginary bird that will stir up different feelings. If your first bird was sinister, for example, your new one might be funny. Follow the same procedures as above. This time, however, wrinkle the tissue paper before applying it to your drawing or add crumpled or three-dimensional pieces. This will add extra texture and surface interest. Compare the completed bird to your earlier one. Which one is more successful? Why?

Lesson 2 *Creating a Fantasy Bird Collage* **267**

Puzzling Paintings

You wouldn't think much of it if you saw a car go by. You might sit up and take notice, however, if the driver were an elephant! Familiar images can seem unfamiliar—even strange—when they are placed in unexpected settings. Artists sometimes surprise viewers by doing just that. They **juxtapose** (**juks**-tuh-pohz), or *place side by side,* objects that look unusual or interesting when viewed together. In this lesson, you will look at two such works.

A PUZZLING PAINTING FROM THE 1930s

Often, the images juxtaposed in an artwork have little in common. In the painting in Figure 14–6, they have *too much* in common. This work was created by a Belgian Surrealist famous for his imaginative use of juxtaposition. His name was **René Magritte** (ren-**ay** mah-**greet**).

Examine this painting. If you were asked to describe it, what would you say? Maybe you would identify its subject simply as a window opening onto a nature scene. Look more closely, however. Find the small object in the shape of an upside-down *T* juxtaposed against a cloud. It takes some viewers a moment to realize that this seemingly out-of-place object is actually part of an easel. On the easel is an unframed landscape painting that blends perfectly with the scene beyond. With your finger, trace the outline of this "painting within a painting." What statement might the artist be making? Notice the title.

Figure 14–6   What two images are juxtaposed in this painting? Would such a juxtaposition be possible in real life?

René Magritte. *The Human Condition.* 1934. Oil on canvas. 100 × 81 × 1.6 cm (39⅜ × 31⅞ × ⅝"). The National Gallery of Art, Washington, D.C. Gift of the Collectors Committee.

Maybe this artwork is a comment on the inability of some people to tell where reality begins and ends. Can you think of advances in our own time that have helped blur the line between fantasy and reality?

A PUZZLING PAINTING FROM THE 1980s

Compare the painting in Figure 14–7 with the one just analyzed. The work on this page was completed fifty years later. Yet, the two share a similar theme. Both, moreover, present "pictures within a picture."

As you study Figure 14–7, you find once again that first impressions can be deceiving. At first glance, this painting appears to be nothing more than a pleasant seascape. On closer inspection, you begin noticing details that are hard to explain. A trio of gently swaying palm trees at the left, for example, appears rooted to a wooden tabletop. On the right side is an open sketchbook propped against a mountain. As if these images weren't puzzling enough, what are we to make of the painting that floats in mid air? How about the one in the sketchbook that continues the scene behind it? Again, the title is a partial key to such mysteries. It hints at the possibility that the work is a picture album of events in the artist's life—past, present, and to come.

✔ Check Your Understanding

1. What does *juxtapose* mean?
2. Name two things that the paintings on these pages have in common.

Figure 14–7 **This artwork reflects the artist's fond memories of a grandmother who introduced her to painting when she was young.**

Lydia Rubio. *Ella Pintaba Paisajes (She Painted Landscapes).* 1989. Oil on canvas. 91.3 × 234 cm (36 × 92"). Private collection.

Creating Your Own Picture Puzzle

Some picture puzzles, as you have seen, make statements of a general nature. Others operate on a more personal plane. What sort of comment or message does the picture puzzle on this page deliver?

Before you attempt an answer, it may help to know that the work is an example of **social protest painting.** Emerging in the 1930s, this was *an art style dedicated to attacking the ills of big-city life.* A frequent target of social protest paintings are current-day problems. Look again at the thought-provoking picture in Figure 14–8. What problem of big-city life do you think this work highlights? What "surreal" or fantasy images and objects can you find?

WHAT YOU WILL LEARN

In this lesson you will create a picture puzzle of your own. Like the painting in Figure 14–8, your work will target a problem of modern life. Begin by thinking about possible themes. Make sketches that juxtapose images that relate to your theme but not ordinarily to each other. Use the best of your sketches as the basis of an oil pastel drawing.

Figure 14–8 Notice the moody sky and downward-pointing arrows. What feelings do they communicate?

George Tooker. *Highway.* 1953. Tempera on panel. 58 × 45.4 cm (22⅞ × 17⅞"). Courtesy of Terra Museum of American Art, Chicago, Illinois. Terra Foundation for the Arts, Daniel J. Terra Collection.

Add images clipped from magazines. Make one image larger than all the others to emphasize its importance.

WHAT YOU WILL NEED

- Pencil and sketch paper
- Sheet of white drawing paper, 9 x 12 inches (23 x 30 cm)
- Oil pastels
- Old magazines
- Scissors
- White glue

WHAT YOU WILL DO

1. Think of a problem you feel strongly about or have learned about. Possibilities include forms of pollution, endangered species, or homelessness. Make a list of images that might be connected with the problem. Be creative.
2. On sketch paper, experiment with juxtaposing images from your list that usually are not related but which, together, make a strong statement. On the theme of air pollution, for example, you might show a factory chimney belching smoke that forms the letters *S.O.S.* Decide on one image that is central to your theme. Draw this image the largest.
3. Transfer your best sketch to a sheet of white drawing paper. Complete your drawing using oil pastels. Choose colors that suit your theme.
4. Thumb through old magazines for additional images. Again, give free rein to your imagination. Clip four or five pictures. Experiment placing these at various points on the surface of your drawing.
5. When you are happy with your arrangement, glue the images in place. Display your finished work. Challenge classmates to solve your picture puzzle.

EXAMINING YOUR WORK

- **Describe** List the images that appear in your work.
- **Analyze** Did you emphasize one image by making it larger than the others? Does your picture contain an interesting juxtaposition?
- **Interpret** What is the mood of your work? What statement does the work make?
- **Judge** Are you pleased with your picture? Were your classmates able to identify the problem your work attacks?

Figure 14–9   Student work. Current-day problem.

STUDIO OPTION

■ Create another picture puzzle, this time using colored pencils or markers. Include nonliving objects that have human properties, such as the scowling automobiles in Figure 14–8. Give your work a title.

Impossible Images

"Seeing," it is said, "is believing." Generally, there is much truth to this statement. Sometimes, however, our eyes play tricks on us. They cause us to see imaginary pools of water shimmering in the distance when the weather is hot. They confuse us by making images appear to shift and change no matter how long we stare at them. You have probably seen optical illusions that will not "stay still."

In this lesson, you will look at an image that, like such illusions, fools the eye. You will examine a second work that looks impossible for entirely different reasons.

AN IMPOSSIBLE BUILDING

Some of the works you have looked at in this chapter contain ghostly beings. Others show eerie, surreal landscapes. The fine art print in Figure 14–10 fits neither of these descriptions. It focuses, rather, on a perfectly straightforward subject. The work may be seen as a kind of **architectural rendering.** This is *a detailed, realistic two-dimensional representation of a proposed three-dimensional structure.* In this case, the proposal is for a **belvedere** (**bel**-vuh-deer), *a building designed to provide a view of its surroundings.* The word is a blend of the Italian roots bel, or "beautiful," and vedere, "view."

Look closely at this print. It doesn't take long before you notice that something is terribly wrong. To pinpoint the problem, locate the two figures—one on each level—gazing out at the scenery. Both stand at a railing along the narrow end on the structure's right. Yet, each faces in a different direction. The first and second floors of the belvedere have been juxtaposed at right angles! Note that a model for this impossible design is located conveniently within the print. It appears in the hands of the perplexed-looking figure seated on the bench near the bottom of the picture. Could such an object really exist in three dimensions? If you were the architect's client, would you approve this plan?

Figure 14–10 The artist was fond of such visual puzzles. Another of his prints appears in Figure 2–10 on page 34. What similarities can you find between these two works?

M. C. Escher. *Belvedere.* 1958. Lithograph. 46.2 × 29.5 cm (18 × 11⅜"). © 1996 Cordon Art, Baarn, Holland. All rights reserved.

AN IMPOSSIBLE CITYSCAPE

In contrast to the confusing world shown in Figure 14–10, the painting on page **273** appears to promise welcome relief. The feeling that you are on solid ground does not last for long, however.

Focus your attention on the triangular shape looming on the horizon. You have probably seen photographs of this structure before. It is one of the great pyramids of ancient Egypt. In and of itself, there is nothing strange about this landmark. It is when we look elsewhere in the painting that a sense of having left reality behind begins to emerge. Notice the building at the left with the sharply pointed steeple. Buildings of this type are not found in or near Egypt. Do you know where such structures are found? Do you know what they are called? Can you understand what makes this cityscape impossible?

Check Your Understanding

1. What is an architectural rendering?
2. What makes the image in Figure 14–10 impossible? How about the painting in Figure 14–11?

✏ STUDIO ACTIVITY ✏

Creating an Impossible City

Browse through a magazine for photographs of unusual buildings. Look for images that show these structures in different sizes and scales. Carefully cut around the contours of each building. Prepare a background for your cityscape by painting a sky at the top of the sheet of white paper. Arrange the images on your background. When you are satisfied with the composition of your portrait, paste the pictures in place with white glue. Paint in trees, cars, or other details if you desire.

P O R T F O L I O

Write an explanation of your results for your portfolio. Tell how your cityscape is "impossible."

Figure 14–11   **Compare the strange juxtapositions in this work with the one in Figure 14–10. Do you recognize any other landmarks in this work?**

Thomas Cole. *The Architect's Dream.* 1840. Oil on canvas. 134.7 × 213.6 cm (53 × 84¹⁄₁₆″). Toledo Museum of Art, Toledo, Ohio. Gift of Florence Scott Libbey.

Creating an "Etching" of a Strange Place

Are you familiar with the game called "hide-and-seek"? Maybe you have played it. If so, it is doubtful your version looked anything like the image in Figure 14–12. Study this work. The central figure is a young barefoot girl with her back to the viewer. She gropes uncertainly through a dark, forbidding place. Can you make out the objects that surround her? Maybe this is all just a bad dream from which the girl will soon awaken. Then again, maybe it is not. Notice the year of the painting. This may help explain the subject matter and tone. Do you know the events of this era that might have prompted such a grim visual commentary?

WHAT YOU WILL LEARN

In this lesson, you will create your own vision of a strange place. You will use your imagination to picture such a place. Create sketches of what your "mind's eye" sees. Use your best sketch as the basis of a crayon drawing. This drawing will be covered in turn with black ink. Finally, you will use a bamboo skewer or other pointed object to scratch a pattern of lines into the inked surface.

WHAT YOU WILL NEED
- Pencil and sketch paper
- Sheet of tagboard or white drawing paper, 9 x 12 inches (23 x 30 cm)

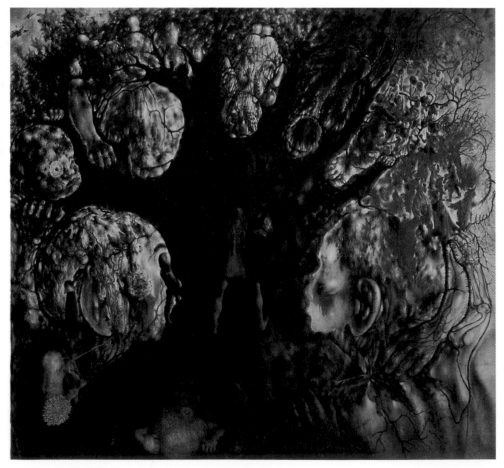

Figure 14–12 Can you identify the figure who is "it" in this game of hide-and-seek? Who or what is the figure seeking?

Pavel Tchelitchew. *Hide-and-Seek.* 1940–42. Oil on canvas. 199.3 × 215.3 cm (6' 6½" × 7'¾"). The Museum of Modern Art, New York, New York. Mrs. Simon Guggenheim Fund.

- Crayons in assorted colors
- Brush, india ink
- Ruler or other straight edge
- Round toothpick or bamboo skewer

WHAT YOU WILL DO

1. With classmates, brainstorm images of imaginary places. The images need not be gruesome, like the one in Figure 14–12. You may, for example, picture a bizarre setting in which ridiculous creatures roam wild. Make notes about the possibilities raised.
2. Choose a location for the subject of an artwork. Let your imagination run away with you. Using pencil, complete several sketches of the images that come to mind.
3. Choose colors that fit the mood of the place you picture in your mind. Fill the entire page of tagboard or paper with a thick layer of crayon. The etching technique you will be using requires a heavy application of this medium.
4. With a brush, paint over your crayon drawing using black india ink, or black tempera paint, with a few drops of detergent added. While the ink or paint is drying, design several different patterns. These should be made up of closely spaced lines.
5. Transfer your best sketch, with pencil, to the india-inked surface. With a pointed object, etch patterns onto the inked surface of your drawing. By carefully scratching through the ink, you will bring out the crayon colors underneath. Using closely spaced lines in your pattern will make it easier to see the crayon images. This will also add visual interest to your picture.

EXAMINING YOUR WORK

- **Describe** Does your picture depict a strange location? What details have you included?
- **Analyze** Did you use closely spaced lines to create an interesting pattern? Do these lines reveal the crayon colors beneath?
- **Interpret** Does your subject communicate a "not-of-this-world" look? Will viewers immediately identify the mood of your picture?
- **Judge** Are you pleased with your picture? If you were to do it again, what would you do to improve it?

Figure 14–13 **Student work. An etching.**

 Try This!

COMPUTER OPTION

■ From the notes you made, choose another "strange" setting. With the Fill tool, flood the entire drawing space with black. Set the line width to thin. Using the Pencil or Brush tool, begin drawing outlines of shapes in your strange world. Change line thickness and color as needed. Add hatching, cross-hatching, stippling, and textures to surfaces.

Lesson 6 *Creating an "Etching" of a Strange Place* **275**

James C. Christensen. *Vanity*. 1994. Acrylic and gold leaf. 41 × 51 cm (16 × 20″). Courtesy of The Greenwich Workshop, Inc. Shelton, Connecticut.

Symbolism in Art and Literature

When you see a red sign with eight sides, what comes to mind? You probably don't even have to see the word *stop* to recognize a stop sign. When you see golden arches, you most likely think of a popular fast-food restaurant. The red octagonal sign and the golden arches are symbols.

Symbolism is a commonly used device in literature and art. In a novel, for instance, the main character may take a journey. On the most basic level, the journey may be a trip across the country. On a secondary level, however, the journey may represent life.

In artwork, an artist cannot use words to explain this secondary level of meaning. Instead, the artist must use images and devices that viewers will recognize. An artist might use the color white, for example, to suggest purity. A dove may symbolize peace.

Look carefully at James Christensen's *Vanity* on this page. The word *vanity* means having an inflated opinion of oneself. It also means being empty or having no value. This work contains many symbols of vanity. Which ones can you find?

MAKING THE CONNECTION

- ✔ Identify five symbols of vanity in this artwork.
- ✔ How does symbolism in art differ from symbolism in literature?
- ✔ What message about vanity do you think the artist is trying to convey in this piece?

INTERNET ACTIVITY

Visit Glencoe's Fine Arts Web Site for students at:

http://www.glencoe.com/ sec/art/students

REVIEW

BUILDING VOCABULARY

Number a sheet of paper from 1 to 6. After each number, write the term from the box that matches each description below.

architectural   juxtapose
    rendering   social protest
belvedere   painting
fantasy art   Surrealists

1. A building designed to provide a view of its surroundings.
2. A detailed, realistic two-dimensional representation of a proposed three-dimensional structure.
3. Group of artists who explored the realm of dreams and the subconscious.
4. Place side by side.
5. An art style dedicated to attacking the ills of big-city life.
6. Art that focuses on make-believe or imaginary subjects.

REVIEWING ART FACTS

Number a sheet of paper from 7 to 13. Answer each question in a complete sentence.

7. What images are juxtaposed to startle the viewer in Figure 14–1?

8. What fantasy images turned up often in art of the Middle Ages?
9. When did the Surrealists work?
10. Who was René Magritte? For what is he best noted?
11. What is the significance of the title of Figure 14–7?
12. What did social protest artists frequently criticize in their works?
13. What makes the print in Figure 14–10 "impossible"?

THINKING ABOUT ART

On a sheet of paper, answer each question in a sentence or two.

1. **Compare and contrast.**   Which of the artworks in this chapter seems to be most disturbing? Which strikes you as the least disturbing? Give reasons for your choices.
2. **Synthesize.**   Choose a work from the chapter and identify the symbols used by the artist. Tell what you think they mean.

MAKING ART CONNECTIONS

1. **Language Arts.**   Look back at Figure 14–4 on page **266.** Notice the manner in which the painting seems almost to suggest a story. Think about the story the work tells. Then write a short poem of six or eight lines that captures the action and emotions. Share your poem with classmates.
2. **Social Studies.**   Use library resources to learn more about the Great Depression and its aftermath. In the course of your research, answer questions such as the following: What caused this economic disaster? Which nations were affected by it? What measures were taken in this country to recover from its effects? Share your findings in an oral report. Find images by Ben Shahn, Reginald Marsh, and other social protest painters to display during your talk.

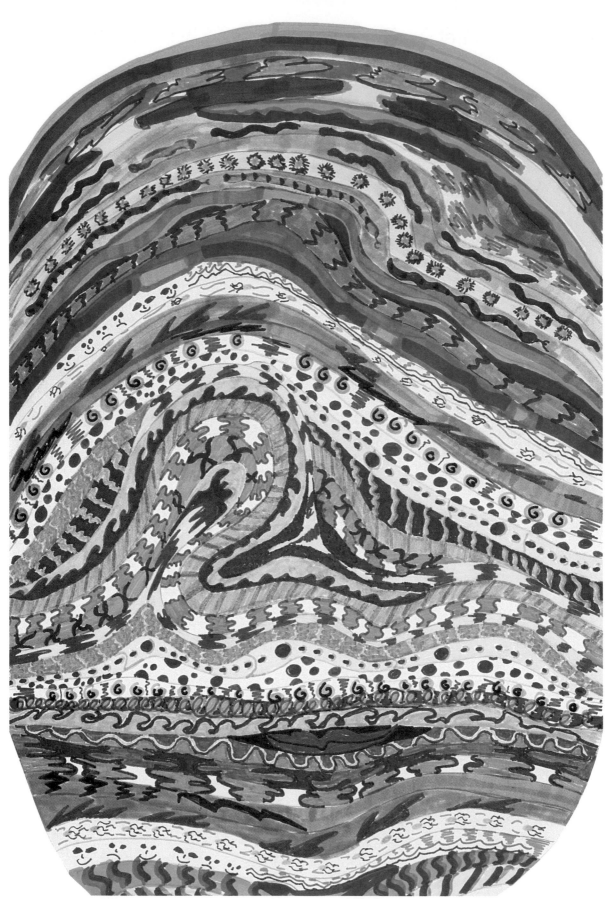

Looking at an object up close can reveal surprising details. This thumbprint was created by a student who tried the Studio Activity "Viewing Objects Up Close" on page 185.

HANDBOOK CONTENTS

PART 3: Career Spotlights

PART 4: Additional Studios

1. Making Gesture Drawings

Gesture drawing is a way of showing movement in a sketch. Gesture drawings have no outlines or details. You are not expected to draw the figure. Instead, you are expected to draw the movement, or what the figure is doing. Follow these guidelines:

- Use the side of the drawing tool. Do not hold the medium as you would if you were writing.
- Find the lines of movement that show the direction in which the figure is bending. Draw the main line showing this movement.
- Use quickly drawn lines to build up the shape of the person.

2. Making Contour Drawings

Contour drawing is a way of capturing the feel of a subject. When doing a contour drawing, remember the following pointers:

- If you accidentally pick up your pen or pencil, don't stop working. Place your pen or pencil back where you stopped. Begin again from that point.
- If you have trouble keeping your eyes off the paper, ask a friend to hold a piece of paper between your eyes and your drawing paper. Another trick is to place your drawing paper inside a large paper bag as you work.
- Tape your paper to the table so it will not slide around. With a finger of your free hand, trace the outline of the object. Record the movement with your drawing hand.

- Contour lines show ridges and wrinkles in addition to outlines. Adding these lines gives roundness to the object.

3. Drawing with Oil Pastels

Oil pastels are sticks of pigment held together with an oily binder. The colors are brighter than wax crayon colors. If you press heavily you will make a brilliant-colored line. If you press lightly you will create a fuzzy line. You can fill in shapes with the brilliant colors. You can blend a variety of color combinations. For example, you can fill a shape with a soft layer of a hue and then color over the hue with a heavy layer of white to create a unique tint of that hue.

If you use oil pastels on colored paper, you can put a layer of white under the layer of hue to block the color of the paper.

4. Drawing Thin Lines with a Brush

Drawing thin lines with a brush can be learned with a little practice. Just follow these steps:

1. Dip your brush in the ink or paint. Wipe the brush slowly against the side, twirling it between your fingers until the bristles form a point.
2. Hold the brush at the beginning of the metal band near the tip. Hold the brush straight up and down.
3. Imagine that the brush is a pencil with a very sharp point. Pretend that pressing too hard will break the point. Now touch the paper lightly with the tip of the brush and draw a line. The line should be quite thin.

To make a thinner line still, lift up on the brush as you draw. After a while, you will be able to make lines in a variety of thicknesses.

5. Making a Grid for Enlarging

Sometimes the need arises to make a bigger version of a small drawing. An example is when you create a mural based on a small sketch. Follow these steps:

1. Using a ruler, draw evenly spaced lines across and up and down your original drawing (Figure T–1). Count

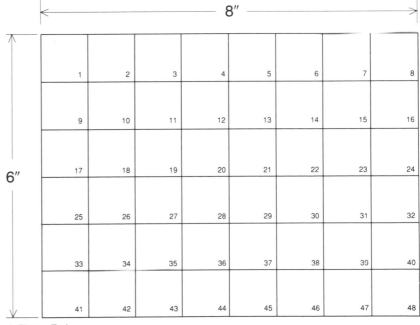

▲ Figure T–1

the number of squares you made from side to side. Count the number of squares running up and down.

2. Measure the width of the surface to which the drawing is to be transferred. Divide that figure by the number of side-to-side squares. The resulting number will be the horizontal measure of each square. You may work in inches or centimeters. Using a ruler or yardstick, mark off the squares. Draw in light rules.

3. Measure the height of the surface to which the drawing is to be transferred. Divide that figure by the number of up-and-down squares. The resulting number will be the vertical measure of each square. Mark off the squares. Draw in pencil lines.

4. Starting at the upper left, number each square on the original drawing. Give the

same number to each square on the large grid. Working a square at a time, transfer your image. (See Figure T–2.)

6. Using Shading Techniques

When using shading techniques, keep in mind the following:

- Lines or dots placed close together create dark values.
- Lines or dots placed far apart, on the other hand, create light values. To show a change from light to dark, start with lines or dots far apart and little by little bring them close together.
- Use care also to follow the shape of the object when adding lines. Straight lines are used to shade an object with a flat surface. Rounded lines are used to shade an object with a curved surface.

7. Using Sighting Techniques

Sighting is a technique that will help you draw objects in proportion.

1. Face the object you plan to draw. Hold a pencil straight up and down at arm's length. Your thumb should rest against the side of the pencil and be even with the tip.

2. Close one eye. With your other eye, focus on the object.

3. Slide your thumb down the pencil until the exposed part of the pencil matches the object's height. (See Figure T–3.)

▲ Figure T–3

4. Now, without moving your thumb or bending your arm, turn the pencil sideways.

5. Focus on the width of the object. If the height is greater, figure out how many "widths" will fit in one "height." If the width is greater, figure out how many "heights" will fit in one "width."

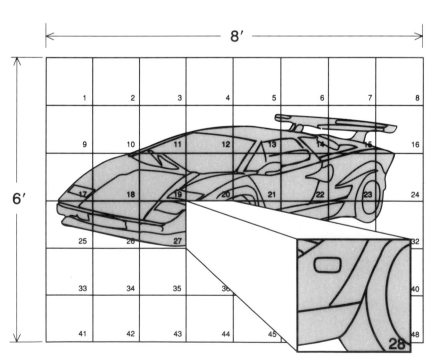

▲ Figure T–2

8. Using a Viewing Frame

Much in the way a camera is used to focus on one area of a scene, you can better zero in on an object you plan to draw by using a viewing frame (Figure T–4). To make a viewing frame do the following:

1. Cut a rectangular hole in a piece of paper about 2 inches (3 to 5 cm) in from the paper's edges.

2. Hold the paper at arm's length and look through the hole at your subject. Imagine that the hole represents your drawing paper.

3. Decide how much of the subject you want to have in your drawing.

4. By moving the frame up, down, sideways, nearer, or farther, you can change the focus of your drawing.

9. Using a Ruler

There are times when you need to draw a crisp, straight line. By using the following techniques, you will be able to do so.

1. Hold the ruler with one hand and the pencil with the other.

2. Place the ruler where you wish to draw a straight line.

3. Hold the ruler with your thumb and first two fingers. Be careful that your fingers do not stick out beyond the edge of the ruler.

4. Press heavily on the ruler so it will not slide while you're drawing.

5. Hold the pencil lightly against the ruler.

6. Pull the pencil quickly and lightly along the edge of the ruler. The object is to keep the ruler from moving while the pencil moves along its edge.

▲ Figure T–4

PAINTING TIPS

10. Cleaning a Paint Brush

Cleaning a paint brush properly helps it last a long time. *Always*:

1. Rinse the thick paint out of the brush under running water. Do not use hot water.

2. Gently paint the brush over a cake of mild soap, or dip it in a mild liquid detergent (Figure T–5).

▲ Figure T–5

3. Gently scrub the brush against the palm of your hand to work the soap into the brush. This removes paint you may not have realized was still in the brush.

4. Rinse the brush under running water while you continue to scrub your palm against it (Figure T–6).

▲**Figure T–6**

5. Repeat steps 2, 3, and 4 as needed.

When it is thoroughly rinsed and excess water has been squeezed from the brush, shape your brush into a point with your fingers (Figure T–7). Place the brush in a container with the bristles up so that it will keep its shape as it dries.

▲**Figure T–7**

11. Making Natural Earth Pigments

Anywhere there is dirt, clay, or sand, there is natural pigment. To create your own pigments, gather as many different kinds of earth colors as you can. Grind these as finely as possible. (If you can, borrow a mortar and pestle.) (See Figure T–8.) Do not worry if the pigment is slightly gritty.

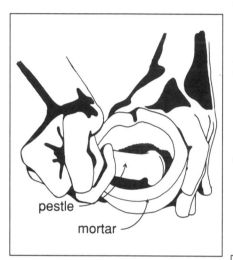

pestle

mortar

▲**Figure T–8**

To make the binder, mix equal parts of white glue and water. Place a few spoonfuls of your powdered pigment into a small jar. Add a little of the binder. Experiment with different amounts of each.

When you work with natural pigments, remember always to wash the brushes before the paint in them has a chance to dry. The glue from the binder can ruin a brush. As you work, stir the paint every now and then. This will keep the grains of pigment from settling to the bottom of the jar.

Make a fresh batch each time you paint.

12. Mixing Paint to Change the Value of Color

You can better control the colors in your work when you mix your own paint. In mixing paints, treat opaque paints (for example, tempera) differently from transparent paints (for example, watercolors).

- *For light values of opaque paints.* Mix only a small amount of the hue to white. The color can always be made stronger by adding more of the hue.
- *For dark values of opaque paints.* Add a small amount of black to the hue. Never add the hue to black.
- *For light values of transparent paints.* Thin a shaded area with water (Figure T–9). This allows more of the white of the paper to show through.
- *For dark values of transparent paints.* Carefully add a small amount of black to the hue.

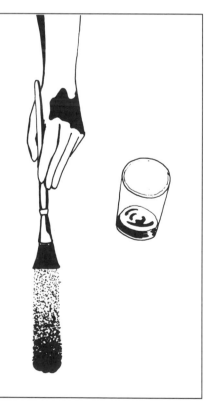

▲**Figure T–9**

13. Working with Poster Paints (School Tempera)

When using poster paints (school tempera) remember the following:

- Poster paints run when wet. To keep this from happening, make sure one shape is dry before painting a wet color next to it.

14. Working with Watercolors

- If you apply wet paint to damp paper, you create lines and shapes with soft edges.
- If you apply wet paint to dry paper, you create lines and shapes with sharp, clear edges.
- If you dip a dry brush into damp paint and then brush across dry paper, you achieve a fuzzy effect.
- School watercolors come in semi-moist cakes. Before you use them, place a drop of water on each cake to let the paint soften. Watercolor paints are transparent. You can see the white paper through the paint. If you want a light value of a hue, dilute the paint with a large amount of water. If you want a bright hue, you must dissolve more pigment by swirling your brush around in the cake of paint until you have dissolved a great deal of paint. The paint you apply to the paper can be as bright as the paint in the cake.

15. Making a Stamp Printing

A stamp print is an easy way to make repetitive designs. The following are a few suggestions for making a stamp and printing with it. You may develop some other ideas after reading these hints. Remember, printing reverses your design, so if you use letters, be certain to cut or carve them backwards.

- Cut a simple design into the flat surface of an eraser with a knife that has a fine, precision blade.
- Cut a potato, carrot, or turnip in half. Use a paring knife to carve a design into the flat surface of the vegetable.
- Glue yarn to a bottle cap or a jar lid.
- Glue found objects to a piece of corrugated cardboard. Make a design with paper-clips, washers, nuts, leaves, feathers, or anything else you can find. Whatever object you use should have a fairly flat surface. Make a handle for the block with masking tape.
- Cut shapes out of a piece of inner tube material. Glue the shapes to a piece of heavy cardboard.

There are several ways to apply ink or paint to a stamp:

- Roll water-based printing ink on the stamp with a soft brayer.
- Roll water-based printing ink on a plate and press the stamp into the ink.
- Apply tempera paint or school acrylic to the stamp with a bristle brush.

16. Working with Clay

To make your work with clay go smoothly, always do the following:

1. Dip one or two fingers in water.
2. Spread the moisture from your fingers over your palms.

Never dip your hands in water. Too much moisture turns clay into mud.

17. Joining Clay

If you are creating a piece of sculpture that requires joining pieces, do the following:

1. Gather the materials you will need. These include clay, slip, (a creamy mixture of clay and water), a paint brush, a scoring tool, (perhaps a kitchen fork) and clay tools.
2. Rough up or scratch the two surfaces to be joined (Figure T–10).

▲ **Figure T–10**

3. Apply slip to one of the two surfaces using a paint brush or your fingers (Figure T–11).

▲ Figure T–11

4. Gently press the two surfaces together so the slip oozes out of the joining seam (Figure T–12).

▲ Figure T–12

5. Using clay tools and/or your fingers, smooth away the slip that has oozed out of the seam (Figure T–13). You may wish to smooth out the seam as well, or you may wish to leave it for decorative purposes.

▲ Figure T–13

18. Making a Clay Mold for a Plaster Relief

One of the easiest ways to make a plaster relief is with a clay mold. When making a clay mold, remember the following:

- Plaster poured into the mold will come out with the opposite image. Design details cut into the mold will appear raised on the relief. Details built up within the mold will appear indented in the relief.
- Do not make impressions in your mold that have *undercuts* (Figure T–14). Undercuts trap plaster, which will break off when the relief is removed. When cutting impressions, keep the deepest parts the narrowest.
- In carving a raised area in the mold, take care not to create a reverse undercut (Figure T–15).

If you want to change the mold simply smooth the area with your fingers.

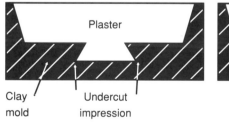

▲ Figure T–14

▲ Figure T–15

19. Mixing Plaster

Mixing plaster requires some technique and a certain amount of caution. It can also be a very simple matter when you are prepared. Always do the following:

- Use caution when working with dry plaster. Wear a dust mask or work in a well-ventilated room.
- Cover your work space to keep the dust from spreading.
- Always use a plastic bowl and a stick for mixing. Never use silverware you will later eat from.
- Always use plaster that is fine, like sifted flour. Plaster should never be grainy when dry.
- Always add the water to the bowl first. Sift in the plaster. Stir slowly.
- Never pour unused plaster down a drain. Allow it to dry in the bowl. To remove the dried plaster, twist the bowl. Crack the loose plaster into a lined trash can.

20. Working with Papier-Mâché

Papier-mâché (**pay**-puhr muh-**shay**) is a French term meaning "chewed paper." It is also the name of several sculpting methods using newspaper and liquid paste. These methods can be used to model tiny pieces of jewelry. They can also be used to create life-size creatures.

In creating papier-mâché sculptures, the paper-and-paste mixture is molded over a support. You will learn more about supports shortly. The molded newspaper dries to a hard finish. The following are three methods for working with papier-mâché:

- **Pulp Method**. Shred newspaper, paper towels, or tissue paper into tiny pieces. (Do not use glossy magazine paper; it will not soften.) Soak your paper in water overnight. Press the paper in a kitchen strainer to remove as much moisture as possible. Mix the mashed paper with commercially prepared papier-mâché paste or white glue. The mixture should have the consistency of soft clay. Add a few drops of oil of cloves to keep the mixture from spoiling. A spoonful of linseed oil makes the mixture smoother. (If needed, the mixture can be stored at this point in a plastic bag in the refrigerator.) Use the mixture to model small shapes. When your creations dry, they can be sanded. You will also be able to drill holes in them.
- **Strip Method**. Tear newspaper into strips. Either dip the strips in papier-mâché paste or rub paste on them. Apply the strips to your support (Figure T–16). If you do not want the strips to stick to your

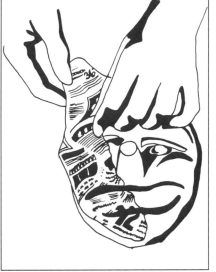

▲ Figure T–16

support, first cover it with plastic wrap. Use wide strips for large shapes. Use thin strips for smaller shapes. If you plan to remove your finished creation from the support, apply five or six layers. (Change directions with each layer so you can keep track of the number.) Otherwise, two or three layers should be enough. After applying the strips to your support, rub your fingers over the surface.

As a last layer, use torn paper towels. The brown paper towels that are found in schools produce an uncomplicated surface on which to paint. Make sure no rough edges are sticking up. Store any unused paste mixture in the refrigerator to keep it from spoiling.

- **Draping Method**. Spread papier-mâché paste on newspaper. Lay a second sheet on top of the first. Smooth the layers. Add another layer of paste and another sheet of paper. Repeat until you have four or five layers of paper. Use this method for making drapery on a figure. (See Figure T–17.) If you allow the lay-

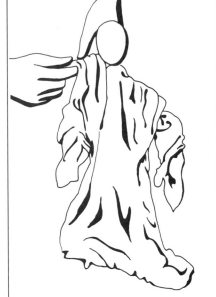

▲ Figure T–17

ers to dry for a day or two, they will become leathery. They can then be cut and molded as you like. Newspaper strips dipped in paste can be used to seal cracks.

Like papier-mâché, supports for papier-mâché creations can be made in several different ways. Dry newspaper may be wadded up and wrapped with string or tape (Figure T–18). Wire coat hangers may be padded with rags. For large figures, a wooden frame covered with chicken wire makes a good support.

▲ Figure T–18

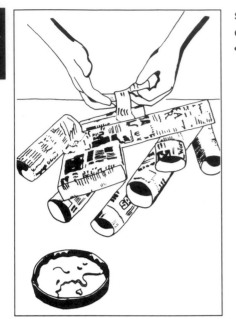

▲ **Figure T–19**

To create a base for your papier-mâché creations, tape together arrangements of found materials. Some materials you might combine are boxes, tubes, and bowls. (See Figure T–19.) Clay can also be modeled as a base. If clay is used, be sure there are no undercuts that would keep the papier-mâché from lifting off easily when dry. (For an explanation of under-cuts, see Technique Tip **18**, *Handbook* page **276**.)

Always allow time for your papier-mâché creations to dry. The material needs extra drying time when thick layers are used or when the weather is damp. An electric fan blowing air on the material can shorten the drying time.

21. Making a Paper Sculpture

Another name for paper sculpture is origami. The process originated in Japan and means "folding paper." Paper sculpture begins with a flat piece of paper. The paper is then curved or bent to produce more than a flat

surface. Here are some ways to experiment with paper.

- **Scoring.** Place a square sheet of heavy construction paper, 12 x 12 inch (30 x 30 cm), on a flat surface. Position the ruler on the paper so that it is close to the center and parallel to the sides. Holding the ruler in place, run the point of a knife or a pair of scissors along one of the ruler's edges. Press down firmly but take care not to cut through the paper. Gently crease the paper along the line you made. Hold your paper with the crease facing upward.

- **Pleating.** Take a piece of paper and fold it one inch from the edge. Then fold the paper in the other direction. Continue folding back and forth.

- **Curling.** Hold one end of a long strip of paper with the thumb and forefinger of one hand. At a point right below where you are holding the strip, grip it lightly between the side of a pencil and the thumb of your other hand. In a quick motion, run the pencil along the strip. This will cause the strip to curl back on itself. Don't apply too much pressure, or the strip will tear. (See Figure T–20.)

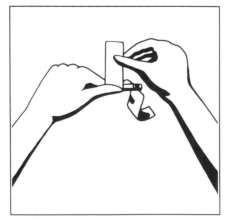

▲ **Figure T–20**

22. Measuring Rectangles

Do you find it hard to create perfectly formed rectangles? Here is a way of getting the job done:

1. Make a light pencil dot near the long edge of a sheet of paper. With a ruler, measure the exact distance between the dot and the edge. Make three more dots the same distance in from the edge. (See Figure T–21.)

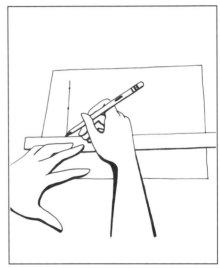

▲ **Figure T–21**

2. Line a ruler up along the dots. Make a light pencil line running the length of the paper.

3. Turn the paper so that a short side is facing you. Make four pencil dots equally distant from the short edge. Connect these with a light pencil rule. Stop when you reach the first line you drew. (See Figure T–22.)

4. Do the same for the remaining two sides. Erase any lines that may extend beyond the box you have made.

5. Trace over the lines with your ruler and pencil.

The box you have created will be a perfectly formed rectangle.

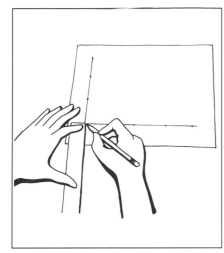

▲ Figure T–22

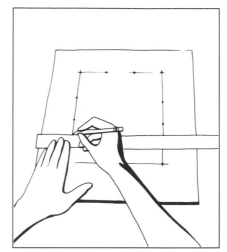

▲ Figure T–23

23. Making a Mat

You can add appeal to an art work by making a mat, using the following steps.

1. Gather the materials you will need. These include a metal rule, a pencil, mat board, cardboard backing, a sheet of heavy cardboard to protect your work surface, a mat knife with a sharp blade, and wide masking tape.
2. Wash your hands. Mat board should be kept very clean.
3. Measure the height and width of the work to be matted. Decide how large a border you want for your work. (A border of approximately 2½ inches on three sides with 3 inches on the bottom is aesthetically pleasing.) Your work will be behind the window you will cut.
4. Plan for the opening, or window, to be ¼ inch smaller on all sides than the size of your work. For example, if your work measures 9 by 12 inches, the mat window should measure 8½ inches (9 inches minus ¼ inch times two) by 11½ inches (12 inches minus ¼ inch times two). Using your metal rule and pencil, lightly draw your window rectangle on the back of the board 2½ inches from the top and left edge of the mat. (See Figure T–23.) Add a 2½ inch border to the right of the window and a 3 inch border to the bottom, lightly drawing cutting guidelines.

   Note: If you are working with metric measurements, the window should overlap your work by 0.5 cm (centimeters) on all sides. Therefore, if your work measures 24 by 30 cm, the mat window measures 23 cm (24 − [2 x 0.5]) by 29 cm (30 − [2 x 0.5]).

▲ Figure T–24

5. Place the sheet of heavy, protective cardboard on your work surface. Place the mat board, pencil marks up, over the cardboard. Holding the metal rule firmly in place, score the first line with your knife. Always place the metal rule so that your blade is away from the frame. (See Figure T–24.) In case you make an error you will cut into the window hole or the extra mat that is not used for the frame. Do not try to cut through the board with one stroke. By the third or fourth stroke, you should be able to cut through the board easily.
6. Working in the same fashion, score and cut through the board along all the window lines. Be careful not to go beyond the lines. Remove the window.
7. Cut a cardboard backing for your art work that is slightly smaller than the overall size of your mat. Using a piece of broad masking tape, hinge the back of the mat to the backing. (See Figure T–25.)

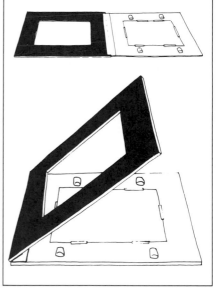

▲ Figure T–25

Position your art work between the backing and the mat and attach it with tape. Anchor the frame to the cardboard with a few pieces of rolled tape.

24. Mounting a Two-Dimensional Work

Mounting pictures that you make gives them a professional look. To mount a work, do the following:

1. Gather the materials you will need. These include a yardstick, a pencil, poster board, a sheet of heavy cardboard, a knife with a very sharp blade, a sheet of newspaper, and rubber cement.
2. Measure the height and width of the work to be mounted. Decide how large a border you want around the work. Plan your mount size using the work's measurements. To end up with a 3-inch (8 cm) border, for example, make your mount 6 inches (15 cm) wider and higher than your work. Record the measurements for your mount.
3. Using your yardstick and pencil, lightly draw your mount rectangle on the back of the poster board. Measure from the edges of the poster board. If you have a large paper cutter available, you may use it to cut your mount.
4. Place the sheet of heavy cardboard on your work surface. Place the poster board, pencil marks up, over the cardboard. Holding the yardstick firmly in place along one line, score the line with your knife. Do not try to cut through the board with one stroke. By the third try, you should be able to cut through the board.

▲ Figure T–26

5. Place the art work on the mount. Using the yardstick, center the work. Mark each corner with a dot. (See Figure T–26.)
6. Place the art work, face down, on a sheet of newspaper. Coat the back of the work with rubber cement. (*Safety Note:* Always use rubber cement in a room with plenty of ventilation.) *If your mount is to be permanent, skip to Step 8.*
7. Line up the corners of your work with the dots on the mounting board. Smooth the work into place. *Skip to Step 9.*
8. After coating the back of your art work, coat the poster board with rubber cement. Be careful not to add cement to the border area. Have a partner hold your art work in the air by the two top corners. Once the two glued surfaces meet, you will not be able to change the position of the work. Grasp the lower two corners. Carefully lower the work to the mounting board. Line up the two corners with the bottom dots. Little by little, lower the work into place (Figure T–27). Press it smooth.

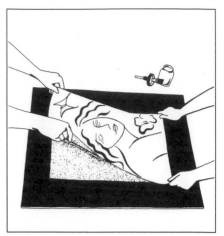

▲ Figure T–27

9. To remove any excess cement, create a small ball of nearly dry rubber cement. Use the ball of rubber cement to pick up excess cement.

25. Making Rubbings

Rubbings make interesting textures and designs. They may also be used with other media to create mixed-media art. To make a rubbing, place a sheet of thin paper on top of the surface to be rubbed. Hold the paper in place with one hand. With the other hand, rub the paper with the flat side of an unwrapped crayon. Always rub away from the hand holding the paper. Never rub back and forth, since this may cause the paper to slip.

26. Scoring Paper

The secret to creating neat, sharp folds in cardboard or paper is a technique called scoring. Here is how it is done:

1. Line up a ruler along the line you want to fold.
2. Lightly run a sharp knife or scissors along the fold line. Press down firmly enough to leave a light crease. Take care not to cut all the way through the paper (Figure T–28).

▲ Figure T–28

3. Gently crease the paper along the line you made. To score curved lines, use the same technique. Make sure your curves are wide enough to ensure a clean fold. Too tight a curve will cause the paper to wrinkle (Figure T–29).

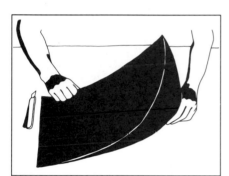

▲ Figure T–29

27. Making a Tissue Paper Collage

For your first experience with tissue, make a free design with the tissue colors. Start with the lightest colors of tissue first and save the darkest for last. It is difficult to change the color of dark tissue by overlapping it with other colors. If one area becomes too dark, you might cut out a piece of white paper, glue it over the dark area carefully, and apply new colors over the white area.

1. Apply a coat of adhesive to the area where you wish to place the tissue.
2. Place the tissue down carefully over the wet area (Figure T–30). Don't let your fingers get wet.
3. Then add another coat of adhesive over the tissue. If your brush picks up any color from the wet tissue, rinse your brush in water and let it dry before using it again.
4. Experiment by overlapping colors. Allow the tissue to wrinkle to create textures as you apply it. Be sure that all the loose edges of tissue are glued down.

28. Working with Glue

When applying glue, always start at the center of the surface you are coating and work outward.

- When gluing papers together don't use a lot of glue, just a dot will do. Use dots in the corners and along the edges. Press the two surfaces together. Keep dots at least ½ inch (1.3 cm) in from the edge of your paper.
- Handle a glued surface carefully with only your fingertips. Make sure your hands are clean before pressing the glued surface into place.
- *Note:* The glue should be as thin as possible. Thick or beaded glue will create ridges on your work.

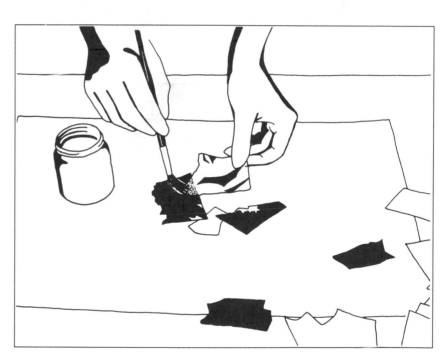

▲ Figure T–30

▲ Artists, down through the ages, have helped us visualize what we learn about history. Art historians are responsible for much of what we know about the artists who have lived in the past.

Romare Bearden

1911–1988
American Painter, Printmaker,
Collage Artist

Saturday Morning
  page 54

"Most artists take some place, and like a flower, they sink roots," Romare Bearden once said. "My roots are in North Carolina." Bearden spent his early childhood near Charlotte, North Carolina. Later, he moved to Pittsburgh, Pennsylvania, and then to New York City. These locations form the background for much of his art.

Bearden's artwork shows not only places but also the people of these areas. His paintings and collages show a rich mix of many aspects of his African-American heritage. His collages have been called quiltlike. They reflect the patchwork quilts made by African-American women in rural areas of North Carolina.

To create his collages, Bearden cut pieces of photographs from newspapers and magazines. Then he arranged them into tight compositions and pasted them on canvas. Like music and literature, Bearden's art tells stories. Some of his collages show the struggle of life in the inner city. Others reveal the joys and sorrow of African-American family life.

In addition to being an artist, Bearden was a musician. He found great inspiration in blues and jazz music. This influence can be seen in the "visual jazz" that he created in his collages.

In the art of printmaking, Katsushika Hokusai is considered the greatest artist of the Japanese style known as Ukiyo-e. The Ukiyo-e style means "pictures of the floating world." Several famous Impressionist painters, including Edgar Degas, Claude Monet, and Henri de Toulouse-Lautrec, collected Hokusai's prints. Hokusai's work had a great influence on the works of these artists.

Hokusai was born to a poor family in Edo (now Tokyo), Japan, in 1760. He studied woodcut printmaking under a Ukiyo-e master. Hokusai created a great number of color prints and book illustrations. These works reflected the lives and customs of the Japanese people. He also painted many landscapes.

Hokusai had done little of the work that has made him famous before he was 60 years old. In his lifetime, Hokusai created an estimated 30,000 pieces of art. Despite producing so much work, Hokusai was a humble man. As he neared death at the age of 89, he said, "If the gods had given me only ten more years I could have become a truly great painter."

Katsushika Hokusai

1760–1849
Japanese Printmaker, Painter

Fishing Boats at Choshi in Shoshu
  page 32

A Gust of Wind at Ejiri
  page 117

Judith Leyster
1609–1660
Dutch Painter

Self-Portrait
page 80

Judith Leyster's name was hardly seen in art history books until 1893, more than 200 years after her death. At that time, workers at the Louvre made an important discovery. While cleaning a painting thought to be by Frans Hals, the workers found Judith Leyster's signature.

Leyster was born in Haarlem, Holland, in 1609. During that time, most female artists were helped by artist fathers. Because Leyster's father was not an artist, she had to rely on talent alone. Leyster also differed from other female painters in her choice of subject matter. Instead of still lifes, Leyster chose to paint *genre* paintings. These were scenes of ordinary life.

Early in her career, Leyster gained recognition. When she was 17, her name was mentioned in a book about Haarlem artists. At 24, she was elected to the painter's Guild of St. Luke. Then she taught painting for several years.

Some of Leyster's most original works are her small genre paintings of women doing household activities. These include scenes in which women are combing their children's hair or sewing by the fireside. Leyster was one of the first artists to paint subjects such as these.

René Magritte was a master of surrealism. When people view his paintings, they often look for hidden symbolism. That is not what the artist wanted, however. Magritte wrote, "People who look for symbolic meanings fail to grasp the inherent poetry and mystery of the image...."

Magritte studied art at the Académie Royale des Beaux-Arts in Brussels, Belgium. To support himself, he worked as a commercial artist for many years and even designed wallpaper.

The objects in Magritte's works are usually ordinary, and they are painted very realistically. What makes the artworks thought-provoking is the unusual placement of the objects. The artist wanted viewers to see the commonplace in a completely different way.

Magritte, however, did not think of himself as an artist. In fact, he did not even have an art studio. Instead, he painted in the living room of his home. Each week, a group of his fellow Surrealist painters came to his home. They would meet to discuss titles for Magritte's unusual paintings.

Today, Magritte's work continues to have a major influence on the world. His images have also inspired many commercial advertisements.

René Magritte
1898–1967
Belgian Painter

The Human Condition
page 268

Claude Monet

1840–1926
French Painter

Stack of Wheat
page **12**

Poplars on the Bank of the Epte River
page **96**

Claude Monet is considered the father of the art movement called Impressionism. He was born in 1840 in a small town in France. Although a poor student, he developed great skill in drawing.

Monet studied at the Paris Academy. To exhibit works at the academy, artists had to follow strict rules. Monet and a group of young artists did not like those rules, so they left to paint out-doors. They painted with dabs of color. When viewed from a distance, the colors blended together.

In 1874 Monet and these other artists held their own exhibit. The paintings in the show shocked the public. One of Monet's paintings in this exhibit was called *Impression: Sunrise*. An angry critic used that title to label the group *Impressionists*.

Monet was interested in the effects of light and how it changed the appearance of objects, particularly their colors. To capture these changes, he made many paintings of the same scene at different times of the day. In this way, he illustrated the changing light and how it affected color.

In 1883 Monet settled at Giverny, France. There he designed his own gardens, including a water lily pond. This pond is fea-tured in many of Monet's paintings.

From the age of 12, Georgia O'Keeffe knew that she wanted to be an artist. She lived to be nearly 100 years old, and she painted for most of those years.

Georgia O'Keeffe was born in Sun Prairie, Wisconsin, in 1887. She studied art with several teachers, learning special techniques from each. From one teacher, she learned how to "fill space in a beautiful way." This sensitivity to space can be seen in all her work, but especially in her flower paintings. O'Keeffe painted flowers of enormous size. She did this because she wanted to surprise viewers and make them take time to see what she saw.

O'Keeffe loved the southwestern United States and lived in New Mexico for many years. She found artistic inspiration in the desert landscape. She saw beautiful form in the plants, mountains, and animals that surrounded her. Some of her paint-ings of the animal bones that she found in the desert shocked people. Eventually, though, they became some of O'Keeffe's most famous works.

Georgia O'Keeffe

1887–1986
American Painter

Red Cannas
page **184**

Marjorie Phillips
1894–1985
American Painter

Night Baseball
page **206**

Although Marjorie Phillips was not an avid baseball fan, two of her most famous paintings feature baseball games. One of her paintings, *Night Baseball,* seemed so authentic that the Baseball Hall of Fame wanted to buy it.

Phillips studied art at the Art Students League in New York. In 1921, she married Duncan Phillips, and the couple founded the Phillips Collection, an art museum. Located in Washington, D.C., the gallery was the first museum of modern art in the United States.

In 1923, Marjorie Phillips had her first one-woman show. Many of her paintings were still lifes and landscapes in the Impressionist style. "I decided to paint the celebration of the wonder of the world," she said. "I didn't want to paint depressing pictures…. That's why my paintings are all on the cheerful side—I felt it was needed."

After her husband's death in 1966, Marjorie Phillips took over as director of the museum. Despite her busy schedule, Phillips always found time to paint. In 1977, at the age of 81, she had a one-woman show in which most of the paintings were less than ten years old.

Mexican painter Diego Rivera believed that art was meant for the working people. He felt that it should be available to everyone, not just people who visited museums. Rivera chose to paint huge murals on the sides of public buildings. His work adorns the walls of the Detroit Institute of Arts in Michigan as well as many buildings in Mexico.

Rivera was born in Guanajuato, Mexico, in 1886. He studied at the Academy of San Carlos in Mexico City. Between 1907 and 1921, he took two trips to Europe. There he studied the paintings of the great masters.

When Rivera returned to Mexico in 1921, he began creating large murals. These works were based on social themes, including the history, culture, and problems of Mexico. Rivera held strong political beliefs, which he sometimes included in his art. He used vivid colors in bold, simple designs.

In 1929, Rivera married Frida Kahlo. She was also a well-known Mexican painter. When he died in 1957, Rivera left his final work unfinished. It was his most ambitious project—a mural showing the history of Mexico for the National Palace in Mexico City.

Diego Rivera
1886–1957
Mexican Painter, Muralist

*The Making of a Fresco
Showing the Building
of a City*
page **232**

Jan Steen
1626–1679
Dutch Painter

The Dancing Couple
page 94

Jan Steen was as much a storyteller as he was an artist. Many of his genre paintings, or scenes of everyday life, tell humorous stories. They have entertained viewers for centuries.

During Steen's time, most artists concentrated on one type of painting, such as still life. Steen, however, did not limit himself in this way. Although he is most well known for his genre paintings, Steen's work also included still lifes, portraits, and biblical subjects.

Other artists of this time, such as Vermeer, also created genre paintings. These artists most often painted calm, quiet scenes with one or two people performing everyday tasks. Steen's works, however, were very different. He painted scenes filled with happy, loud people enjoying themselves. To create an added sense of realism, Steen often included himself and his wife and children in the paintings.

There is a Dutch expression, "a Jan Steen household," that is still used today. It refers to a home filled with happy chaos, similar to the homes depicted in Steen's paintings.

Leonardo da Vinci is probably most famous for his paintings of the *Mona Lisa* and *The Last Supper*. He was more than just an extraordinary artist, however. Leonardo was also a great scholar. He was well educated in many subjects, including anatomy, physics, geography, and architecture.

Showing talent for drawing as a young child, Leonardo trained under the artist Andrea del Verrocchio. He soon rejected both the egg tempera and fresco media that were commonly used. Instead, Leonardo turned to oil paints, which had recently been invented by the Flemish painter Jan van Eyck.

In many ways, Leonardo da Vinci was well ahead of his time. He was constantly inventing, searching, and trying new ideas. His notebooks fascinate us with ideas for ways to fly, complex machines, and studies of the human body.

Unfortunately, Leonardo's passion for experimenting did not always work out. When he painted the *The Last Supper*, Leonardo mixed oil with the fresco medium. Fresco is painted with water-base paint on freshly laid plaster. Because oil and water do not mix, the oil he added would not stick to the wall. The mural had begun to fade and flake even during Leonardo's lifetime. With continual efforts to preserve it, however, it remains one of the most well-known works of all time.

Leonardo da Vinci
1452–1519
Italian Painter

Oak Leafs and a Spray of Greenwood
page 108

Advertising Artist

Advertising artists design the artwork that is used in advertisements. They usually work for an advertising agency. They may also work for a publication, such as a magazine or newspaper. Some advertising artists work in the ad department of a large corporation, such as a store or restaurant chain.

Advertising artists work as part of a design team. This team includes an art director, designers, and writers. First, the art director develops a concept, or idea, for an advertisement. The copywriters write the words that will appear in the ad. Then the artist creates a design that works with both the art director's concept and the words. Many advertising artists use computers when creating their artwork.

A career as an advertising artist usually requires a college education in art or design. Courses in computer design techniques are very valuable. Once they are hired, advertising artists may also receive on-the-job training.

Architect

An architect is an artist who designs buildings and other structures. Your home, school, and local shopping mall were all designed by architects. An architect prepares plans that show both the interior and exterior of a building. These sketches include floor plans that show the placement of rooms, hallways, doors, windows, closets, and other features. They also show the exterior walls on all sides of the building and a top-down drawing of the roof.

A building design must be not only visually pleasing but also functional and safe. When planning a building, architects must consider how the structure will be used. For example, the design for a home would be very different from the design for a restaurant or hospital. Architects must also keep in mind the needs of the people who will use the building. This includes such subjects as traffic patterns, living and work areas, and storage space. They must also know about heating and cooling, ventilation, and plumbing.

Architects need a college degree in architecture. They take courses in math, engineering, and drafting. In addition, they must pass an exam to become licensed.

Art Director

Art directors are responsible for the look of the advertisements that you see in newspapers, in magazines, and on television. They are also responsible for the style and design of magazines, and of books like this one. Art directors most often work in the fields of advertising and publishing.

An art director studies the information that needs to be presented. He or she must decide how that information can be shown in a visually appealing way. The art director then works with a design team that includes artists, designers, and copywriters. The art director oversees the team's work and checks to make sure that the final printed material is satisfactory.

Most art directors have a college education. Courses should provide a well-rounded background in art and design. Art directors study graphic design, drafting, layout, photography, and computer design. Several years of on-the-job training are required before a person can become an art director.

Art Teacher

Art teachers instruct students in the use of various art materials and techniques. They also educate students in the theories and principles of art criticism, aesthetics, and art history. In middle schools, art teachers provide general art instruction. Art teachers in high schools may specialize in a specific area, such as painting, drawing, or crafts.

In a classroom, the art teacher helps students create their own artwork. Students are taught how to use a wide variety of media, such as pencils, charcoal, pastels, paints, and clay. The teacher encourages students to analyze their own work as well as the works of master artists.

Art teachers must have a college degree. Their educational background includes courses in both art and teaching. Many art teachers continue to study and exhibit their own artwork throughout their teaching careers. An essential part of being an art teacher is a love of art and a desire to encourage this appreciation in others.

Artist

Artists create works of art. Their work is usually classified as either fine art or applied art. Fine art, such as a painting, is created simply to be viewed and appreciated. Applied art, such as ceramics or other crafts objects, serves a more practical purpose.

The work of an artist may involve a variety of media. The media are the materials used to create the art. A painter, for instance, might use oil, watercolor, or acrylic paint. A sculptor might create art out of stone, clay, or wood. Other artists might create jewelry, pottery, or furniture from such materials as metal, clay, or plastic.

Although not all artists have a college education, almost all have had formal art instruction. This training includes studio art classes, such as drawing, painting, and design. It also includes courses in art history. One of the most important requirements for a career as an artist is a natural talent in art.

Graphic Artist

Graphic artists design artwork for many types of products. These products might include packaging and promotional displays, brochures, advertisements, magazines, and books like the one you are reading. Graphic artists are often employed in the publishing or advertising fields. However, they may also work in other areas, such as designing the boxes that hold videos and computer games. They frequently work as a member of a design team.

Most graphic artists use computers to help in the creation of their artwork. Computer technology saves time by performing some of the tasks that artists previously had to do by hand. For example, artists can use computer graphics to easily experiment with a variety of colors, shapes, and designs.

A career in graphic art generally requires a college education and formal art training. In addition, graphic artists must have an in-depth knowledge of computer graphics. Because the computer field changes so rapidly, graphic artists must continually learn about new technology.

Illustrator

The work of an illustrator revolves around drawing. Illustrators may create many different types of artwork. Most specialize in one field, such as technical illustration. Illustrators often work in the publishing and advertising industries.

A technical illustrator specializes in drawing diagrams. These might be included in instructional manuals. They help explain how to use appliances or equipment, such as a computer or VCR. A fashion illustrator draws sketches of clothing and accessories. Fashion illustrations might appear in catalogs, advertisements, or magazines.

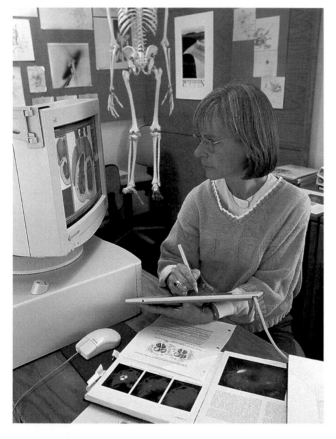

Most illustrators have a college degree in art. Besides drawing, they learn about design, composition, and perspective. Illustrators who want to concentrate on one area must also take courses related to that subject. For example, a medical illustrator must study biology and medicine.

Industrial Designer

Have you ever wondered who designed your favorite toys and electronic games? Those are the work of industrial designers. They design manufactured products, such as computers, kitchen appliances, and cars. Industrial designers usually work for large companies, such as toy, equipment, or machine manufacturers.

Industrial designers develop new products. They also make improvements to existing products, such as adding new features or changing the design of an automobile. When developing a product, industrial designers first do research. The designers need to know who will use the product and how they will use it. Industrial designers also must evaluate similar products that are already available. Then they combine this knowledge with their artistic ability. Their goal is to create products that will work well and be popular with the consumers who purchase them.

A career in industrial design requires a college education. In addition to art courses, industrial designers study computer-aided design. Many designers use computer technology when developing products.

Interior Designer

Interior designers plan the interior space of buildings. These buildings might include homes, offices, hotels, or restaurants. Sometimes interior designers plan upgrades to existing buildings. In addition to preparing drawings, interior designers choose furniture, carpeting, and window coverings. They also select lighting and color schemes. Interior designers must make sure that all of these individual parts work together as a whole and are aesthetically pleasing.

When planning an interior space, the interior designer must always consider the client's needs, tastes, and budget. Many designers use computer programs to create several versions of an interior plan. Using a computer also allows the designer to easily make changes to suit the client's wishes.

To be an interior designer, you need a college education. Courses include drawing, design, and art history. Interior designers also must show creativity, a flair for color, and an eye for detail.

Landscape Architect

Landscape architects combine their love of nature and the environment with their artistic ability. They design outdoor areas such as those surrounding houses or apartment complexes, shopping centers, and office buildings.

Landscape architects choose which types of trees, bushes, and flowers are best suited for the location. Then they draw sketches of how these plants should be arranged. One goal of a landscape architect is to make sure that the design is not only functional but also attractive. Another goal is to make sure that the design works well with the natural environment. As in all design fields, more and more landscape architects are using computers to complete their work more efficiently.

A career in landscape architecture requires a college education. Courses include landscape design and construction, surveying, and city and regional planning. In addition, landscape architects study science and nature and take studio art courses.

Museum Worker

Some people combine their love of art and museums to become museum employees. There are a wide variety of museums across the country. Some show artwork, such as paintings, sculpture, or photographs. Others house objects of historical value, such as antique clothing or furniture. Still others display items related to science or natural history, such as dinosaur skeletons.

People who work in museums may have several different types of jobs. A curator chooses and obtains the objects that will be displayed in the museum. An assistant curator helps the curator set up the museum exhibits. A conservator cares for and preserves the objects kept in the museum. A tour guide provides information about exhibits to the museum's visitors and answers their questions.

The degree of education required for a museum worker varies depending on the type of work. Most museum workers, however, are highly educated. Many have advanced college degrees and are considered experts in their field.

Photographer

Photographers are skilled artists who use their cameras to create artwork. Their work varies greatly depending on what type of photographs they take. For example, a catalog photographer works in a studio and takes pictures of objects such as food, clothing, or jewelry. A newspaper or magazine photographer works in the field, taking pictures of people and events in the news.

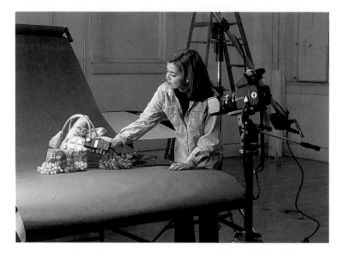

The work of photographers involves more than just taking the pictures. Photographers must first visualize the shot or set it up in an artistic way. After the pictures are taken, many photographers develop their own film in a darkroom. Then they print the slides or photographs.

A career as a photographer requires formal training in photography. Many photographers have a college degree in art. Photographers who specialize in certain areas, such as science, may need additional courses in that field. Beginning photographers sometimes receive training on the job by assisting a professional photographer.

Textile Designer

The fabric of the clothes you are wearing was designed by a textile designer. The word *textile* refers to cloth or fabric. Textile designers create and draw patterns for fabric. The fabric may be used in clothing, furniture upholstery, draperies, or rugs. Textile designers sometimes create their own original designs. At other times, they may adapt a design or develop one based on a certain theme. Textile designers work for companies that manufacture fabric.

Like other artists, textile designers must have creativity and artistic skill. They must also understand how fabric is constructed and manufactured. In addition, they need to be aware of current fashion trends. With this knowledge, they are better able to create popular designs.

Textile designers generally need a college education. They study art, design, and textiles. Many textile designers also take courses in computer technology, including computer-aided design.

Web-Site Designer

A web site is a location on the World Wide Web, which is part of the Internet. The Internet is a network of computer systems. It allows computer users to communicate with other users around the world. Web sites may be sponsored by companies, organizations, or individuals. They are most often used to provide information, promote products, and answer questions.

Web-site designers use computer software to create and maintain these sites. The work involves laying out web pages, designing graphic elements, and creating electronic links to other sites. Web-site designers may create sites for a large company or organization. They may also work for a design firm that creates sites for many companies.

To be a web-site designer, a person must have a background in art, with an emphasis on design. A web-site designer must also have technical training in computers and computer programming. Keeping current with the latest technology is an important part of the job.

LESSON 1

Making A Color Wheel

Are you amazed at a rainbow's colors every time you see one? It might have been such an experience that inspired the colorful painting in Figure S–1. Examine this work. It is an example of a twentieth-century style of painting known as Hard-Edge painting. Works of this style use simple shapes and vivid colors. Like a rainbow, this painting features bands of color that change and blend. Why do you suppose the artist has included thirteen bands in all? Which color contains the extra panel?

WHAT YOU WILL LEARN

You will create a one-of-a-kind color wheel. Rather than use simple geometric shapes, as the Hard-Edge artist has done in the work on this page, you will choose a basic free-form shape. This will represent a real or imaginary plant, animal, or other object. As in Figure S–1, you will repeat the same shape. You will arrange your shapes in a circle on construction paper, placing the shapes in their correct order on the color wheel.

WHAT YOU WILL NEED

- Sketch paper and pencil
- Scissors
- Sheets of construction paper in primary, secondary, and intermediate hues, 6 x 9 inches (15 x 23 cm)
- Black construction paper, 18 x 24 inches (46 x 60 cm)
- White glue or glue stick

Figure S–1   **Identify the primary, secondary, and intermediate hues. How much skill did Kelly need to paint these panels without any visible brush strokes?**

Ellsworth Kelly. *Spectrum II*. (Thirteen panels). 1966–67. Oil on canvas. 203.2 x 693.4 cm (80" x 22'9"). Saint Louis Art Museum, St. Louis, Missouri.

WHAT YOU WILL DO

1. With classmates, brainstorm a list of plants, animals, people, or objects that would be good subjects for a color wheel. Discuss which shapes might be the most interesting for this artwork.

2. Working by yourself, make several sketches of one of the shapes discussed. Choose your best sketch, and cut out the shape. This shape is to be a *template*, or stencil.

3. Place the template on a sheet of construction paper in one of the primary hues—blue, red, or yellow. Carefully trace around the shape using pencil. Place sheets of construction paper in the remaining two hues beneath the first. Line the sheets up. Carefully cut out the shape penciled on the first sheet. You will now have three copies of your template, one for each of the primary hues. Repeat this step, once for the secondary hues and again for the intermediate hues.

4. Note the arrangement of hues on the color wheel on page **8**. Arrange the shapes you have created in a circle in the order shown. Experiment with "flipping," or turning the shapes in different positions, being careful to maintain the color-wheel positions. When you are satisfied with your composition, glue the shapes in place.

EXAMINING YOUR WORK

- **Describe**   Identify the shape that appears in your color wheel. Tell whether it is a real, imaginary, or stylized shape.
- **Analyze**   Identify the sets of primary, secondary, and intermediate hues. Show where you have used the principle of repetition with respect to a single shape.
- **Interpret**   Explain why you chose this shape. Tell why it makes an interesting color wheel. What mood does it create?
- **Judge**   Decide whether you think your work is successful. Tell what you would do differently to improve the design.

ADDITIONAL STUDIOS

Figure S–2   Student work. Color wheel.

COMPUTER OPTION

■ Use the Pencil or Brush tool to draw the contour of your favorite shape. Choose the Lasso tool to select your shape. Make copies, and use the Rotate command to angle these. Arrange the copies in a circular fashion. Choose the Fill tool and color the shapes with the correct hues in their position on the color wheel on page **8.** Title, save, and print.

Creating a "Clan" Robe

Have you ever heard people with similar backgrounds or interests described as "birds of a feather"? To the Tlingit of the American Northwest, this expression was taken quite seriously. The object in Figure S–3, in fact, displays the "bird of a feather"—in this case, thunderbird—that served as a family crest to Tlingit of the Shungookeidi clan. Study this object. Notice the rich use of pattern and recurring motifs. Have you seen other Native American artifacts that made use of similar designs? What kind of balance has been used to organize this object?

WHAT YOU WILL LEARN

You will work with a group of classmates to create a blanket that represents your class. Begin by choosing an animal that symbolizes a quality you would like to emphasize. Design and cut your animal's shape from Kraft paper. Then cut and paste rounded geometric shapes, called *ovoids* and *U-forms*, to represent facial features and small details. You will add variety and contrast by alternately leaving thick and thin spaces between shapes.

Figure S–3 **This Chilkat robe repeats ovoid and U-form shapes that represent the inside and outside view of an animal.**

Naaxein (Tlingit) *Chilkat Woven Robe.* c. 1880. Mountain goat wool, yellow cedar bark, natural dyes. 131 x 170 cm (51⁵⁄₁₆ x 66¹⁵⁄₁₆"). Seattle Art Museum, Seattle, Washington.

WHAT YOU WILL NEED

- Sketch paper and pencil
- Sheet of Kraft paper in a dark hue, approximately 30 x 45 inches (76 x 114.3 cm)
- Scissors
- Construction paper in assorted colors, 12 x 18 inches (30 x 46 cm)
- White glue or glue stick

WHAT YOU WILL DO

1. With a group of four or five classmates, brainstorm a list of animals that symbolize different qualities. Possibilities include owl (for wisdom) and lion (for bravery). From the list, choose an animal that you feel represents a quality your class as a whole exhibits.
2. Each group member is to make several large sketches of your animal. Choose the best features from several drawings. Transfer the outline of this "composite," or group, sketch to the sheet of Kraft paper. Cut out the animal's shape.
3. Transfer body parts from your design to contrasting hues of construction paper. Make parts large enough to fill the body.
4. Cut rounded shapes (ovoids)—rectangles and squares—for facial features and for smaller details. Cut U-shaped forms for ears, ribs and feathers. Since your robe is to be formally balanced, you will need to make a copy of each shape. You can easily accomplish this by cutting through two sheets of paper for each feature.
5. Arrange all features and details on the body outline before gluing any of them down. Add variety to your design by alternating the distance between features.

EXAMINING YOUR WORK

- **Describe**   Tell what animal your group chose for your blanket. What features and body parts did you include?
- **Analyze**   Explain how you created variety. How did you achieve contrast?
- **Interpret**   How do the characteristics of your animal match the identity of your class?
- **Judge**   Tell whether you think your work is successful. What part worked best?

Figure S–4   **Student work. Clan robes.**

![Try This!] ## COMPUTER OPTION 🖥

■   Select the Brush tool, and draw the outline of an animal shape. As you work, vary the line thickness of your brush to create contrast and variety. Fill all of the spaces within the animal shape. Use the Mirror tool, if available, to make a mirror image. Otherwise, use the copy and paste and Rotate commands for this purpose.

Contour Drawing

Look at Figure S–5. Notice how lifelike the subject looks for a drawing made almost totally of line. A first step toward doing work like this is learning to do contour drawing. **Contour drawing** is *drawing an object as though your drawing tool is moving along all the edges and ridges of the form.* This technique helps you become more perceptive. You are concerned with drawing shapes and curves.

In contour drawing, your eye and hand move at the same time. Imagine that the point of your pen is touching the edge of the object as your eye follows the edge. You never pick up your pen. When you move from one area to another, you leave a trail. Look at the model and not at the paper.

WHAT YOU WILL LEARN

You will make a series of contour drawings with a felt-tipped pen. First, you will draw different objects. Second, you will use your classmates as models. Finally, you will make a contour drawing of a classmate posed in a setting. (See Technique Tip **2**, *Handbook* page **281.**)

WHAT YOU WILL NEED

- Felt-tipped pen with a fine point
- Sheets of white paper, 12 x 18 inches (30 x 46 cm)
- Selected objects provided by your teacher

WHAT YOU WILL DO

1. Take one of the items from the collection on the display table. Place it on the table in front of you. Trace the lines of the object in the air on an imaginary sheet of glass. As you look at the object, you must concentrate and think. Notice every detail indicated by the direction and curves of the line.

Figure S–5   **Notice how the artist gives a feeling of form by changing the thickness of the line. What ways do you know of making lines thicker and darker?**

Juan Gris. *Max Jacob.* 1919. Pencil on paper. 36.5 x 27.7 cm (14⅜ x 10½"). Museum of Modern Art, New York, New York. Gift of James Thrall Soby.

2. Make a contour drawing of the object on a sheet of paper using a felt-tipped pen. Do several more drawings on the same sheet of paper. Turn the object so you are looking at it from a different angle. Make another contour drawing. Keep working until your drawings begin to look like the object.

3. Next, exchange objects with your classmates. Do a contour drawing of your new object. Work large, letting the drawing fill the page. Do not worry if your efforts look awkward. Complete several drawings of different objects.

4. Work with a partner. Take turns posing for each other. Each model should sit in a comfortable pose. The first contour will look distorted. Remember, you are drawing the pose. Work large and let the drawing fill the page.

5. Finally, make a contour drawing of one person sitting in a setting. Include background details. You may stop and peek at the drawing. When you do, do not pick up the pencil. Do not take your eyes off the model while drawing.

6. Display the final drawing. Discuss how contour drawing has improved your perception.

EXAMINING YOUR WORK

- **Describe** Show the different kinds of contour drawings you did. Identify the media you used.
- **Analyze** Compare your first contour drawing to your last. Explain how using contour drawing has changed your perception skills.
- **Judge** Evaluate your final contour drawing. Tell whether you feel your work succeeds. Explain your answer.

Figure S–6 Student work. This is an example of a contour drawing that shows background details.

 Try This!  **STUDIO OPTIONS**

■ Make a contour drawing of a chair in your classroom using colored markers or a black felt-tipped pen.

■ Use a piece of wire that bends easily and make a three-dimensional contour "drawing" of a foot or hand.

Performing Arts Handbook

The following pages of content were excerpted from *Artsource®: The Music Center Study Guide to the Performing Arts,* developed by the Music Center Education Division, an award-winning arts education program of the Music Center of Los Angeles County.

The following artists and groups are featured in the Performing Arts Handbook.

Tandy Beal is a dancer, choreographer, actress, comic, and dreamer. Born into a theatre family, she recalls her father's advice to struggling artists: "The most important thing about performing is that you must be truthful." Following his advice, her dance "Dust to Dust" explores the idea that although people look and act in ordinary ways, they can have a rich inner world of imagination. In a dramatic section of the piece, the dancers, wearing everyday clothing, tear through large sheets of paper that have projected images of themselves dressed as performers. The work ends when the dancers disappear, replaced by tall columns of sand and glitter falling lightly onto the stage.

Tandy Beal & Company. *"Dust to Dust."* Photo courtesy of Tandy Beal & Company.

■ DISCUSSION QUESTIONS

1. The photo on this page depicts a moment from the dance "Dust to Dust." Describe the positions of the dancers and the feelings you think they are expressing.
2. In thinking about the brief description of the dance, what do you think the choreographer was trying to show when she chose to replace the dancers with columns of sand and glitter? Discuss your ideas and give reasons to support them.
3. People can easily see the daily activities we do but cannot know what goes on in the world of our imagination. Discuss this idea and give examples from your own life.

■ CREATIVE EXPRESSION ACTIVITIES

Technology   Using a camera, take close-up slides of different members of the class. Project these onto butcher paper in a darkened room and have people do simple movements, such as walking, skipping, jumping, and swaying in front of them so that the projections move back and forth from the paper to the people. Wear white for the best effect.

Language Arts   Although people look ordinary and act ordinary in their daily lives, they can have a rich inner world of imagination. Write about this concept with regard to yourself.

George Gershwin. Photo courtesy of The Music Center Operating Company Archives, Otto Rothchild Collection.

George Gershwin is one of America's most celebrated composers and pianists. According to Encyclopedia Britannica, Gershwin "created a new type of urban American music." The song "I Got Rhythm" was introduced in the Broadway musical *Girl Crazy* in 1930. It is an upbeat, fun song based on a simple four-note rhythmic motif. "Variations for Piano and Orchestra: I Got Rhythm" is full of clever ideas. A lone clarinet introduces the basic theme, or melody. The piano plays a little flurry, followed by the full orchestra. The piano then states the theme in solo. All in all there are four variations and a finale, where the melody alternates between different sections of the orchestra and the piano.

■ DISCUSSION QUESTIONS

1. The term *variations on a theme* refers to a basic technique composers use to change a musical theme. Using creative skills and musicianship, composers change the way a melody is played. Each version introduces a variation while keeping the basic character of the melody or theme. Discuss how this is similar to the way a visual artist works.

2. Discuss the four-note rhythmic motif on which the melody "I Got Rhythm" is based. Listen to the Artsource audio cassette or other recording for the way that the simple motif is developed into different variations. Discuss the differences between the variations.

■ CREATIVE EXPRESSION ACTIVITIES

Music   Take a familiar, simple song like "Three Blind Mice" and see if you can create three variations in the way you sing or play it. Suggestions might include changing the tempo (speed), unison or in a round, alternating loud with soft dynamics or change of pitch.

History   Read about New York and its performing and visual arts scenes in the 1920s and 1930s. Compare the artistic movements in the visual arts, literature and poetry, drama and dance with what was happening in music during this period.

Dance   Learn a popular dance or dance step from the 1920s or 1930s (Charleston, Lindy Hop, Truckin', Suzy Q). Compare its style with a popular dance of today.

For over 25 years, the Ballet Folklorico de Mexico has presented authentic folk dances from different ethnic groups within Mexico. Amalia Hernández, the featured director of the dance group shown on this page, creates exciting dances based on ancient traditions. From the time of the Olmec Indians to the birth of modern Mexico, more than thirty distinct cultures have influenced Mexican culture. The dance shown in this photo is called "Los Mitos" and features the pageantry and ritual of these cultures before the arrival of the Spaniards.

Ballet Folklorico de Mexico. "Los Mitos." Amalia Hernández, artistic director.

■ DISCUSSION QUESTIONS

1. Compare the headdress of the dancers to the headdress on page 182 in your book. What similarities do you see in the patterns and symbols?
2. What symbolism do you see in the photo on this page that inspired ancient cultures of Mexico? What characteristics of the symbol can you name?
3. After viewing the video, describe how the dancers used geometric spatial designs.

■ CREATIVE EXPRESSION ACTIVITIES

Dance   Stand in an open area with 6–8 students and organize yourselves into three different geometric shapes, selecting from a circle, square, triangle, or the letter X. After your designs are organized, choose two that you like and walk or skip from one figure into another using eight counts to travel.

Language Arts   Write a personal reflection of your impressions and feelings about either the images you see in the illustration on this page or of the dance in the video.

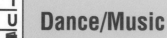

AMAN International Folk Ensemble. "Danse des Balais" from *Suite of French Canadian Dances.* Photo courtesy of AMAN International Folk Ensemble.

The AMAN International Folk Ensemble, based in Los Angeles, is a cultural and educational organization. It is dedicated to researching, preserving, and presenting the traditional dance, music, and folklore of many ethnic groups, particularly those representing North American immigrants. Choreographers Yves Moreau and France Bourque-Moreau were asked to show a wide range of dances from the richly varied heritage of French Canadian culture. They chose to choreograph a suite of five dances to represent both rural and urban traditions. The one shown here is a broom dance called "Danse des Balais" from Chicoutimi in Quebec.

■ DISCUSSION QUESTIONS

1. Study the photo of "Danse des Balais" and describe the differences in the costumes worn by the men as well as the movement being done.
2. Imagine you were given an assignment to make a statement about today's teen culture through dance, music, and costumes in a ten-minute performance piece. What would you choose to include?
3. The names of the instruments used to play the traditional music are: piano, button accordion, fiddle, guitar, and an Irish drum called a *bodhram*. How are these instruments similar or different from those found in a popular rock band?

■ CREATIVE EXPRESSION ACTIVITIES

History   Interview your parents or grandparents to find out what folk dances they know that represent their cultural heritage. Find out what country they came from and what traditions they relate to within the culture. If possible, learn a part of the dance and teach it to the class.

Dance   Use the Artsource audio cassette or find the directions and music to the French Canadian folk dance "Les Saluts." It is a simple circle dance that is fun and gives a flavor of the traditional music and dance style.

Tandy Beal, a dancer and choreographer, and Bobby McFerrin, a musician, combined their artistic talents in a creative process called improvisation. Improvisational work is very challenging. It requires a great deal of trust, alertness, and the ability of each to respond fully to the other in the present moment.

Improvisation is about playing in a serious way. Someone sets out an idea, and others who know the rules and boundaries of the improvisational process can join in the play. It is much like professional sports where the players, working within certain rules and boundaries, think and respond to the actions of each other, using great alertness and skill to achieve a goal.

Tandy Beal and Bobby McFerrin. *Voice/Dance.* Photo courtesy of Tandy Beal & Company.

■ DISCUSSION QUESTIONS

1. Name all the ways you can communicate without speaking in words. Demonstrate each as you identify them.
2. Discuss why artistic improvisation as described above is different from simply playing or fooling around.
3. Discuss other situations when people improvise to solve problems or create something (scientists, advertising writers, sports players, computer programmers, parents). Is brainstorming related to improvisation? If so, discuss the relationship.

■ CREATIVE EXPRESSION ACTIVITIES

Communication With a partner, communicate using only vocal sounds, gestures, and body percussion. Experiment for one minute and then share your reactions to the experience. Focus on how the length of the sound or motion, rhythm, dynamics, and energy affected the improvisation. Try it again.

Technology Selectively record sounds from the environment, such as children jumping rope, video games, a sports event, machines, and so on. Use this recording to motivate a writing assignment that uses sounds to trigger emotions and thoughts that lead to a story.

Music

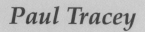

International troubadour Paul Tracey draws upon his cultural heritage to communicate ideas about life through original songs. Working on his father's farm with his father and a Swazi foreman named Simon Shabalala, he learned about farming, building, and appreciating nature. He now realizes he has been an environmentalist his whole life.

He has written a show called *Our Little Blue Planet,* which stresses the uniqueness of this planet and the delicate balance between all the species in nature. His song "Dead as a Dodo" points out that it is too late to save the dodo, for they are now extinct. However, there is still time to protect other endangered species.

Paul Tracey, minstrel. *Our Little Blue Planet.* Photo © 1995 Craig Schwartz.

■ DISCUSSION QUESTIONS

1. Make a list of endangered species, such as the condor, some species of whales, the panda, and the rhino. Select one and make a case as to why it should be preserved, or play the role of the "Devil's Advocate" and say why it should be eliminated.
2. Paul's farm in Africa has been declared a Nature Reserve. Local children and students come there to learn about nature, how to perceive its beauty, and to respect the overall balance of nature in the environment. Discuss ways that you could beautify something in your neighborhood that would also improve the environment.

■ CREATIVE EXPRESSION ACTIVITIES

Language Arts There is a saying, "Think globally and act locally." Write a jingle that incorporates this idea into a catchy tune.

Art What if the creatures who became extinct were redesigned so that they could survive. Select one extinct creature and redesign it so that it would have a better chance for survival. For example, if whales could develop armor-plated skin, they could repel harpoons.

The Robert Minden Ensemble. Drawing by Nancy Walker.

"The Boy Who Wanted to Talk to Whales" is a modern folk tale about the adventure of a boy who had a powerful desire to talk to the great whales. He meets a curious musician "playing" a carpenter's hand saw and begins a musical journey filled with possibility and discovery. Eventually, the boy gets his chance to communicate with the whales in a way he never imagined. The original score is performed without the use of synthesizers or electronically generated sounds. Instead, an odd assortment of ordinary objects are transformed into musical instruments: empty tin cans, wood, vacuum cleaner hoses, and a Slinky. Also included are conch shells and a Waterphone, which create a magical sound for his journey.

■ **DISCUSSION QUESTIONS**

1. Have you ever tried to mimic the language or song of a particular animal or bird? Can you demonstrate? Discuss the types of language and sounds made by other living creatures.

2. Have you had moments in your life when you felt truly connected to nature or all living things? Describe your experiences.

3. Study the artwork and see if you can identify the ordinary materials that are being used as instruments. Can you think of other possibilities?

■ **CREATIVE EXPRESSION ACTIVITIES**

Science   Select a species of whale to study, such as the Orca, or killer, whale. Find a scientific recording of sounds made by killer whales and see if you can find recycled materials to help you imitate it.

Music   Discover a new sound from an ordinary household object and bring it in to share with the class. Create an environment of sounds with all the students participating. Working with sensitivity, vary the loud and soft dynamics, rhythm and balance between the sounds in order to create something that works and sounds interesting.

The Chameleons: Keith Berger and Sharon Diskin. *Life Cycle.* Photo © 1990, Craig Schwartz.

*L*ife Cycle follows the relationship of two characters, one female and one male, from infancy through childhood, adolescence, courtship, marriage, parenthood, middle-age, old age, death, and finally, rebirth. On a bare stage and without costumes or props, Berger and Diskin use pantomime and mime techniques to project a variety of human emotions and enact the rituals of friendship, love, and separation. Their work began with a desire to do a story about universal relationships. They began by improvising ways to create age changes by altering their posture, expressions, and attitudes.

■ DISCUSSION QUESTIONS

1. Why do you think Keith Berger and Sharon Diskin titled their mime piece *Life Cycle*? What does the term *cycle* mean, and how does this relate to the stages of life?
2. Study the photo on this page and describe the situation and what you think is being communicated by the two mimes.
3. Identify situations where people use gestures to communicate ideas rather than words. Discuss why this is done in each of the situations.

■ CREATIVE EXPRESSION ACTIVITIES

Pantomime Imagine that you are watching the following things, using primarily your eyes to show each idea: a tennis match, an airplane flying high, a spider crawling near your toes, and a butterfly flying around you and landing on a part of your body.

Pantomime Show the following ideas in mime movement: fishing, writing a letter, stirring cake batter, dealing cards, getting dressed, sewing a button on a shirt, and bowling.

Playwriting Create a mime scenario about a day in the life of a specific character. Then write an outline of the action to use as a mime script.

Danais and Ara Tokatlian base their personal and professional lives on the principles of universal brotherhood. They try to help people accept and understand different cultural values and styles of artistic expression. Communicating these ideas through their exciting music, they combine ethnic instruments, rhythms, and melodies from various areas of the Americas with contemporary sounds. Their composition "Peace Pipes" is drawn from the music of the Quechua and Aymara people of Peru and Bolivia.

Arco Iris: Danais and Ara Tokatlian. Photo by Deborah Allison.

■ DISCUSSION QUESTIONS

1. Think of the titles "Peace Pipes" and "Soaring Over the High Plains." What kind of musical sounds, melody, or rhythms would you create if you were able to compose music to bring these images to life?
2. Arco Iris uses instruments that are made from materials found in the environment. What instruments might you be able to create from natural objects or sources?
3. Think of three different cultures you know about. What instruments from each can you suggest that could combine to form a fusion of new sound?

■ CREATIVE EXPRESSION ACTIVITIES

Science Explore the scientific basis for sound production of the following instruments: drums, glockenspiel (steel bars), xylophone (wood bars), and flutes.

Language Arts Think of an instrument you find interesting. Write a paragraph, poem, or short story from the point of view of the instrument. Describe yourself in specific detail including shape and color, how you are held, treated, and produce sound to express your feelings. You might ask yourself these questions: How do I make sound? What am I made of? What kind of music do I play?

EVERYBODY BE YOSELF

CHIC STREET MAN

SING-ALONG FUN FOR THE ENTIRE FAMILY

Chic Street Man is clever at communicating ideas through his music. He often combines storytelling in his compositions, as in *Rag Man.* He skillfully uses his guitar, his singing voice, and his speaking voice to tell the tale of a rag man, as seen through the eyes of a boy. This is a true story-song of an old man who used a horse and wagon to come into Chic's neighborhood looking for rags. The song is sung in a style derived from African cultural traditions, combining storytelling and poetry with music.

Chic Street Man. *Rag Man.* Photo by Neil Ricklen.

■ DISCUSSION QUESTIONS

1. Chic Street Man calls his *Rag Man* performance a "rap recitation." Why do you think he calls it that?
2. In *Rag Man* Chic weaves a story about a man who advertised his work by riding through the streets calling and singing to his potential customers. Do vendors still come to your neighborhood? If so, discuss what they sell and how they call to their customers.
3. Discuss how songs and music are used to advertise and sell products. Recall some songs that are memorable or are being currently used.

■ CREATIVE EXPRESSION ACTIVITIES

Language Arts   Select three commercials using music or song that are memorable. Demonstrate and describe them, discuss the various music styles used, and suggest what type of audience the companies wish to reach.

Art/History/Culture   Examine the artworks of African-American artists who, like their counterparts in music, have portrayed the historical, cultural, social, and political lives of their people. Look for the messages they convey, and describe how the artists communicated their messages through visual art.

Dr. Jester Hairston was born in 1901 and has lived through more than 90 years of history. Although he was musically trained, he didn't become interested in the music of his own people until he was an adult. He composed "Goin'Down That Lonesome Road" as a "protest song without hatred." Although a feeling of dissatisfaction is expressed in some of the lyrics, the melody, tempo, rhythm, and styling of the song convey a positive spirit. The lyrics also contain phrases that transmit a feeling of hope with a confident look to the future. This song uses a swing style that gives it an uplifting and lively mood.

Dr. Jester Hairston. "Goin' Down That Lonesome Road."
Photo courtesy of Jester Hairston.

■ **DISCUSSION QUESTIONS**

1. Why do you suppose a composer would choose an upbeat swing style of music when composing a protest song?
2. Think of something that you strongly protest. Discuss the ideas you would include in a song or poem to communicate your main ideas and feelings.
3. Research songs of social conscience today. What are people feeling strongly about? Do these issues vary from group to group, or are these issues universal?

■ **CREATIVE EXPRESSION ACTIVITIES**

Language Arts   Think of contemporary popular songs that convey similar messages or themes, for example "We Are the World," It's a Small World," and "Teach the World To Sing." Recall and write down as many titles as you can. Then write a title for an idea you believe in and would like people to sing. Write song lyrics to go with your title.

Music   In small groups, select a simple child's story, such as "Goldilocks" or "The Three Little Pigs." Write a rap style song for one of the characters to do, or tell the basic story in rap style. Perform for each other.

Nobuko Miyamoto and members of Great Leap. "Joanne Is My Middle Name" from *A Slice of Rice.*

For "Joanne Is My Middle Name," Nobuko Miyamoto went deep inside herself to dramatize the dilemma of being a third generation Japanese-American searching for a way to belong. She found the theme of trying to adapt her name and examined her trail of name changes. As a young girl, she connected with the magic of the arts through music, which in turn awakened her passion to dance and dramatically tell stories. This song/story begins with her childhood experiences of living in Japanese internment camps during World War II. It continues through her various rites of passage to the acceptance of her heritage and her name.

■ DISCUSSION QUESTIONS

1. Many immigrants who come to this country change their names in order to fit into the American culture. Discuss the pros and cons of doing this.
2. Discuss the symbolic importance of names in relationship to our identity. What do names tell about us? Where did your name come from? Were you named after a relative or famous person? What do you feel that your name tells about you?
3. Make a list of the names of people in your class and what cultural heritage they represent. What are the advantages of having a name which in some way connects you to your heritage?

■ CREATIVE EXPRESSION ACTIVITIES

Language Arts Ask your parents how your name was chosen for you, and find out any interesting background related to your name and its original history. Write down this information, and then write your feelings about your name.

Theatre Assume the role of playwright and write a monologue or solo speech about an important event in your life. There should be a beginning, middle, climax, and conclusion with a clear emotional progression. Use the script for a classroom presentation.

Paul Salamunovich, Director of the Los Angeles Master Chorale.
Photo: Robert Millard, Courtesy of the Los Angeles Master Chorale.

Paul Salamunovich is the Director of the Los Angeles Master Chorale. The job of a choral director is to guide a choir, made up of individual voices, to collectively capture the mood of each piece they sing. A choral conductor serves, in a sense, as a translator. According to Salamunovich, the conductor must understand why the composer wrote as he or she did and the effect of that historical time and place on the work. Then he works to accurately interpret the intent, meaning, and technical and aesthetic requirements of the music.

■ DISCUSSION QUESTIONS

1. Have you ever been in a choir or heard a choir perform? Discuss the things that you think a choir member must do to successfully contribute to the group effort.
2. "America" is a song of celebration of our American history. What other songs do you know that celebrate American life or the qualities of other cultures?
3. Discuss the importance of "America" as one of our country's most loved and respected patriotic songs. Name occasions when this song is sung or played.

■ CREATIVE EXPRESSION ACTIVITIES

Music   Experiment in combining vocal sounds with a partner or in a small group, seeing how you can transform the isolated vocal sounds into music.

Language Arts   Think of something that you would like to celebrate, and write lyrics or a poem to express your feelings of joy, pride, and honor. Think of words and images that could be metaphors for your feelings, for example, rockets burst forth from my heart; rainbows paint over this day; my thoughts take wings.

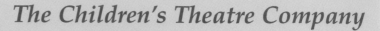

The Children's Theatre Company. *The Story of Babar, the Little Elephant.* 1996 Season. Courtesy of the Children's Theatre Company.

The Children's Theatre Company in Minneapolis, Minnesota is known for its ability to vividly re-create the storybook page on stage. The play featured on this page is *The Story of Babar, the Little Elephant,* based on the children's story by Jean de Brunhoff. The biggest challenge in bringing a book off the page and onto the stage lies in expanding two-dimensional art to three dimensions. In this case, it was important to create an accurate scale of the elephant characters to the human ones. The costumes for Babar and his elephant friends needed to look exactly like those in the book but be flexible enough so the actors could move and dance! The play's creative team left nothing to chance, inventing action and dances for every scene in the story.

■ DISCUSSION QUESTIONS

1. Select a specific animal as a character in a play. If you were a costume designer, how might you go about creating a costume that would transform a person into this animal? What would you have to consider?
2. How might you actually construct a costume for your animal?
3. Think about how short a children's book is. When you bring it from the page to the stage, how would you go about creating additional dialogue, songs, and dances for a dramatic performance?

■ CREATIVE EXPRESSION ACTIVITIES

Language Arts Read *The Story of Babar, the Little Elephant,* or another book in the Babar series such as *Travels of Babar* or *Babar the King.* Divide the book up into different scenes that could be portrayed in a play.

Visual Arts/Theatre Design a basic structure for the animal costume. Consider such things as weight and frame, and the mathematical proportions of the different pieces. Draw to correct scale, and make suggestions for types of materials and fabrics to be used.

Artists and Their Works

ARTISTS AND THEIR WORKS

Allah, Habib, Persian, c. 15th century, painter
Concourse of the Birds, 132, *Fig. 7–10*

Assa, Fred, American, 1936–, painter
Spring Cleaning, 166, *Fig. 9–4*

Bearden, Romare, American, 1911–1988, painter,
printmaker, collage artist
Saturday Morning, 54, *Fig. 3–16*

Benton, Thomas Hart, American, 1882–1975, painter
July Hay, 102, *Fig. 6–1*
The Sources of Country Music, 260

Biggers, John, American, 1924–, painter
Starry Crown, 222, *Fig. 12–1*

Borglum, Gutzon, American, 1871–1941, sculptor
Theodore Roosevelt (Mt. Rushmore), 204,
Fig. 11–2

Brancusi, Constantin, Rumanian, 1876–1957, sculptor
Bird in Space, 134, *Fig. 7–12*

Brett, Dorothy, English, 1883–1979, painter
San Geronimo Day, Taos, 202, *Fig. 11–1*

Bronzino, Agnolo di Cosimo, Italian, 1502–1572,
painter
Eleonora of Toledo and Her Son, 144, *Fig. 8–2*

Brown, Everald, Jamaican, 1917–, painter
Instrument for Four People, 200
Victory Dance, 249, *Fig. 13–7*

Brown, Roger, American, 1941–, muralist
Homesick-Proof Space Station, 214, *Fig. 11–12*

Bruegel, Pieter, Dutch, 1530–1569, painter
The Fall of Icarus, 240
The Hunters in the Snow, 113, *Fig. 6–11*

Burchfield, Charles, American, 1893–1967, painter
Night of the Equinox, 118, *Fig. 6–16*

Butterfield, Deborah, American, 1949–, sculptor
Horse, 20, *Fig. 1–20*

C

Calder, Alexander, American, 1898–1976, sculptor
Sow, 5, *Fig. 1–3*

Cassatt, Mary, American, 1845–1926, painter
Margo in Blue, 48, *Fig. 3–10*

Cézanne, Paul, French, 1839–1906, painter
The Basket of Apples, 4, *Fig. 1–2*

Chagall, Marc, Russian, 1887–1985, painter
Green Violinist, 262, *Fig. 14–1*

Christensen, James, American, 1942–, painter
Vanity, 276

Cole, Thomas, American, 1801–1848, painter
The Architect's Dream, 273, *Fig. 14–11*

Corot, Jean Baptiste Camille, French, 1796–1875,
painter
View of Genoa, 178, *Fig. 9–17*

Craig, Franck, French, 1874–1918, painter
"La Pucelle!" Jeanne d'Arc Leads Her Army, 158,
Fig. 8–16

D

Daumier, Honoré, French, 1808–1879, painter
Family Group, 44, *Fig. 3–6*
The Young Courier, 148, *Fig. 8–6*

Davies, Arthur B., American, 1862–1928, painter
Dances, 149, *Fig. 8–7*

Davis, Bing, American, 1937–, painter
Puberty Ritual Image #10, 258, *Fig. 13–6*

Demuth, Charles, American, 1883–1935, painter
Eggplant and Green Pepper, 190, *Fig. 10–8*
The Figure 5 in Gold, 38

Dillon, Leo and Diane, American, both 1933–,
illustrators
"Marie and Redfish," 237, *Fig. 12–15*

Doolittle, Bev, American, 1947–, painter
The Sacred Circle, 122, *Fig. 7–1*

Dove, Arthur, American, 1880–1946, painter
Fog Horns, 64, *Fig. 4–3*

Dubuffet, Jean, French, 1901–1985, painter
The Reveler, 150, *Fig. 8–8*

Dürer, Albrecht, German, 1471–1528, painter,
printmaker
The Great Piece of Turf, 109, *Fig. 6–7*
Melencholia 1, 74, *Fig. 4–10*

E

Escher, M. C., Dutch, 1898–1972, printmaker
Belvedere, 272, *Fig. 14–10*
Day and Night, 34, *Fig. 2–10*

Estes, Richard, American, 1932–, painter
Paris Street, 17, *Fig. 1–17*

Exekias, Greek, 550–525 B.C., potter, painter
Group E. Quadriga Wheeling Right, 83, *Fig. 5–3*

Artists and Their Works   **327**

Glossary

Abstract   Having a recognizable subject that is shown in an unrealistic manner. (Ch. 4–6)

Adenla (uh-**den**-luh)   A sculpted ceremonial head-dress used in rites of passage. (Ch. 13–5)

Aesthetics (es-**thet**-iks)   The study of the nature of beauty and art. (Ch. 4–1)

Aesthetic view   An idea or school of thought on what is most important in a work of art. (Ch. 4–1)

Ancestor figure   An image carved in wood that was used as the resting place of a spirit. (Ch. 8–5)

Applied art   Works of art made to be useful as well as visually pleasing. (Chs. 5–1, 10–5)

Appliqué (ap-lih-**kay**)   An art form in which cutout shapes are attached to a larger surface. (Ch. 7–3)

Architects   Artists who plan and create buildings. (Ch. 9–2)

Architectural rendering   A detailed, realistic two-dimensional representation of a proposed three-dimensional structure. (Ch. 14–5)

Architecture   The art of planning and creating buildings. (Ch. 5–5)

Art critic   A person whose job is studying, understanding, and judging works of art. (Ch. 4–2)

Art historians   People who study art of different ages and cultures. (Ch. 5–1)

Artist   A person who uses imagination and skill to communicate ideas in visual form. (Ch. 1–1)

Art medium   A material used to create a work of art. (Ch. 3–1)

Art movement   A trend formed when a group of artists band together. (Ch. 5–7)

Assemblage (ah-sem-**blahzh**)   A three-dimensional artwork consisting of many pieces assembled together. (Ch. 6–2)

Balance   A principle of art concerned with arranging the elements so that no one part of the work overpowers, or seems heavier than, any other part. (Ch. 2–1)

Belvedere (**bel**-vuh-deer)   A building designed to provide a view of its surroundings. (Ch. 14–5)

Binder   A liquid that holds together the grains of pigment. (Ch. 3–3)

Bust   A sculpture that shows a person's head, shoulders, and upper chest. (Ch. 5–1)

Calligraphy (kuh-**lig**-ruh-fee)   The art of beautiful writing. (Ch. 7–5)

Camcorder   A small hand-held video camera. (Ch. 11–7)

Caricature (**kar**-ih-kuh-chur)   A humorous drawing that exaggerates features of a person to make fun of or criticize him or her. (Ch. 11–4)

Cartouche (kar-**toosh**)   An oval or oblong containing an important person's name. (Ch. 12–1)

Cityscape   A drawing or painting focusing on large buildings and other objects found in cities. (Ch. 9–5)

Color   What the eye sees when light is reflected off an object. (Ch. 1–3)

Columns   Vertical posts that rise to support another structure. (Ch. 9–4)

Composition   The way the principles are used to organize the elements of art. (Ch. 4–1)

Content   The message, idea, or feeling expressed by a work of art. (Ch. 4–1)

Contour drawing   Drawing an object as though your drawing tool is moving along all the edges and ridges of the form. (Handbook)

Contours   Outlines and surface ridges. (Ch. 5–2)

Credit line   A listing of important facts about an artwork. (Ch. 4–2)

Cutaway   A view in which an outside wall has been removed to reveal the scene within. (Ch. 12–5)

Diorama (dy-uh-**ram**-uh)   A scenic representation in which miniature sculptures and other objects are displayed against a painted backdrop. (Ch. 5–6)

E

Eight, The   A group of American realists who worked at the beginning of the twentieth century. (Ch. 9–6)

Elements of art   The basic visual symbols an artist uses to create works of art. (Ch 1–1)

Elevation   A drawing of an outside view of a building. (Ch. 9–4)

Glossary

Embroidery The art of making ornamental designs with needle and thread. (Ch. 12–5)

Emphasis Making an element or an object in a work stand out. (Ch. 2–3)

Environment Surroundings. (Ch. 7–1)

Façade (fuh-**sahd**) The front of a building. (Ch. 9–4)

Fantasy art Art that focuses on make-believe or imaginary subjects. (Ch. 14–1)

Figure study A drawing that focuses on the human form. (Ch. 8–3)

Fine art Art made to be enjoyed visually, not used. (Ch. 5–1)

Folk art Art made by artists who have had no formal training. (Ch. 7–8)

Font Typeface. (Ch. 12–8)

Form An element of art that refers to an object with three dimensions. (Ch. 1–5)

Fresco (**fres**-koh) A painting created when pigment is applied to a section of wall spread with fresh plaster. (Ch. 12–5)

Frieze (**freez**) A decorative band running across the upper part of a wall. (Ch. 11–5)

G

Gesture drawing Moving a drawing medium quickly and freely over a surface to capture the form and actions of a subject. (Ch. 3–2)

Gold leaf A very thin layer of gold glued to a surface for decoration. (Ch. 12–7)

Gouache (**gwash**) A form of watercolor that uses non-clear pigments. (Ch. 11–1)

H

Harmony Combining the elements of art to accent their similarities. (Ch. 2–3)

Hieroglyphic (hy-ruh-**glif**-ik) An early form of picture writing. (Ch. 5–2)

Hue A color's name. (Ch. 1–3)

I

Illumination Hand-painted book illustration. (Ch. 7–5)

Intaglio (in-**tahl**-yoh) A printmaking technique in which the image to be printed is cut or scratched into a surface. (Ch. 3–5)

Intensity The brightness or dullness of a hue. (Ch. 1–3)

J

Jewelry Art, and the craft of making art, to be worn. (Ch. 10–7)

Juxtapose (**juks**-tuh-pohz) Place side by side. (Ch. 14–3)

K

Kachina (kuh-**chee**-nuh) Hand-crafted statuette that represents spirits in Pueblo rituals. (Ch. 12–4)

Kiln A special hot oven in which pottery objects are fired. (Ch. 10–6)

Kinetic (kuh-**net**-ik) **art** An art style in which parts of a work are set into motion by a form of energy. (Ch. 13–4)

L

Landscape A drawing or painting of mountains, trees, or other natural scenery. (Ch. 6–1)

Line The path of a dot through space. (Ch. 1–2)

Line quality The unique character of any line. (Ch. 1–2)

Mascot An animal or person used by a group as a sign of luck. (Ch. 7–1)

Monoprint A print made by applying ink or paint to a plate and then transferring the image by hand-rubbing. (Ch. 6–7)

Mosaic (moh-**zay**-ik) Small bits of colored glass and jewels set in cement. (Ch. 11–5)

Movement The principle of art that leads the viewer to sense action in a work, or it can be the path the viewer's eye follows through the work. (Ch. 2–4)

Murals Large two-dimensional works painted on walls. (Ch. 8–7)

N

Nature study A drawing used to help artists sharpen their perception of natural objects. (Ch. 6–3)

Negative space Empty spaces between the shapes or forms in two- and three-dimensional art. (Ch. 1–5)

Non-objective Having no readily identifiable subjects or objects. (Ch. 4–3)

Old Stone Age The historical period that occurred between 30,000 and 10,000 B.C. (Ch. 7–1)

Painted screen An art object used as a wall or room divider. (Ch. 5–3)

Pan A slow, steady, sideways movement of the video camera to capture details in a panorama. (Ch. 11–8)

Panorama A complete view of an area in all directions. (Ch. 9–7)

Pendant A jewelry item worn suspended from the neck on a string or chain. (Ch. 10–5)

Perception An awareness of the elements of an environment by means of the senses. (Ch. 3–1)

Perceive Become aware through the senses of the special nature of objects. (Ch. 10–1)

Petroglyph (**peh**-truh-glif) Symbolic rock carving or painting. (Ch. 12–1)

Photography The art of making images by exposing a chemically treated surface to light. (Ch. 11–1)

Pictogram A small picture that stands for a word or an idea. (Ch. 12–1)

Picture plane The flat surface of a painting or drawing. (Ch. 2–3)

Pigment A finely ground powder that gives paint its color. (Ch. 3–3)

Point of view The angle from which the viewer sees the scene in an artwork. (Ch. 4–4)

Porcelain (**por**-suh-lihn) A fine-grained, high-quality form of pottery. (Ch. 7–3)

Portfolio A carefully selected collection of artwork kept by students and professional artists. (Ch. 1–Opening)

Portrait A visual representation of a person at rest. (Ch. 3–4)

Portraiture (**pohr**-tray-chur) The art of making portraits. (Ch. 8–5)

Pottery Art, and the craft of making art, from clay. (Ch. 10–6)

Principles of art Guidelines that govern the way artists organize the elements of art. (Ch. 2–1)

Printmaking Transferring an image from an inked surface to create a work of art. (Ch. 3–5)

Proportion How parts of a work relate to each other and to the whole. (Ch. 2–3)

Public art Art to be displayed in and enjoyed by a community. (Ch. 8–7)

Pueblo (**pweh**-bloh) Dried-clay dwelling. (Ch. 13–3)

R

Renaissance (**ren**-uh-sahns) Period of rebirth. (Ch. 5–5)

Resist An art medium, such as crayon, that serves as a protective coating. (Ch. 6–6)

Rhythm The repetition of an element to make a work seem active. (Ch. 2–4)

Rococo (roh-**koh**-koh) An art style of the 1700s that emphasized graceful movement, curving lines, and delicate colors. (Ch. 9–3)

S

Sculpture A three-dimensional work of art. (Ch. 3–6)

Seal Symbolic image or emblem. (Ch. 13–1)

Seascape A drawing or painting of the ocean and objects found on or around it. (Ch. 9–7)

Self-portrait A painting or drawing of an artist's own image. (Ch. 8–1)

Shadow puppet An art object in the shape of an animal or human attached to a wand or a stick. (Ch. 13–4)

Shape An area clearly set off by one or more of the other five visual elements of art. (Ch. 1–5)

Sketchbook A pad of drawing paper on which artists sketch, write notes, and refine ideas for their work. (Ch. 2–Opening)

Slip Clay with enough added water to give it a runny, liquid consistency. (Ch. 10–6)

Social protest painting An art style dedicated to attacking the ills of big-city life. (Ch. 14–4)

Solvent A liquid used to control the thickness or thinness of the paint. (Ch. 3–3)

Space   The distance or area between, around, above, below, and within things. (Ch. 1–5)

Staged photograph   A photographic composition that makes use of artificial images or processes. (Ch. 9–1)

Still life   A painting or drawing of nonliving objects. (Ch. 1–5)

Story board   A frame-by-frame plan of a video production. (Ch. 11–7)

Study   A drawing used to plan a painting or other large project. (Ch. 6–3)

Style   An artist's personal way of using the elements and principles of art to express feelings and ideas. (Ch. 8–1)

Stylized   Simplified or exaggerated. (Ch. 6–1)

Subject   An image viewers can easily identify. (Ch. 4–1)

Surrealists   The group of artists who explored the realm of dreams and the subconscious. (Ch. 14–1)

Symbol   An image used to stand for a quality or an idea. (Chs. 5–2, 7–7)

T

Tapestry   A woven wall hanging with decorative designs or colorful scenes. (Ch. 7–7)

Texture   How things feel, or look as though they might feel if touched. (Ch. 1–7)

Totem   An object that serves as an emblem or respected symbol. (Ch. 7–2)

Trait   A personal characteristic. (Ch. 7–1)

Tricolor   A flag with three broad bands of color. (Ch. 13–1)

Trompe-l'oeil (trohmp-**loy**)   A style of painting in which objects are depicted with photographically realistic detail. (Ch. 8–5)

U

Unity   The arrangement of elements and principles of art to create a feeling of completeness or wholeness. (Ch. 2–6)

V

Value   The lightness or darkness of a hue. (Ch. 1–3)

Variety   Combining one or more elements of art to create interest. (Ch. 2–3)

Vessel   A hollow utensil made to hold something. (Ch. 10–5)

Video documentary   An in-depth study of a person, place, thing, or event. (Ch. 11–7)

Videographer   Person who operates a video camera. (Ch. 11–8)

W

Watercolorist   A painter who works in watercolor. (Ch. 10–4)

Glosario

A

Abstract/Abstracto   Mostrar un sujeto reconocible de forma no realista. (Cap. 4–6)

Adenla/Adenla   Tocado ceremonial usado en rituales de transición. (Cap. 13–5)

Aesthetics/Estética   Estudio de la naturaleza de la belleza y el arte. (Cap. 4–1)

Aesthetic view/Punto de vista estético   Idea o escuela de pensamiento sobre qué es lo más importante en una obra de arte. (Cap. 4–1)

Ancestor figure/Figurín de un ancestro   Imagen tallada en madera que se usaba como el lugar de descanso de un espíritu. (Cap. 8–5)

Applied art/Arte aplicado   Obras de arte hechas con un fin utilitario además de ser agradables a la vista. (Caps. 5–1, 10–5)

Appliqué/Appliqué   Forma de arte en la que se adhieren recortes de material a una superficie más grande. (Cap. 7–3)

Architects/Arquitectos   Artistas que planean y crean edificios. (Cap. 9–2)

Architectural rendering/Perspectiva arquitectónica realista   Representación bidimensional realista y detallada de una estructura tridimensional propuesta. (Cap. 14–5)

Architecture/Arquitectura   Arte de planear y crear edificios. (Cap. 5–5)

Art critic/Crítico de arte   Aquel que se ocupa de estudiar, comprender y juzgar obras de arte. (Cap. 4–2)

Art historians/Historiadores del arte   Aquellos que se ocupan de estudiar el arte de las distintas épocas y culturas. (Cap. 5–1)

Artist/Artista plástico   Aquel que usa su imaginación y su habilidad para comunicar ideas de una forma visual. (Cap. 1–1)

Art medium/Medio artístico   Material utilizado en la creación de una obra de arte. (Cap. 3–1)

Art movement/Movimiento artístico   Tendencia que se manifiesta cuando se une un grupo de artistas. (Cap. 5–7)

Assemblage/Assemblage   Obra de arte tridimensional que consiste de muchas piezas ensambladas entre sí. (Cap. 6–2)

B

Balance/Equilibrio   Principio del arte que se refiere al arreglo de los elementos de manera tal que ninguna parte de la obra abrume o parezca más pesada que cualquier otra parte. (Cap. 2–1)

Belvedere/Mirador   Edificio diseñado para proveer una vista de sus alrededores. (Cap. 14–5)

Binder/Sustancia aglutinante   Líquido que une los granos de pigmento. (Cap. 3–3)

Bust/Busto   Escultura que muestra la cabeza, hombros y parte superior del pecho de una persona. (Cap. 5–1)

C

Calligraphy/Caligrafía   El arte de escribir con letra bella. (Cap. 7–5)

Camcorder/Cámara de video   Cámara de video pequeña y manuable. (Cap. 11–7)

Caricature/Caricatura   Dibujo humorístico que exagera los rasgos de una persona para ridiculizarla o criticarla. (Cap. 11–4)

Cartouche/Tarjeta   Forma oval u oblonga donde está inscripto el nombre de una persona importante. (Cap. 12–1)

Cityscape/Paisaje urbano   Dibujo o pintura que muestra grandes edificios y otros objetos que se hallan en las ciudades. (Cap. 9–5)

Color/Color   Lo que ve el ojo cuando la luz se refleja de un objeto. (Cap. 1–3)

Columns/Columnas   Postes verticales que se elevan para proveer apoyo a otra estructura. (Cap. 9–4)

Composition/Composición   Forma en que se utilizan los principios para organizar los elementos del arte. (Cap. 4–1)

Content/Contenido   Mensaje, idea o sentimiento expresado por una obra de arte. (Cap. 4–1)

Contour drawing/Dibujo de contorno   Dibujar un objeto como si el instrumento de dibujo delineara los bordes y líneas en la supersicie de la forma. (Technique Tips Handbook)

Contours/Contornos   Bordes y aristas de una superficie. (Cap. 5–2)

Credit line/Resumen de datos   Listado de información importante acerca de una obra de arte. (Cap. 4–2)

Cutaway/Sección   Vista en la que se ha quitado una pared exterior para mostrar la escena del interior. (Cap. 12–5)

Glosario

D

Diorama/Maqueta   Representación de una escena en la que esculturas en miniatura y otros objetos se muestran contra un fondo pintado. (Cap. 5–6)

E

Eight, The/Los Ocho   Grupo de realistas estadounidenses que trabajaron a principios del siglo veinte. (Cap. 9–6)

Elements of art/Elementos del arte   Los símbolos visuales básicos que usa un artista para crear obras de arte. (Cap. 1–1)

Elevation/Alzado   Dibujo de la fachada de un edificio. (Cap. 9–4)

Embroidery/Bordado   Arte de realizar diseños decorativos con aguja e hilo. (Cap. 12–5)

Emphasis/Énfasis   Hacer que resalte un elemento o un objeto en una obra. (Cap. 2–3)

Environment/Ambiente   Lo que rodea algo. (Cap. 7–1)

F

Façade/Fachada   El frente de un edificio. (Cap. 9–4)

Fantasy art/Arte de fantasía   Arte que se enfoca en sujetos ficticios o imaginarios. (Cap. 14–1)

Figure study/Estudio de figuras   Dibujo que se enfoca en la figura humana. (Cap. 8–3)

Fine art/Bellas artes   Obras hechas para el disfrute visual, no para ser utilizadas. (Cap. 5–1)

Folk art/Arte folklórico   Obras realizadas por artistas que no han tenido entrenamiento formal. (Cap. 7–8)

Font/Fundición   Conjunto de todos los moldes o letras de un tipo para imprimir. (Cap. 12–8)

Form/Forma   Elemento del arte que se refiere a un objeto con tres dimensiones. (Cap. 1–5)

Fresco/Fresco   Pintura creada al aplicar pigmento a una sección de una pared revocada con yeso fresco. (Cap. 12–5)

Frieze/Friso   Banda decorativa ubicada a lo largo de la parte superior de una pared. (Cap. 11–5)

G

Gesture drawing/Dibujo de gestos   Mover un instrumento de dibujo en forma rápida y espontánea sobre una superficie para captar la forma y las acciones de un sujeto. (Cap. 3–2)

Gold leaf/Dorado a la hoja   Una capa fina de oro adherida a una superficie con fines decorativos. (Cap. 12–7)

Gouache/Aguada   Un tipo de acuarela que usa pigmentos no transparentes. (Cap. 11–1)

H

Harmony/Armonía   Combinar los elementos del arte para acentuar sus similitudes. (Cap. 2–3)

Hieroglyphic/Jeroglífico   Forma antigua de escritura por medio de dibujos. (Cap. 5–2)

Hue/Tono   El nombre de un color. (Cap. 1–3)

I

Illumination/Iluminación   Ilustración-a-mano de libros. (Cap. 7–5)

Intaglio/Entallar   Técnica de impresión en la cual se raspa o se corta sobre una superficie la imagen que ha de imprimirse. (Cap. 3–5)

Intensity/Intensidad   Luminosidad u opacidad de un matiz. (Cap. 1–3)

J

Jewelry/Joyería   Arte y oficio de realizar obras de arte que se llevan puestas. (Cap. 10–7)

Juxtapose/Yuxtaponer   Poner lado a lado. (Cap. 14–3)

K

Kachina/Kachina   Estatuilla hecha a mano que representa a los espíritus en los ritos de la cultura Pueblo. (Cap. 12–4)

Kiln/Horno   Horno especial para cocinar objetos de alfarería. (Cap. 10–6)

Kinetic art/Arte cinético   Estilo artístico en el que se ponen en movimiento partes de una obra por medio de energía. (Cap. 13–4)

L

Landscape/Paisaje   Dibujo o pintura de montañas, árboles u otra escena natural. (Cap. 6–1)

Line/Línea   La trayectoria de un punto a través del espacio. (Cap. 1–2)

Line quality/Cualidad de la línea   El carácter único de cualquier línea. (Cap. 1–2)

M

Mascot/Mascota   Animal o persona utilizados por un grupo como signo de buena suerte. (Cap. 7–1)

Monoprint/Monocopia   Estampa hecha al aplicar tinta o pintura sobre una plancha y luego transferir la imagen frotando con la mano. (Cap. 6–7)

Mosaic/Mosaico   Pequeños trozos de vidrio de colores y joyas asentados sobre cemento. (Cap. 11–5)

Movement/Movimiento   Principio del arte que hace que el espectador vea acción en una obra; o la trayectoria que sigue el ojo al mirar una obra. (Cap. 2–4)

Murals/Murales   Obras bidimensionales grandes pintadas sobre paredes. (Cap. 8–7)

N

Nature study/Estudio del natural   Dibujo utilizado para ayudar al artista a realzar su percepción de los objetos naturales. (Cap. 6–3)

Negative space/Espacio negativo   Espacios vacíos entre las formas o figuras de una obra bidimensional o tridimensional. (Cap. 1–5)

Non-objective/No objetivo   Que no tiene sujetos u objetos inmediatamente identificables. (Cap. 4–3)

O

Old Stone Age/Edad de Piedra   El período histórico que abarca del año 30,000 al 10,000 [A.C.] (Cap. 7–1)

P

Painted screen/Biombo   Objeto de arte utilizado como pared o para dividir una habitación. (Cap. 5–3)

Pan/Toma panorámica   Movimiento lateral lento y regular de la cámara de video para captar los detalles de un paisaje. (Cap. 11–8)

Panorama/Panorama   Vista completa de un área en todas las direcciones. (Cap. 9–7)

Pendant/Pendiente   Artículo de joyería que se lleva alrededor del cuello colgado de un hilo o cadena. (Cap. 10–5)

Perception/Percepción   Toma de conciencia de los elementos de un ambiente por medio de los sentidos. (Cap. 3–1)

Perceive/Percibir   Tomar conciencia a través de los sentidos de la naturaleza particular de los objetos. (Cap. 10–1)

Petroglyph/Petroglifo   Grabado o pintura simbólicos sobre una piedra. (Cap. 12–1)

Photography/Fotografía   Arte de hacer imágenes al exponer a la luz una superficie tratada con sustancias químicas. (Cap. 11–1)

Pictogram/Pictograma   Figura pequeña que representa una palabra o una idea. (Cap. 12–1)

Picture plane/Plano   La superficie plana de una pintura o dibujo. (Cap. 2–3)

Pigment/Pigmento   Polvo fino molido que da color a la pintura. (Cap. 3–3)

Point of view/Punto de vista   Ángulo desde el cual el espectador ve la escena de una obra de arte. (Cap. 4–4)

Porcelain/Porcelana   Forma de alfalería de grano fino y alta calidad. (Cap. 7–3)

Portfolio/Carpeta de trabajos   Colección cuidadosamente seleccionada de obras que tienen los estudiantes y artistas profesionales. (Cap. 1–Introducción)

Portrait/Retrato   Representación visual de una persona en reposo. (Cap. 3–4)

Portraiture/Pintura de retratos   El arte de hacer retratos. (Cap. 8–5)

Pottery/Alfarería   Arte y oficio de hacer objetos de arte con arcilla. (Cap. 10–6)

Principles of art/Principios del arte   Lineamientos que gobiernan el modo en que los artistas organizan los elementos del arte. (Cap. 2–1)

Printmaking/Grabado   Acción de transferir la imagen desde una superficie cubierta de tinta para crear una obra de arte. (Cap. 3–5)

Proportion/Proporción   Manera en que las partes de una obra se relacionan entre sí y con el todo. (Cap. 2–3)

Public art/Arte público   Obra de arte expuesta para el disfrute de una comunidad. (Cap. 8–7)

Pueblo/Pueblo   Vivienda de arcilla reseca. (Cap. 13–3)

R

Renaissance/Renacimiento   Period de renacimiento. (Cap. 5–5)

Resist/Capa protectora   Medio artístico que sirve como capa impermeable, como los lápices de cera o crayones. (Cap. 6–6)

Rhythm/Ritmo   Repetición de un elemento para que una obra parezca activa. (Cap. 2–4)

Glosario

Rococo/Rococó Estilo artístico del siglo dieciocho que enfatizaba la gracia del movimiento, las líneas curvas y los colores delicados. (Cap. 9–3)

Sculpture/Escultura Obra de arte tridimensional. (Cap. 3–6)

Seal/Sello Emblema o imagen simbólica. (Cap. 13–1)

Seascape/Paisaje marino Dibujo o pintura del océano y los objetos que se encuentran en él o a su alrededor. (Cap. 9–7)

Self-portrait/Autorretrato Dibujo o pintura de la imagen del propio artista. (Cap. 8–1)

Shadow puppet/Marioneta Objeto de arte de forma animal o humana unido al extremo de una varilla. (Cap. 13–4)

Shape/Contorno Área claramente delimitada por uno o más de los otros cinco elementos visuales del arte. (Cap. 1–5)

Sketchbook/Cuaderno de bocetos Bloc de papel de dibujo donde los artistas bosquejan, toman apuntes y pulen ideas para su trabajo. (Cap. 2–Introducción)

Slip/Arcilla blanda Arcilla con suficiente agua agregada como para darle una consistencia resbaladiza y blanda. (Cap. 10–6)

Social protest painting/Pintura de protesta social Estilo artístico dedicado a atacar los males de la vida en los grandes centros urbanos. (Cap. 14–4)

Solvent/Solvente Líquido usado para regular el espesor de la pintura. (Cap. 3–3)

Space/Espacio Distancia o área entre, alrededor, sobre, debajo y dentro de las cosas. (Cap. 1–5)

Staged photograph/Foto de estudio Composición fotográfica que usa imágenes o procesos artificiales. (Cap. 9–1)

Still life/Naturaleza muerta Dibujo o pintura de objetos no vivientes. (Cap. 1–5)

Story board/Tablero de historieta Plan toma por toma de una producción de video. (Cap. 11–7)

Study/Estudio Dibujo usado para planear una pintura u otro proyecto grande. (Cap. 6–3)

Style/Estilo Modo personal que tiene el artista de usar los elementos y principios del arte para expresar ideas y sentimientos. (Cap. 8–1)

Stylized/Estilizado Simplificado o exagerado. (Cap. 6–1)

Subject/Sujeto Imagen que el espectador puede identificar fácilmente. (Cap. 4–1)

Surrealists/Surrealistas Grupo de artistas que exploraron el mundo de los sueños y el subconsciente. (Cap. 14–1)

Symbol/Símbolo Imagen utilizada para representar una cualidad o una idea. (Caps. 5–2, 7–7)

Tapestry/Tapiz Paño tejido con diseños decorativos o escenas coloridas que se cuelga de la pared. (Cap. 7–7)

Texture/Textura La forma en que algo se siente al tocarlo, o como parece que se sentiría al tocarlo. (Cap. 1–7)

Totem/Tótem Un objeto que sirve como emblema o símbolo respetado. (Cap. 7–2)

Trait/Rasgo Característica personal. (Cap. 7–1)

Tricolor/Tricolor Una bandera con tres franjas anchas de color. (Cap. 13–1)

Trompe-l'oeil/Trompe-l'oeil Estilo de pintura en que se representa a los objetos detalladamente, con realismo fotográfico. (Cap. 8–5)

Unity/Unidad El arreglo de elementos y principios del arte para lograr una sensación de consumación y totalidad. (Cap. 2–6)

Value/Opacidad La claridad u oscuridad de un color. (Cap. 1–3)

Variety/Variedad Combinar uno o más elementos del arte para generar interés. (Cap. 2–3)

Vessel/Recipiente Utensilio cóncavo destinado a guardar algo. (Cap. 10–5)

Video documentary/Documental de video Estudio en profundidad de una persona, lugar, cosa o evento. (Cap. 11–7)

Videographer/Camarógrafo Persona que opera una cámara de video. (Cap. 11–8)

Watercolorist/Acuarelista Pintor que trabaja con acuarelas. (Cap. 10–4)

Bibliography and Resource List

The following resources provide information in various areas of art and education. The entries are organized by subject and each title is followed by a brief description to help you choose the subjects you wish to read about.

Art History

Anderson, Bjork. *Linnea in Monet's Garden.* New York: R and S Books, 1985. When Linnea visits Claude Monet's garden in Giverny, she gets to stand on the bridge over his lily pond and walk through his house. Later, when she sees his paintings in Paris, she understands what it means for a painter to be called an Impressionist. This delightful book contains photographs of Monet's paintings as well as old family snapshots.

Avi-Yonah, Michael. *Piece by Piece! Mosaics of the Ancient World.* Minneapolis, Minn.: Lerner, 1993. This book describes ancient and modern techniques as well as early Greek, Roman, and Byzantine mosaics.

Barnicoat, John. *Posters: A Concise History.* New York: Thames and Hudson, 1985. The importance of the poster, including its role in various artistic movements.

Capek, Michael. *Artistic Trickery: The Tradition of Trompe L'Oeil Art.* Minneapolis, Minn.: Lerner, 1995. From the ancient Greeks to contemporary designers, artists have long been inspired to play visual jokes. This book lets the reader in on some of the gags.

Davidson, Rosemary. *Take a Look: An Introduction to the Experience of Art.* New York: Penguin, 1993. This book introduces the history, techniques, and functions of art through discussion and reproductions of paintings, photographs, drawings, and design elements. It also includes valuable diagrams and information about seeing and looking at art.

"Introduction to the Renaissance," *Calliope: World History for Young People.* Peterborough, N.H.: Cobblestone Publishing, May/June 1994. This issue of *Calliope* deals with many aspects of the arts and sciences during the Italian Renaissance. It features articles on artists such as Michelangelo and Leonardo da Vinci, rulers such as Isabella d'Este, and composers such as Monteverdi.

Biography

Gilow, Louise. *Meet Jim Henson.* New York: Random House, 1993. The creator of the Muppets, puppet stars of television and the movies, is the subject of this biography.

Greene, Katherine, and Richard Greene. *The Man Behind the Magic: The Story of Walt Disney.* New York: Viking, 1991. This biography of Walt Disney discusses his boyhood on a Missouri farm, his struggles as a young animator, and his building of a motion picture and amusement park empire.

Heslewood, Juliet. *Introducing Picasso: Painter, Sculptor.* Boston: Little, Brown, 1993. By examining the life of the well-known modern painter and the historical and artistic influences on his work, this book gives young readers a sense of who Picasso was and how his art developed. Photographs illustrate his work and his life.

Kastner, Joseph. *John James Audubon.* New York: Harry N. Abrams, 1992. This biography chronicles the life of Audubon from his childhood in France to his adventures in the New World, and shows how he captured these adventures in his artwork.

Neimark, Ann E. *Diego Rivera: Artist of the People.* New York: HarperCollins, 1992. Diego Rivera is brought to life in this comprehensive biography. It is illustrated with reproductions of Rivera's artwork.

Newlands, Anne. *Meet Edgar Degas.* New York: Lippincott, 1988. Degas talks to the reader about 13 of his paintings, describing what it's like to be a young artist in Paris.

Careers

Gordon, Barbara. *Careers in Art: Graphic Design.* VGM Career Horizons, 1992. Provides descriptions of careers in the graphic design field including art directors, book and magazine publishers, industrial designers and production artists. Information on courses and training requirements, job opportunities, and portfolio preparation.

Kaplan, Andrew. *Careers for Artistic Types.* Brookfield, Conn.: Millbrook, 1991. The author interviews 14 people who work in careers that are of interest to young people who like art.

Bibliography and Resource List

Media and Techniques

James, Jane H. *Perspective Drawing: A Point of View.* 2d ed. Englewood Cliffs, N.J.: Prentice Hall, 1988. For students who want to learn more about perspective.

Kehoe, Michael. *A Book Takes Root: The Making of a Picture Book.* Minneapolis, Minn.: Carolrhoda, 1993. This book traces the process of making a picture book from idea to manuscript to final production. Color photographs accompany the text and make this a fun-to-read and informative book.

Lauer, David A. *Design Basics.* 2d ed. New York: Holt, Rinehart and Winston, 1985. A resource for design students.

Mayer, Ralph. *The Artist's Handbook of Materials and Techniques.* 5th ed., rev. and updated. New York: Viking-Penguin, 1991. An up-to-date reference on art materials and techniques.

Meilach, Dona Z., Jay Hinz, and Bill Hinz. *How to Create Your Own Designs: An Introduction to Color, Form and Composition.* New York: Doubleday and Co., 1975. An excellent introduction to the elements of design.

Patterson, Freeman. *Photography and the Art of Seeing.* Rev. ed. San Francisco: Sierra Club Books, 1990. This book offers good advice on creative photography and is of particular interest to the beginning photographer.

Porter, Albert W. *Expressive Watercolor Techniques.* Worcester, Mass.: Davis Publications, 1982. A useful resource with valuable information on techniques and processes.

Sheaks, Barclay. *Drawing Figures and Faces.* Worcester, Mass.: Davis Publications, 1987. A helpful resource for students who wish to expand their drawing techniques.

Weldon, Jude. *Drawing: A Young Artist's Guide.* London: Dorling Kindersley, 1994. This well-designed and beautifully illustrated book guides the young artist through a wide variety of artistic experiences. Each idea is illustrated with master drawings and paintings. Topics include light and shade, color, imagination, and storytelling.

Multimedia Resources
Laserdiscs

American Art from the National Gallery A collection of 2,600 paintings and sculpture by American artists spanning three centuries.

Louvre Compendium Includes more than 5,000 works of art and 35,000 detailed images in a three-volume series.

Videodisc Volume I: Painting and Drawings

Videodisc Volume II: Sculpture and Objets d'Art

Videodisc Volume III: Antiquities

The National Gallery of Art A guided tour of the National Gallery featuring more than 1,600 masterpieces. A printed catalog and on-screen captions identifying each work are included.

The National Gallery of Art Laserstack Use this laserstack to create your own notes or slide lists for presentations. Works may be arranged by artist, nationality, period, style, date, medium, or subject.

Regard for the Planet A resource for 50,000 photographs documenting world cultures, places, and events of the last 40 years.

CD-ROMs

Art and Music Series Focuses on art and music from medieval times to Surrealism, with text linked to 24-volume student encyclopedia and glossary. Events, challenges, and achievements of each time period are highlighted. (lab packs available) WIN & MAC

National Museum of Women in the Arts Access to 200 artworks from the collection. Available on CD-ROM or videodisc.

With Open Eyes Access to images through time line, geographical location, and close-ups. View 200 multimedia and multicultural artworks from the collection of the Art Institute of Chicago. View any object in a virtual-reality gallery to get a sense of scale. Includes games, music, poetry, and sound effects. WIN & MAC

Index

Index

Credits